SILVER VEINS, DUSTY LUNGS

THE MEXICAN EXPERIENCE

William H. Beezley, series editor

SILVER VEINS, DUSTY LUNGS

MINING, WATER, AND PUBLIC HEALTH IN ZACATECAS, 1835–1946

ROCIO GOMEZ

University of Nebraska Press
Lincoln

Parts of two chapters were originally published as "Fuentes de progreso: Agua, minería y salud pública en Zacatecas, 1884–1894," in "Historias Ambientales," ed. Michael K. Bess and Raúl Pacheco-Vega, trans. Adrian Hinojos, *ISTOR: A Journal of History* 69 (Summer 2017): 9–24.

Library of Congress Cataloging-in-Publication Data
Names: Gomez, Rocio (Professor of Latin American history), author.
Title: Silver veins, dusty lungs: mining, water, and public health in Zacatecas, 1835–1946 / Rocio Gomez.
Description: Lincoln: University of Nebraska Press, [2020] | Series: The Mexican experience | Includes bibliographical references and index.
Identifiers: LCCN 2019053581
ISBN 9781496221117 (paperback)
ISBN 9780803290891 (hardback)
ISBN 9781496221568 (epub)
ISBN 9781496221575 (mobi)
ISBN 9781496221582 (pdf)
Subjects: LCSH: Water-supply—Health aspects—Mexico—Zacatecas (State)—History. | Silver mines and mining—Environmental aspects—Mexico—Zacatecas (State)—History. | Silver mines and mining—Health aspects—Mexico—Zacatecas (State)—History. | Public health—Mexico—Zacatecas (State)—History. | Environmental health—Mexico—Zacatecas (State)—History. | Zacatecas (Mexico: State)—Environmental conditions.
Classification: LCC RA593.M6 G66 2020 | DDC 363.6/1097243—dc23
LC record available at https://lccn.loc.gov/2019053581

Set in Garamond Premier Pro by Mikala R. Kolander.

Contents

Illustrations

Figures

Maps

Tables

Acknowledgments

IT TAKES A VILLAGE TO PRODUCE A BOOK. WHILE RE-
search and writing have proved to be solitary, I am indebted to a
pueblo of friends, colleagues, and organizations in the research and
writing of this book. It began under the supervision of William
Beezley at the University of Arizona. While I am thankful for his
guidance, I am also glad I did not take his advice and write on Mexico City. My thanks to the scholars who shared my enthusiasm in
exploring the environmental history of modern Zacatecas: Kevin
Gosner, Bert J. Barickman, Douglas Weiner, and especially Katherine Morrissey. The idea for a history of environmental health in
modern Mexico emerged in Martha Few's class on the history of
medicine, and for her sustained encouragement I am grateful. At
the University of Arizona, I had the privilege of having a wonderful
cohort of graduate student colleagues, and I am thankful to those
who encouraged the nascent stages of this book: Ryan Alexander,
Natasha Varner, Diana Montaño, Luis Coronado Guel, Pete Soland,
Shayna Mehas, Lisa Munro, and Anna Rose Alexander.

At the University of Arkansas, special thanks go to Kathryn Sloan,
Tricia Starks, Lynda Coon, Kirstin Erickson, and Yvette Murphy-
Erby—five outstanding mentors and scholars who encouraged this
research. Kathryn Sloan and Kirstin Erickson in particular have
known me since I was a doctoral student, and I am especially thankful to them for their guidance and mentorship. Not to be outdone,
my thanks to Elliott West for discussing mining and mining amalgamation with me over several lunches. No doubt the wait staff at

Ella's restaurant is now well versed in the history of cinnabar and mercury poisoning in both California and Zacatecas. Brenda Foster and Melinda Adams scanned and rescanned many of the images found here. I am thankful for their time.

At Virginia Commonwealth University, I am grateful to join a community of scholars whose research on science, technology, and society has helped me situate this work in the broader historiography of global science and technology studies. A special thanks to colleagues in the Department of History and elsewhere— John Powers, Antonio Espinoza, Karen Rader, Carolyn Eastman, Michael Dickinson, Leigh Ann Craig, McKenna Brown, Gabriela León-Pérez, and Kathryn Shively—who have offered support and encouragement since my arrival in August 2019. My sincere thanks to Harold and Laura Greer, who made my professorship possible at VCU through their generosity and commitment to Latin American History. My colleagues in the VCU Migration Studies Initiative and other Latinx faculty at VCU have been invaluable in providing me with the headspace I needed to complete this work. I hope I can do the same for them in their research.

This research was supported in part by a Humanities Research Grant from the J. William Fulbright College of Arts and Sciences at the University of Arkansas. The publication of this book was funded in part by a generous Scholarship Catalyst and Seed Award from the Dean's Office in the College of Humanities and Sciences at Virginia Commonwealth University.

This book would not have been possible without the time, hard work, and generosity of archivists and librarians in Zacatecas and Mexico City. At the Archivo Histórico del Estado de Zacatecas, my eternal gratitude to Genóveva Raquel Andrade Haro, who worked closely with me to identify sources, even as the archive was undergoing an extensive remodeling. Cristina del Río and Cristina Morales helped orient me and made a number of suggestions regarding holdings. Finally, Directora María Auxilio Maldonado Romero has my sincere thanks for allowing me to proceed with my research despite the extensive wiring work and painting during my visit. At the Archivo Histórico Municipal de Zacatecas, Angelia Medina Arteaga provided invaluable suggestions during our discussions of sources to pair with those found across town in the state archive. Lic. Olga Manuel Castillo served as a guide at the Archivo Histórico del Agua in Mexico City while making phone calls on my behalf to track down additional sources in libraries across the city. All of these women played a fundamental role in this research, and this book is a testament to their dedication and belief in free, open archives.

Conference and presentation audience members contributed valuable feedback on portions of this research. They include attendees at meetings of the Rocky Mountain Council of Latin American Studies, Reunión de Historiadores Mexicanos, Southeastern Council of Latin American Studies, and the Latin American Studies Association, as well as individuals who gathered for scholarly events at Arkansas State University and Virginia Commonwealth University. Friends and colleagues have shared their time and read drafts of this work. This work benefited in its early stages from a careful reading by Emily Wakild, who offered advice on how to improve it. Justin Castro read the introduction. Lisa Munro carefully copyedited chapter 5. C. T. Goode tracked down additional sources at AGN. In addition, this project is made richer through further discussions with and feedback from other scholars, including Justin Castro, Pete Soland, Diana Montaño, Scott Whiteford, Edward Beatty, Juan José Saldaña, Sonia Robles, Dana Velasco Murillo, Raúl Pacheco-Vega, Michael K. Bess, Carlos Dimas, Casey Lurtz, Beau Gaitors, Nicole Pacino, Brian Leech, Mica Jorgenson, Andrew Wood, Omar Escamilla, Elizabeth Manley, Sterling Evans, Thomas Rogers, Mikael Wolfe, Anton Rosenthal, and Elizabeth Kuznesof.

At the University of Nebraska Press, my thanks to the staff and team that put this book together. Bridget Barry guided me through the first steps of manuscript development, and Joeth Zucco shepherded this project along. Emily Wendell, Tish Fobben, and Ann Baker showed tremendous patience with this first-time author. Freelancer Maureen Bemko's careful edits have made this book better. Overall,

I cannot overstate my gratitude to this pueblo for all of their wisdom and time. All errors and omissions are of course my own.

This work benefits from the influence and mentorship of Myrna Santiago. As a fellow Latina in academia, I cannot overstate her influence on myself and my scholarship.

My deepest thanks to my parents, Rafael and Eugenia, as well as my siblings, Vanessa and Alberto, for their tireless support. This book is for Matthew Moscato, for his steadfast love and encouragement during the graduate school, research, job market, and tenure-track gauntlet. Sybil and Pru, my scrappy terriers and writing companions, are included in this dedication because they too traveled to Zacatecas with me during my research year.

A Note about Mine Names

MANY OF THE MINES DISCUSSED IN THIS WORK HAVE names. *Mina* is the Spanish word for "mine." Therefore, many of the mine names in the documents appear as Mina followed by a name (e.g., Mina San Rafael). I have generally left the names in this format. In some instances I use the name of the mine first followed by the English word "mine." Thus, I may also reference the San Rafael mine.

SILVER VEINS, DUSTY LUNGS

Introduction

The Ecology of Extraction

> *Patria*: your face is of maize,
> Your mines the palace of the King of Gold,
> And your sky, the storks slipping through
> And the green lightning of parrots.
> The Christ-Child left you a stable
> And the springs of petroleum, the devil.
> —Ramón López Velarde (1888–1921), "La Suave Patria"

THIS IS A STORY ABOUT THE EARTH, HOW DIFFERENT groups used it, and how it made them sick. This is a story that begins in underground mines but soon moves to the surface to involve people like Emilia Reina. Reina lamented the loss of flowers along the Río Mexicapam in a 1954 letter to engineer Antonio Rodríguez. She recalled how she had once enjoyed fruit from the trees along the river before the water turned thick and foamy. The mine poisoned the water when contaminated runoff flowed into the waterway. Now the cattle died when they drank from it, and it was no longer safe for humans to consume. The sheep and goats died too. She beseeched the engineer to relate her pueblo's problem to federal officials in order to receive compensation or access to other water sources. Her pleas for help largely fell on deaf ears.[1]

The silver veins of Zacatecas have long been a blessing and a curse for the city in the state of the same name. On its main thoroughfare, locals and tourists walking on the cobblestones are surrounded by colonial buildings and baroque architecture. An impressive aque-

1. A view of La Bufa and the aqueduct. Library of Congress, Prints and Photographs Division, George Grantham Bain Collection, L C-B 2-2103-3.

duct gives the cityscape a utilitarian beauty as it stretches toward the mountain known as La Bufa, but the structure ends abruptly, as if to signify the finite quantity of water. While the city has grown alongside mining, the consequences of extraction have also grown to include water scarcity and a toxic landscape. Despite the riches it produced, the mining industry also consumed considerable water and threatened human health. Caught between mineral wealth and exploitation, the environmental history of Zacatecas offers insight into two worlds: one working to carve out the earth underground and the other striving to build a city aboveground. To emphasize only one at the expense of the other ignores the inexorable ties between soil and sky, labor and the body, nature and culture.

The shared space between a city population and nearby mines provides a framework for explaining how industrial operations consumed resources and what those activities left behind. While mining extracted minerals and other resources, it also affected water, workers, and the surrounding environment. The inseparable spatial relationship between mining and residents creates multiple ecologies affecting the biochemical compositions of humans, plants, and animals while informing new ideas regarding extractive industries. For the city of Zacatecas, its long-standing tie to mining shapes not only its industrial heritage and identity but also its economy. The city stemmed from the colonial business of mining, which grew into an industry in the nineteenth century and quickly shifted to foreign ownership in the twentieth century.[2] The resulting romantic landscape of the city with a "silver heart"—the aqueduct, the towering La Bufa, the baroque-style cathedral, the colonial buildings—underscores an interdependence on mining, which has shaped perceptions of the industry as well as the resulting environmental consequences of its presence. While most mining now occurs in the hinterlands, far from urban centers, the city of Zacatecas offers a contrast, as it grew alongside mining, with homes, streets, and markets placed next to open mine entrances.

Silver Veins, Dusty Lungs discusses how the mining industry affected water sources and the human body through the lens of political and social ecology in order to situate the dynamic exchange against the backdrop of modern Mexican history. This work thus views ecology through water management, miasma and germ theory, and technology to suggest how *zacatecanos*, or the people of Zacatecas, perceived illness as a consequence of industrial extraction. Because of the inseparability of the human organism from its natural surroundings, this book explores the far-reaching repercussions of extraction, going beyond the mining site and into the physiological details of environmental health. It places industry and its ecological consequences at the center of revolutions in both medical science and the political sphere. With the renewed interest in mining in the United States and the ever-present Canadian extraction companies in Latin America, this book shows that the ecological effects of mining often prove detrimental not just to the environment but to humans as well.

This book examines water, public health, and mining according to the ecology of extraction. The ecology of extraction in Zacatecas touched all of nature, human and nonhuman alike, as workers hauled rocks to the surface to begin the process of turning them into silver. Within this space, the human organism experienced frequent exchanges with the surrounding environment, as well as with the social, economic, and political consequences of these interactions. Dust, water, materials used in converting the ore to silver—they all form part of this ecology and contribute to the interactions between nature and other organisms in the sphere. However, the ecology of extraction is not unidirectional but rather is in constant flux, while also being subject to nuances in the environment. Specifically, the ecology of extraction weighs not only the materials excavated during mining but also those left behind. The mining waste, debris, and runoff proved to be part of a cycle in which humans extract ore, refine what they need from it (i.e., silver and other metals), and then release the contaminated remains back into the environment and into this shared space.

The Ecology of Extraction

The ecology of extraction employs a framework of political and social ecology in order to show how silver mining in Zacatecas affected nature, human and nonhuman alike. While fluid methodologically and thematically, political ecology examines power dynamics, particularly in how a society uses resources, how it distributes them, and who wins in an unequal system. In addition, political ecology analyzes how extractive industries affect the lives of locals by studying things like the quality of their water and the environmental health consequences of contaminated soil. Political ecologists also recognize that extractive industries are subject to global markets and that workers face the exploitive character of mining as well. Historians such as Myrna Santiago and Matthew Vitz have employed this form of analysis in order to explain how power shapes ecological problems and the solutions proposed to address them.[3]

The history of Zacatecas is closely intertwined with mining and illustrates the colonial legacy of silver. In the colonial period mines typically belonged to local or domestic investors, but their ownership increasingly shifted into foreign hands in the nineteenth and twentieth century. However distant from Mexico City it may be, Zacatecas has remained subject to the forces of capitalism, competition, and extraction through the centuries. Political ecology explains how mining consumed resources, but grasping the extent of the ecological ramifications requires a historical understanding of how the city grew around and within extraction sites. Consequently, I ask, How does power shape the city and mining when they exist so close together? How does power inform the illnesses and disease that emerge from extractive industry? The close spatial relationship between the two encompasses human bodies, water, animal bodies, ideas of governance, and concepts on nonhuman nature—an intricate web to consider in how extraction affects the multitude of beings it involves. In this dynamic exchange the interconnected relationship between nature and society demonstrates a foundation for the environmental challenges facing a specific community, a crucial part of social ecology.

Social ecology shapes the local (and lateral) narratives of how Zacatecanos used nature, as well as how they conceptualized their relationship to it. In addition to the proximity of mining operations, the people of Zacatecas relied on the mining economy to sustain the city. Consequently, they tolerated the use of heavy metals for amalgamation near their homes and the leaching of toxins into waterways. Miners, well aware of the risks, ventured daily into the mines. These dangers inspired *corridos*, or Mexican folk songs, about the fear of not returning home at the end of the day. Because of the long-standing links between the city and mining, locals possessed an inherent knowledge, via word of mouth and family histories, about these dangers. They knew from stories and cautionary tales of the ways mining affected nature—the same nature they interacted with daily. They spoke of how the mercury from the patio amalgamation pits eroded horses' hooves, of how miners died of hacking coughs after a lifetime in the mine, of how plants growing near mine runoff had died. How did this relationship between workers and labor proceed given the former's full knowledge of the toxicity in their surroundings? Whereas modern science typically emphasizes difference by isolating organisms to study them individually, empirical observation revealed connections in nature through ordinary activities such as food and water gathering, agriculture, and even nonmechanized extraction. As the anthropologist Mary Douglas has posited, "A separating, disembedding process of analysis had to go completely counter to the kind of thinking which assumed the connectedness of everything in the universe, as pairs or as opposites of everything else."[4] Despite their awareness of the dynamic ecology of mining, Zacatecanos have continued to rely on it undeterred since 1546. Consequently, this has been a relationship of risk. Risk existed in sharing water sources with mining operations upstream, in digging the ore out of the depths of mountains, in living near the dusty environs of amalgamation sites. In Zacatecas, the interconnectedness of nature, human and nonhuman alike, has manifested itself in local knowledge as well as in the physiological consequences of this close relationship.

I employ the phrase "ecology of extraction" to demonstrate how water, public health, and mining interacted in this shared space. Water illustrates the ecology of extraction in three ways. First, residents of Zacatecas used it domestically and consumed it in their daily life, absorbing its contaminants. Because of their spatial proximity to mines, Zacatecanos encountered waste from the mines or refining operations not only in their water but also through other environmental consequences of mining, such as mudslides. Water served as a lifeline to industry as well as community, since both needed it for survival. With the steep topography and arid climate, locals had little choice but to share their water with the industry. Moreover, many mining operations in Zacatecas hit the water table fairly quickly, as the state sits on ancient aquifers. As a result, even with minimal surface water in the form of streams or rivers, residents counted on access to wells, springs, or reservoirs near mines to access the resource. Consequently, residents developed a mutually beneficial relationship with extractive industries early in the city's history: the populace tolerated the shared space with mining while at the same time benefiting from open access to underground water sources. Likewise, the mining industry wanted to remove water from mines, and a willing population armed with buckets volunteered to take the water. This arrangement existed well into nineteenth century, until the concept of water management and subsoil rights altered it. Second, farmers used the waterways for their crops and animals in the rural areas outside the state capital. Farmers and ranchers relied on water pumped from mines to irrigate their fields and to use in their homes. In the process, they and their farm animals ingested or absorbed heavy metals in the mine runoff. When that water became contaminated with the slurry, the liquid resource quickly became a fountain of discord among all parties, particularly during the twentieth century when mining spread farther into the hinterlands. Lastly, I use the ecology of extraction framework to examine the role of the national government as it tightened its grip on waterways, consolidating control of the resource in the late nineteenth century and into the twentieth. While locals lost control over water sources, the federal government dictated the management of the resource through legislation upholding the "federalization/centralization" of water.[5] While scholars of environmental history and water in Mexico emphasize the legislation that limited local use of water sources, this book examines how farmers in Zacatecas resisted and employed legal means in order to have water for their land.[6] Specifically, many farmers and townspeople challenged mining companies' claims to rivers, employing the language of the Constitution of 1917 even as additional legislation provided private companies more leeway. Environmental historians of extraction also highlight the dynamic exchange that occurs between the human body and its surroundings in extraction sites.[7] In particular they underscore how this exchange occurs through labor and emphasize the effects of toxic labor on the human body. In short, the ecology of extraction involves not only the trade-offs between human and nonhuman nature but also the understood dangers that belie this connection.

This is a story of continuities. I agree with other historians of Mexico who dispute the idea that the Porfiriato and the Mexican

Revolution illustrate two distinct eras in Mexican history. This narrative of a shift in Mexican history at the time of the revolution primarily focuses on the political center of the country and excludes smaller cities like Zacatecas. The continuity of mining in Zacatecas, from the colonial period to today, offers a framework for understanding the long-term consequences of the use of contaminated water and its effects on public health. While mining profits had ups and downs, the industry has persisted, even to today. With regard to periodization, this environmental history of Zacatecas, Mexico (1835–1946), begins with a cholera pandemic, which spurred the desire to invest in a water distribution system, and ends with the presidency of Manuel Ávila Camacho. Despite these parameters, the book begins in a bygone geologic era to explore the creation of silver and follows the element through its important role in colonial history. The book ends with a discussion of the dismantling of revolutionary protections with regard to water and occupational health outlined in the Constitution of 1917.

The geography of Zacatecas complicates its relationship with extraction. Trapped between the steep slopes of the Sierra Occidental and Sierra Oriental, the city sits at an elevation of roughly eight thousand feet (map 1). Without any major rivers in the area, the city relies on reservoirs, wells, and, in desperate times, water from mines to quench its thirst. An arid landscape makes competition for water fierce, particularly during droughts. While hills in the city create a stunning landscape, they make water transport and accessibility difficult. Despite the seeming isolation, small pueblos and villages dot the arid landscape, subsisting on their own mining (map 2).

Silver Mining in Context

Historians have emphasized the role of mining largely during the colonial period in Zacatecas while ignoring much of its history after independence. The viability of the silver veins in the city concentrated a diverse group of settlers, including people of Spanish, indigenous, and African descent.[8] Economic histories describe the ups and downs of the mining industry during the colonial period

COAHUILA

DURANGO

SIERRA MADRE OCCIDENTAL

Río de Aguanaval

SAN LUIS POTOSÍ

Río Jiménez del Teul

Santa Rosa

Ramón López Velarde

La Zacatecana

Sierra de Guadalupe

Río Grande

Río Jerez

JALISCO

AGUASCALIENTES

Sierra de Morones

NAYARIT

JALISCO

GUANAJUATO

0   100 mi

Map 1. Geographical features of the state of Zacatecas.
Map designed by Mapping Specialists Ltd.

Map. 2. Cities and towns of the state of Zacatecas.
Map designed by Mapping Specialists Ltd.

as well as the fallout from the 1893 crash of the silver market.[9] With regard to colonial mining, most scholars focus on Potosí, the South American mining city that along with Zacatecas mined silver for the Spanish Empire. Featuring the dangers of silver mining and the oppressive draft labor system of South America, the environmental history of Potosí outlines how silver mining in that region affected the health of indigenous workers, especially because of heavy mercury use in refining.[10] This study challenges the narrative that mining disappeared from Zacatecas with the Spanish Empire. On the contrary, it continued and flourished despite questionable results for city residents.

In the late nineteenth century, doctors and technocrats alike in Mexico City viewed water as a conduit for disease and floods as an affront to attempts at modernization. Technocrats designed the Gran Canal del Desagüe, a large-scale project that attempted to empty the remnant lakes surrounding Mexico City while carrying any waste away from the city. Many of the same officials joined public health specialists to plan infrastructure that would provide water for domestic use.[11] While this effort served as a model for other cities to follow, regional factors limited the implementation of such reforms, especially with water. Zacatecas engineers in particular struggled to apply these standards to water supply in the city. For example, they faced alternating mudslides and droughts in the 1890s, which shifted priorities. On the national level, politicians during the Porfiriato (1876–1910) and the revolutionary period (1910–46) passed several pieces of legislation dealing with water rights and resource access. The Porfiriato exacerbated the ecology of extraction by allowing mining companies to excavate for silver ore while gaining additional rights to water. The revolutionary period, for all its bluster, subsequently allowed mining companies to continue using waterways and water sources in the name of production, exposing farmers and their animals to contamination while further complicating the relationship between the human body and the industry.

Because mining is not a contained industry, the ecology of extraction also involves the human body and endangers human health.

I explore the effects of this industry not only by examining how mining contributed to water contamination in Zacatecas but also by showing how disease swept through the region because of an itinerant population. In addition to the toxic material entering waterways, disease also came into Zacatecas through workers who labored in mines and agriculture on haciendas that surrounded the city in the late nineteenth century. These large estates typically belonged to the well-heeled and drew profit from mixed agricultural activities, mining, or refining. Along with ranching and seasonal work in the fields or haciendas, many laborers worked in extraction seasonally or in different mines over many years. This created an itinerant workforce that lived in the state capital or its surroundings but that wandered for work. The people of Zacatecas in the mid-nineteenth century faced the arrival of new germs and viruses traveling with mining speculators from other parts of the country, as well as from the United States and Great Britain. Cholera, typhus, diphtheria, and the Spanish flu—all of these diseases entered the city of Zacatecas with itinerant populations. In the cases of both peripatetic disease and water-caused illnesses, local officials pushed for preventive measures to protect the health of the population, with varying degrees of success. These public officials cited doctors and methods that worked to limit the spread of illness in the national capital. Officials called for the use of lye or carbolic acid as disinfectant and for isolating the more "unhealthy" sectors of society. Disease was an important social question and not simply illness experienced by individuals. Municipalities, families, and unions responded differently to disease and illness, revealing their loyalties, concerns, and priorities. For example, after cholera skulked into the city in 1833, city officials increasingly pushed for a water distribution system that separated contaminated effluvia from water for domestic use. Although the city did not achieve this goal for another sixty years, the devastating epidemic gave birth to the early plans for the system's design. Disease also revealed the struggle to grasp how and where the cholera bacillus emerged, as well as the social and environmental factors that supported it. In another case, typhus arrived via lice on the clothes worn by *campesinos* in the early twentieth century as the workers came to the city during a drought. With agriculture devastated by the lack of rain, the rural poor arrived en masse in the city, leading municipal officials to isolate them and scramble to contain the disease.

By the late nineteenth century, politicians and technocrats had created public health measures to curb the spread of disease while often fixating on water as the source of maladies. Developments in water infrastructure coincided with shifts in medical theories as physicians identified germs as the cause of disease, even as miasma theory lingered into the twentieth century. The germs, or "little creatures," in water spurred physicians to advise governments on cautionary measures to limit the exposure of the population and provide lessons on how to avoid an epidemic.[12] The global cholera pandemic in the 1830s forced cities and towns to initiate plans to install water distribution systems. During this era the seeds of modern public health institutions germinated. In Mexico City, technocrats and politicians engineered the Gran Canal, in part as a precautionary measure to avoid the spread of seasonal waterborne or mosquito-borne diseases. Through legislation drafted during the Porfiriato, water became one of the most protected resources. Farmers, ranchers, and mine owners fought contentiously over it, yet the federal government that emerged with the revolution hesitated to take sides because it was desperate to preserve investments in the country after the conflict. Thus, legislation to protect individual resources did not limit the fallout from the relationship between nonhuman nature and the extractive industry but instead exposed communities to toxic environments and conflicts.

Mining emerged as the constant in the history of Zacatecas, a continuity from the colonial period to the present. With mining, the ecology of extraction underscored the importance of not just what the industry removed but also what it injected into the local water system, air, and other ecologies. The industry relied on the excavation of ores of silver and other precious metals, as well as on the refining of the materials. During excavation, miners entered the belly of mountains to remove large chunks of earth but then left mercury, lead, and other heavy metals in the waterways near refining operations. Whether or not humans consumed this water, the toxins remained to affect other organisms. Likewise, the integration of the human body into that exchange created a link between the environment and mammalian physiology. Workers died when handling toxic metals during long careers as miners. Animals died after drinking from streams near a mine. The ecology of extraction framework made Zacatecas and silver mining biologically intertwined and indistinguishable.

During the Porfiriato and the revolutionary period that followed, the people of Zacatecas witnessed legislation that changed mining and water access as well as public health measures. Individually, these three—mining, public health, and water—proved significant in driving the goals of the Porfiriato and the revolutionary project, but an examination reveals that over time the federal government increasingly favored extractive industries, setting the precedent for today. Porfirio Díaz opened the door for foreign extraction of Mexican resources, but the revolution did little to curb such exploitation. The continued presence of mining corporations in Zacatecas illustrates this point. Technocrats applied changes to water management in order to help support public health measures in the early twentieth century. On the local level municipal officials faced the daunting task of holding mining operations to account for the polluted waterways. Even after revolutionary reforms, farmers and ranchers received little help from municipal officials to settle their disputes over water.

Ore Bodies and the Body Politic

The proximity of an extractive industry to a population raises questions as to how the human organism experienced this dynamic exchange, an interaction that began in 1546 and has continued into the twenty-first century. What characterized the interaction during the Porfiriato and the revolution is the greater emphasis on water infrastructure and public health measures to protect the community as well as workers. With public health, the overlapping of spaces served as an extension of the human organism, which internalized traces of the raw materials extracted. Porous and permeable, the human body absorbs its surroundings through inhalation, consumption, and touch. This permeability allows both nutrients and microscopic foes to affect the health of an individual. Just as armies marched across Zacatecas, so did diseases. The pathological armies include cholera, typhus, diphtheria, Spanish flu, and silicosis-tuberculosis.

Microbial militaries had devastating effects in the region and often affected the physiologies of miners or soldiers. Cholera coincided with the sacking of Zacatecas by Antonio López de Santa Anna in 1835. Typhus spread after the onset of drought, while diphtheria attacked children in the pre-vaccine era. Likewise, the Spanish flu arrived in the small pueblos of Zacatecas in 1918, raising alarm with its extreme levels of morbidity and mortality. The microbes and physiological details play a central role in illustrating how disease debilitated large sectors of the population. Knowing the "blood and guts" of infirmities highlights the susceptibility of the human body to environmental factors or microbial agents. Moreover, the telltale signs of particular diseases provide an empirical testimony to what doctors saw in patients at the time.

Physicians and patients alike suffered the social and economic conditions of Zacatecas, including a lack of medical infrastructure, poor hygiene, and the legacies of colonialism.[13] Likewise, disease ecology and social medicine underscore the role of water even in salubrious conditions, as potability served as a signifier for an orderly and healthful society. In the late nineteenth century, doctors believed that miasmas contributed to disease, and that theory spurred efforts to drain lingering, malodorous pools. In Zacatecas, residents contended with the bowl-like layout of the city and the frequent use of water sources for silver refining processes, which created unwanted pools. These conditions led to a common understanding of water during this time: standing water versus flowing water. Did stagnant water harbor miasmas or did it flow? Did it come from a mine or did it have a healthy provenance? The cultural construction of water changed according to the needs of the city or the capriciousness of climate. Farmers and mine operators interpreted waterways differently. The former used water for cattle, crops, or parched throats. The latter employed water as a tool in refining, and because of frequent excavations below the water table, miners and mine operators viewed it as an annoying obstacle to the veins of ore. In both aspects of mining, miners disposed of wastewater in existing streams, leading to contentious relationships with locals. Because mining took place in the city of Zacatecas and because farming occurred on the outskirts, water became a central issue to all concerned parties.

The intersection of silver mining and human health underscored the role of workers. In refining, miners employed a process known as patio amalgamation to turn the raw rock ore into silver, a method used since the inception of the industry in Zacatecas. Mining operators and engineers attempted to introduce newer methods in the colonial era in Zacatecas, with limited success, initially making the region an outlier in refining techniques.[14] Pneumatic drills and excavation techniques changed the landscape dramatically. Drill work in the mines kicked up dust that workers inhaled. Silicosis and its derivative ailment, silicosis-tuberculosis, sparked a discussion among unions, politicians, and medical doctors about the mining companies' degree of responsibility for the illness and those affected by it.[15] The combination of mining and new technology spawned a public health crisis among miners and mining communities during an era of union activity and workers' rights. Meanwhile, medical doctors did little to advance the workers' cases against mining companies, as occupational health science was in its infancy and had yet to offer consistent evidence about the relationship between silicosis and tuberculosis.

An examination of occupational health and environmental factors not only reiterates the susceptibility of the human body to contaminants but also underscores how the organism serves as a barometer of the surrounding environment. Workers often suffered the lingering effects of their labor, particularly in industries heavy with chemical use or offering few safety measures. In Mexico, Article 123 of the Constitution of 1917 codified workers' rights by outlining a minimum wage in addition to defining the workday and workweek. The subsequent Ley Federal de Trabajo in 1931 created a running list of occupations and the most common diseases associated with those professions. For miners, raw materials and extraction methods formed the foundation for their labor in the mines. Workers' awareness grew via their understanding about nature through labor: handling raw materials in agriculture, excavating subterranean silver ores, and wrangling animals, among others.[16] Yet this knowledge does not consider the microscopic interactions between nature and workers' bodies. In the case of Zacatecas, the term "workscape" offers better insight, as it makes the worker and the mine inseparable through the intersections of the land, water, air, and dirt, thus establishing a dynamic relationship.[17] Notably, miners took their "workscape" with them when they left the mines, exposing others to the dust and heavy metals on their clothes. The term also encapsulated the area surrounding a mine, which extended the microscopic exchange between industry and locals even further. Miners and families living near work sites drank the water pumped from mines, planted crops near work sites, and recognized the effluvia of refining. Thus, the shared biome of residents and labor influenced the health of locals and the ideas people had about the body and health. The body became a tool as well as an extension of the environment, a subject in a "landscape of exposure."[18] Their labor exposed them to exchanges on the microscopic level that led to an internalizing of the surrounding dirt, air, and water. The landscape of exposure also made specific sectors of the population more vulnerable. Miners and their families, residents living near mines, and farmers all faced economic hardships, which made their bodies expendable in the eyes of mining companies.[19]

After the ousting of Porfirio Díaz, revolutionary governments incorporated medical knowledge into their efforts to control workers' reforms outlined in the Constitution of 1917. Paralleling the effort by revolutionary governments to control water, an expert few medical

scientists garnered diagnostic power through education and professionalization. Locals in Zacatecas often pointed to putrid ponds as
sources of dangerous miasmas, reflecting the common perception in
the nineteenth century that disease spread through invisible wafting clouds of toxic air. Moreover, physicians cited Louis Pasteur's
achievements in rabies research and germ theory as a model for how
modern countries tackled disease, a message echoed by Mexico's
apostle of public health, Eduardo Liceaga.[20] Through these changes,
Zacatecas miners witnessed how occupational diseases became the
subject of debates surrounding their symptoms, the causes of their
illness, and the official diagnosis. While miners interpreted diseases
such as silicosis-tuberculosis in colloquial terms such as "miners'
cough," doctors and public health specialists linked diseases to the
specific environs of an occupation. However, the application of this
diagnosis to public policy suggested a "centralization" of medical
knowledge in government doctors. In controlling disease narratives,
government officials limited compensation claims along with what
fell under the category of "occupational disease," a move that satisfied
mining company doctors.

In addition to human bodies, animal bodies also interacted with
the ecology of extraction, further illustrating the presence of nature
in the city. For example, there is Emilia Reina's description of the loss
of cattle and sheep, cited at the beginning of this introduction. Yet
animal bodies also illustrated how the country began to understand
disease and its epidemiology. Before the advent of antibiotics and
the regular use of vaccines, disease vectors arrived in the form of
animals, a phrase used inclusively here to refer to dogs, insects, and
cattle. Similarly, the shift from miasma theory to an understanding of germs ignited the formation of public health institutions to
limit the spread of animal-borne contagions. In Zacatecas, public
health officials attempted to stop rabies in dogs and hydrophobia
in humans through a vaccination campaign, an effort that came
less than twenty years after little Joseph Meister received a series of
successful injections from Louis Pasteur in 1885. Stumbling out of
the mountains and rural areas, rabid animals typically encountered

domestic animals during periods of drought. Livestock and pets then spread the disease to unfortunate humans who crossed their path. Drought also brought the scourge of typhus via the unassuming louse. Endemic to the region, the disease came in waves over decades and often traveled along with human migrants as they sought to escape the disease in the countryside, only to encounter it in the city as well. Typhus launched public health efforts that redrew the lines between private and public. Engineers and politicians alike raided locals' homes to check for lice, dusting with lye and carbolic acid in order to rid the homes of the vectors. In turn, they excoriated any residents whose homes they deemed slovenly and who seemed disinclined to help their public health crusade. Meanwhile, cattle presented a conundrum similar to mining. Beef production formed a crucial part of the economy in the region, often sustaining the city even when mining floundered, with haciendas nearby raising cattle to supplement crops or mining on the property. Because the sale of cattle took place in the city center, the slaughterhouses operated at the bottom of the bowl-like setting. During the culling season, blood and entrails filled the streets, thus threatening the population with "miasmas," according to local complaints. At the same time, the sudden deaths of cattle and other ungulates indicated the presence of toxins in water sources near mines, alerting farmers to possible contaminants. When animals died after consuming the effluvia, animal owners demanded compensation for their losses. The growing outcry regarding the loss of cattle to mining contamination led to the intervention of federal ministers, who exerted pressure on foreign mining companies. Overall, the bodies of animals became subject to the public health measures outlined by municipal governments as medicine transitioned from superstition to science.

The Center of Power and the Center of Extraction

The uneven application of sweeping legislation to water and public health problems across the country in this era underscored the difference between the center and the periphery. Some regions succeeded in applying public health reforms that provided access to water to a large portion of their citizenry, and other cities built public wells or fountains to distribute water across various neighborhoods. Yet, with mining present in Zacatecas since its founding, municipal officials struggled to apply a feasible solution to distributing usable water to the city's population without crossing paths with mining, highlighting a growing divide between the goals of Zacatecas and of Mexico City. This rift signaled a changing of the power dynamics that had been established after independence. Although it rejected Spanish rule in 1821, the national capital continued to rely to some extent on the old industries built by colonialism. Cities like Zacatecas, Guanajuato, Pachuca, and Taxco emerged as important sites that eventually funded the republic. While the commodity focus in silver mining proved attractive in this research, the history of how Zacatecas and mining undermined the paradigm laid out by Mexico City in public health and water further emphasized the violence of extraction on nature—human and nonhuman alike. Local ecologies became the focus rather than tangents in the historical narrative. Moreover, natural resources mined in Zacatecas became part of national history: rocks and earth removed from mountains became the silver that financed an empire. This process provided historical weight to the city's relationship with nature, even if it served as the periphery and not the center. After independence, this role as a peripheral but important extraction site continued to be reflected in the historiography of Zacatecas.

However, the city served as a mining giant in contrast to Mexico City and also established itself as a storied center in the industry in three principal ways. First, Zacatecas served as the jewel on the Camino Real, the trail of silver towns that connected colonial Mexico City to its hinterland mines in what became New Mexico and the U.S. Southwest. Through this extractive umbilical cord, the seat of the viceroyalty received its wealth. The trail was also a link useful in monitoring the missions in the far north. Second, Zacatecas routinely produced silver of higher quality than the mines of Potosí in South America, which generated higher quantities.[21] The purity of Zacatecas silver spurred not only settlement but also investment in milling and amalgamation operations in the city. The emphasis on converting the raw ore to silver in the region gave the city further importance, since it became not the center for ore production but rather a center for silver production. Lastly, the quality of the silver spurred scientists and engineers to devise new methods of amalgamation and new refining technology, igniting a scientific scramble to create a more efficient means of production. In the process, engineers such as Miguel Bustamante introduced nuanced changes into the patio system of ore processing in order to extract the maximum amount of silver, with minimal waste. His efforts to limit the amount of mercury spilled in the process fell by the wayside as intractable workers refused to change their methods. Similarly, by the late nineteenth century, cyanide amalgamation was all the rage in Mexican mining, save in the state of Zacatecas. Despite the push to increase the efficiency of production, refiners and workers accustomed to the patio system hesitated to abandon the age-old process. Along with this stubborn refusal to acquiesce to the demands of external engineers and techniques, refining and patio workers exerted a degree of authority in the conversion of ore to silver, often citing the region's centuries of experience and their own faith in the patio system. This challenge further entrenched the city in its industrial heritage while dismissing the push from the peripheral industrial power (i.e., Mexico City) to increase efficiency and production. In sum, the city's industrial authority made it a center of extraction and provincialized the capital's power when it came to silver mining, at least until the early twentieth century.

From its position on the geographic periphery relative to Mexico City, the state of Zacatecas has continuously thumbed its nose at the will of the national capital. In 1835 conservative politicians in Mexico City pushed to limit state militias in order to consolidate military might in the national army. With twenty thousand men to protect a city of three hundred thousand residents, as well as artillery, the state militia of Zacatecas refused to disband, even with congressional legislation aimed directly at them. After a fierce debate led by Pedro Ramírez, who represented the state of Zacatecas in

Congress, conservative legislators passed the law ordering militias to disband. In turn, Zacatecas interim governor Manuel Cosío accused Congress of interfering in state affairs, without disclosing that only four thousand rifles were available for the state's twenty thousand militia troops.[22] Later that spring General Santa Anna, fresh from his resignation as president, charged into the city and leveled it in retribution for the state's insolence. Similarly, Jesús González Ortega, the Zacatecas governor and military hero who defended the besieged city of Puebla for two months in 1863, challenged the authority of the revered president Benito Juárez two years after that battle. González Ortega argued that the president had overstayed his electoral term, citing the four-year term limit outlined in the Constitution of 1857. Despite anger and despondency, Juárez and González Ortega called an uneasy truce to their enmity.

This is a story of the long game. Extraction has proceeded over centuries, and this book examines not only what mining took out of the ground but also what it left behind. In order to understand the various continuities and lingering toxic legacies, this work begins by examining underground mines first, then working its way out to the city and then the nation. In the process, the themes of water and human health remain central to the discussion of the ecology of extraction.

Chapter 1 details the silver mining industry during the Zacatecas secessionist crisis and the cholera epidemic that plagued the city in 1835. It begins with the mountains that give the region its unique terrain. Mining techniques—both indigenous and Spanish—differed in their use of timber and water, illustrating how early settlers quickly became acculturated to extraction. During the colonial period, technology became a contentious topic as the science behind refining sought to make the processes more efficient and profitable for the Crown. However, local miners resisted and continued to rely on the patio amalgamation method into the twentieth century. To examine mining interests in the nineteenth century, chapter 1 uses *denuncios*, or public claims to mines, to show how mining investors negotiated their use of resources. These denuncios also reveal fights over land as owners challenged potential buyers on their nationality, wealth, and age. The flurry of mining activity saw mines constructed in various directions, resulting in a cavernous network under the city. In the quest to find productive veins in these subterranean bodies, miners often hit aquifers. They then faced a dilemma: pump out the water and continue digging or stop mining that location. Both decisions yielded consequences for the mining companies and residents relying on mines for water access.

Chapter 2 addresses the environmental impacts of mining and the public health ramifications. After centuries of mining, the treeless landscape contributed to mudslides and floods that spilled into the city from hills above. Locals, citing offenses to their honor, responded with angry letters to city officials and linked having a clean home to decency. Furthermore, they claimed that runoff from refineries and mines produced miasmas that imperiled human health. In order to remedy these problems, the city attempted to hire engineering companies to install a water distribution system like that of the national capital. Faced with an increasingly desperate populace, municipal officials invested in wells to tap underground bodies of water and built public fountains to provide access. The discussion in chapter 2 analyzes the cultural construction of water through letters and petitions detailing the notable difference between standing water and flowing streams. In both cases, residents cite the mining industry as encroaching on water sources, to the detriment of public health.

The next few chapters outline the social and cultural dimensions of mining, water, and public health. Chapter 3 explores the broad definition of violence: not only violence between individuals but also the violence, or industrial trauma, committed on the human body. Accidents and falls had been widespread in mining sites since the beginning of the industry. However, violence with intent also took place as mines became crime scenes. Mines often functioned as liminal spaces, away from the scrutinizing gaze of city authorities but close enough to the city to remain in its jurisdiction. Chapter 3 views violence as an act centered on the body, whether brutality between humans or an industrial accident at work. Accidents and fatalities increased in tandem with the introduction of new excavating equipment and refining techniques. In some industrial accidents, the human body suffered so much damage that the incidents were investigated as criminal cases. Using criminal cases, flyers, and gubernatorial *memorias*, this analysis also addresses public health measures undertaken to combat the violence of diseases related to water conditions, especially rabies. While violence between individuals divides, public health campaigns that attempt to heal serve as a cultural salve and reaffirmation of community.

Zacatecas becomes a site of epidemics and public health debates in chapter 4, with analysis spanning the period from the Porfiriato to the 1930s. The epidemics of typhus and diphtheria prompted officials to undertake preventive measures while also renewing their commitment to the health of the community, particularly its youngest members. While *científicos* debated water infrastructure in Mexico City, Zacatecas council members attempted to quash epidemics by emphasizing cleanliness and education. Their concerns stemmed from the lack of water in the region due to drought, which exacerbated conditions that favored the louse-born illness of typhus. In addition, insalubrious conditions and weakened immune systems intensified diphtheria epidemics. Porfirian-era efforts to improve public health in the national capital attempted to pressure smaller cities into following their lead in creating a modern city. Topographical differences and omnipresent mining limited that possibility in the state capital of Zacatecas and in surrounding pueblos. Based on examinations of letters of complaint, telegrams to federal officials, and engineers' reports, this chapter also delves into the petitions of surrounding mining communities in the state of Zacatecas.

Chapter 5 explores the history of occupational health in Mexico with a focus on lung ailments. In addition to examining silicosis, the chapter also discusses how workers sought to have tuberculosis recognized as a disease of the mining profession, under the Ley Federal de Trabajo's guidelines for protecting workers. This chapter argues that the medical debate surrounding the illness gave political and private interests the counterweight needed to dismantle revolutionary social programs for workers. Similar to the status of silicosis, the addition of tuberculosis to the list of illnesses covered in the federal legislation drew scrutiny from medical doctors, politicians, and mining company executives. In their quibbling, these parties neglected the similarities in symptoms between silicosis and tuberculosis. Meanwhile, the miners saw their claims engulfed in a global debate on the pathologies and physiologies of the two diseases. Medical doctors insisted that repeated exposure to the dusty confines of a mine contributed to the chronic, debilitating disease of silicosis, which, coupled with a secondary infection of tuberculosis, signified a death sentence.

Finally, the conclusion examines the present-day toxic legacies surrounding the state capital. Foreign investment in mining renewed the industry in the state but shifted to open-pit mining. At the same time, a new type of extraction moved in. Water extraction outside the state capital has added to the calamities, as the city has struggled to balance business investment with the water demands of its own growing population.

1

Underground Bodies

Extraction, Exposure, and Dissection

THE ECOLOGY OF EXTRACTION EMERGES IN THE POWER struggles over silver mining and access to water, while informing ideas on the role of the industry in the city. Changes to legislation after independence limited access to mines to an exclusive few and by the late nineteenth century had concentrated mineral rights in the hands of foreign investors. In addition to extracting the raw rock from the mountain, miners and speculators faced another challenge in both amalgamation and refining, two processes that required space and expensive resources. Among these resources, amalgamation and refining required water as well as investors. Caught in the middle, farmers saw water sources lost to the industrial needs of silver. Zacatecanos had to contend with the presence of mining activity and the fortune seekers it drew, as well as the impacts they and the mining activities themselves had on public health. The responsibility for determining who or what harbored dangerous miasmas fell to a few municipal officials. Those officials often accused bystanders, such as tavern patrons, of harming public health, rather than addressing industry's role in damaging health by releasing toxic substances. Economic and social powers supported the idea that mining and extraction were normal activities and not subject to question. The creation of this paradigm developed over a long trajectory, beginning with the settling of the city. It involved not only colonialism but also how the mining industry colonized the minds of locals, convincing them that the encroachment of toxins was both inevitable and acceptable.

Extraction and environmental degradation illustrated the continuity from colonial Mexico to modern Mexico, with dangerous health implications for the populations of Zacatecas over centuries. The ecology of extraction was manifested in the human body through contact with mines, amalgamating contaminants, or their runoff into the water systems in the region. The science of extraction embraced European methods to maximize efficiency and wealth, with little attention paid to informing workers about potential dangers. With silver mining taking place in and around the city, the barriers between the population and industry faded amid the growth of the region's population and extraction activities during the sixteenth century. With the city resting atop three silver ore veins, the residents of Zacatecas lived over extraction sites where mines and tunnels made up the underground infrastructure. Unwittingly, they participated in the dynamic exchange between the industry and the human body through water, a conduit for harmful effluvia from mining. Due to amalgamation and refining practices, water emerged as a point of contention for both the industry and the city, as both depended on the same streams for their survival. The use of shared water sources blurred the lines between the human organism and its surroundings in air, water, and earth.

This chapter explores the process in which the city of Zacatecas became engulfed by the mining industry, from the first European settlement in the region to the late nineteenth century. It argues that the activities of the underground affected life in the city and shows how the ongoing relationship shaped the use of water sources. It also considers the reason why Europeans settled in the region: silver. It offers a background to the element in the context of "big history," examining how silver developed in the crevices of mountains. The discussion then moves to indigenous and Spanish miners' extraction techniques. Technology serves as an undercurrent in this chapter, with special attention to European ideas of engineering as well as resistance to making the process more efficient with colonializing contraptions. In addition, the mining codes and laws give insight into how landowners used water sources and brought other concerned parties into the mix. Lastly, the importance of public health underpins the discussion of water and mining, as federal reforms in water infrastructure pushed communities to model themselves after the canals or fountains of Mexico City despite local conditions. Public health awareness evolved as physicians shifted from the miasma theory to germ theory in the late nineteenth century.

The Geology of Zacatecas

Volatile geological activity marked the creation of the mountains surrounding the city of Zacatecas, as tectonic events forced peaks upward. Ancient ocean beds made up the lower levels of this landscape, while the mountains created the backbone of the North American continent. Through the bedrock, the peaks forming the Sierra Madre Occidental, to the west of the city of Zacatecas, emerged during this era. This upward push gave the city its elevation of more than 8,000 feet, situating it in the *altiplano*. The altiplano, or high-elevation plateau, created an arid environment, which foreshadowed the precarious presence of water sources in the region; vast expanses of desert surround the city. Likewise, to the northwest, a quartzitic sandstone layer that heaved upward revealed the fossils of mollusk-bearing phyllites, a foliated rock often composed of mica and quartz.[1] The bivalves of the pre-Triassic and Triassic period (250 million years ago) survived only long enough to experience an extinction-level event that left layers of volcanic rock and ash, signaling the presence of high temperatures. The resulting Lower Volcanic Complex formed part of the largest silica-based, igneous sections on earth during the Cenozoic era (beginning roughly 65 million years ago).[2] A volcanic belt from the late Paleocene to the Eocene (65–57 million years ago) stretched the width of Mexico's midsection, from the Pacific to the Bay of Campeche. Even today, it frequently belches into activity with the Volcán de Colima and the temperamental Popocatépetl, near Mexico City. With major crustal structures presented in layers of silica, the geological record in surrounding mountains details the layers of pyroclastic floes dating back 46 million years to the Jurassic period, with earlier strata of marine sediments and silica formations. In the convergence of these structures, together with geologic volatility, pressure, and time, fault lines rippled away from the city of Zacatecas through the high-elevation desert, signaling the rugged beginnings of the Sierra Madre Occidental. Today the city today sits north of the San Luis–Tepehuanes fault system, with minimal seismic rumblings.[3]

The volatility continued during a volcanic period. The Sierra Madre Occidental, to the west of the city of Zacatecas, formed part of a larger spine of North America, which pulsated with magma and tectonic activity.[4] Volcanic belts included not only granite formations but also silica-based, igneous sections. With changing temperatures, the volcanic activity and the disparity of cooling across the region led to pockets with a high quartz presence, making the soils especially sandy in places. Moreover, the igneous traces throughout the Sierra Madre Occidental signaled a global cool-down during the shift from the Eocene to the Oligocene (approximately 34 million years ago).[5] Asteroid collisions in North America and Asia contributed to the winter-like conditions, as revealed by soil samples in the region.

As a metal, silver lacks gold's value or liquid mercury's malleability, but it often emerges in the presence of other precious metals. Born from secondary nuclear reactions in the creation of stars, silver appears in its pure elemental form in the earth's crust as a remnant from the formation process of other metals, including gold (Au) and palladium (Pd).[6] In geological formations, silver (Ag) is typically found alongside metals such as gold, lead, copper, zinc, or tin. Although the metal does not react with oxygen or water, it occasionally has been found exposed on the surface with a smooth coating, called acanthite (Ag_2S). Furthermore, the economic value of silver deposits depends largely on the presence of other metals, specifically lead, gold, and copper, to offset the initial investment in excavating for silver. With other metals to pique financial interest, the mining industry weighs not only the economic benefits of exploration in silver but also the possible bonanza of finding additional metals in the same mine. Notably, the silver-producing states in Mexico today now host copper or tin mines as well.

From an industrial perspective, silver production relies heavily on access to mercury in order to concentrate the precious metal and separate it from others in the same ore. Without mercury (*azogue*), there would be no silver.[7] Mercury served to bind itself to silver and other metals. Mercury (Hg) or mercury sulfide (HgS) often occurs naturally in oxidation zones near silver deposits, or rather in porous zones near the surface with unstable compounds. Mercury binds with silver to create an alloy, creating a higher-quality, more concentrated silver. Indeed, Spanish silver mining in the Americas initially remained largely isolated from European technologies because the Crown benefited from owning both silver- and mercury-producing mines. As a result, silver production often had a higher yield when mercury from cinnabar mines in Almadén, Spain, or Huancavelica, Peru, produced a steady stream of the binding metal. Cinnabar, or rather a red mercury sulfide (HgS), required its own refining method, using sodium hydroxide (NaOH) and sulfur (S), in order to convert the reddish powder to liquid mercury. Access to cinnabar mines assured a contained process, from mining to refining, within the empire while limiting production access to outsiders.

First Arrivals, First Excavations

The first arrivals into the region of Zacatecas incorporated the environment into their regional identity. Inhabitants of the settlement near the archaeological ruins of La Quemada, about thirty miles north of the present-day city of Zacatecas, dominated the region around 500 CE. They lived near the imposing structure of a rudimentary pyramid with pillars surrounded by ceremonial sites as well as evidence of agricultural production. Near the site, four indigenous groups established their territory in the region: the Caxcanes near the state capital, the itinerant Zacatecos to the north, and to the south the Tepehuanes and the Guachichiles.[8] Notably, the Caxcanes established an outpost in the sierra to the south of present-day Zacatecas on what became known as the Cerro del Teúl. An archaeological dig revealed a ceremonial site and ballcourt along with several steles depicting ballplayers, suggesting an influence of the Toltecs. Moreover, the ceremonial post indicated a continuous presence beginning in 200 CE as evidenced by tools and landscape changes.[9]

Indigenous communities in the region also practiced metalworking, or the shaping of metals, to some degree. Despite sparse archaeological evidence of mining activity, indigenous material culture featured the use of gold, silver, and precious stones dating back to the seventh century.[10] In addition to religious purposes, excavated materials also had utilitarian value. Indigenous miners, without the benefit of metal tools, used stones as hammers, wood pieces as shovels, and deer horns to loosen dirt, as in the case of an Andean group.[11] Other groups in western Mexico used what could be described as "fire mining," in which miners built a fire near a wall of untapped ore. As the fire heated the earth, the indigenous miners splashed water on the wall to cause a rupture in the earth and, they hoped, expose silver or gold.[12] Moreover, while the materials produced largely came from alluvial deposits, the indigenous miners inadvertently drew Spaniards' attention to the precious metals underground by presenting them with nuggets of gold or chunks of silver. This material evidence of indigenous mines largely disappeared under the inevitable excavation spurred by the Spanish "discovery" of these materials.

The indigenous communities' use of silver and gold, as well as their excavation for the metals, illustrated the continuum of mining history from pre-Columbian experiences to the present. Nonetheless, this use of materials by indigenous populations underscored two points of mining history. First, indigenous communities shaped the landscape and earth around them. In excavation and even in alluvial dredging, early groups began the journey into subterranean extraction, effecting environmental change in the vicinity of their mining activity. Moreover, while scholars highlight this activity as contrary to the ecologically noble indigenous archetype, indigenous communities engaged in mining to provide items for religious ceremonies or everyday material culture.[13] Second, despite this archetype, the indigenous peoples of pre-Columbian Mexico did not have the benefit of iron, steel, or mechanized machines. Indigenous miners pursued the metals even before Europeans arrived, yet their search for them did not reach the level of extraction the Spanish settlers pursued. The process of mining underscored the value of precious metals in different cultures, in different eras, making the environmental changes a consequence of the cultural weight carried by metal. In other words, the labor invested in mining illustrated how intensively an individual's or a society's pursuit of the metal propelled them to excavate. The collective lust for the metal drove humans underground into the mines. Indeed, indigenous miners opened the silver veins of the Americas yet planted the dysplasia that eventually grew into a cancer.

In an attempt to quash indigenous rebellions after the fall of Tenochtitlan in 1521, Spaniards saw indigenous communities use the landscape in an effort to resist the Spanish march northward toward Zacatecas and beyond. While potential mines served as a draw for Europeans, indigenous communities in the region presented a growing resistance. As the Spanish moved across the newly christened New Spain, they found scars of indigenous mining in Nueva Galicia, or the vice-principality that eventually included the states of Jalisco and Zacatecas. Confident in the submission of regional groups, Cristóbal de Oñate established the city of Guadalajara in 1531, using it as a home base from which to explore the region.[14] As the Europeans advanced to the northeast, they met a strong collective of indigenous groups, sparking what eventually became the Mixtón War. In El Teúl, a small group known as the Teultecos killed a large number of the Spanish troops, before retreating to the central *cerro*, or hill.[15] That hill held religious significance, as archaeological digs have uncovered a stele representing a deity. Moreover, the indigenous people used the sheer rock cliffs to prevent the Spanish from launching an attack, while other indigenous defenders provided support from the ground and surrounding areas. Despite the initial clashes, the Spanish brought in additional troops and continued their northern push even as they encountered increasingly fierce opposition. In El Teúl, the Teultecos called for allies, often launching attacks from the top of the Cerro del Teúl. Notably, they chose obsidian swords as their weapons, indicating extensive trade with regions that had access to the volcanic rock.[16] Joining forces with Franciscan friar Juan Pacheco, Juan Delgado laid the cornerstone of the church in that town in 1536, with a stone edifice completed a year later. To celebrate the momentous occasion for the town that became San Juan Bautista del Teúl, Pacheco lured the cacique's son and daughter down from the ceremonial hill to be converted and baptized.[17]

Along with the protracted siege in El Teúl and the violent upheaval of the Mixtón War (1540–42), Francisco Tenamaztle also demonstrated a counternarrative to the whitewashed discovery of silver and settlement in the region. The rebellion pitted the Caxcanes and Zacatecos, alongside other groups in the region, against the Spanish forces from Guadalajara, as supervised by Viceroy Antonio de Mendoza and thirty thousand indigenous allies from Tlaxcala and the Valley of Mexico.[18] Slowing the advance of the Spanish in the hills between Zacatecas and Jalisco, Tenamaztle claimed to be the rightful king of the Caxcan people, having established his reign in the southwestern city of Nochistlán de Mejía. The Spanish attempted to appease Tenamaztle but faced considerable opposition even after the indigenous leader adopted Christianity. Stubborn and bellicose in the face of growing odds, Tenamaztle represented a tenacious character in holding back the Spanish advance, in contrast to the recurring narrative of European-indigenous relations. Moreover, Tenamaztle and the Mixtón War represented the first of a string of violent uprisings as the Spanish attempted to forge El Camino Real de Tierra Adentro, the thousand-mile trail connecting Mexico City to the silver cities in north-central Mexico and into present-day southwestern U.S. states such as New Mexico.

The European founding of the city of Zacatecas came just twenty-five years after the fall of Tenochtitlan in 1521 to Hernán Cortés and his men. Cortés encouraged his lieutenant to follow the river systems westward and north, particularly the Lerma-Santiago waterways.[19] While Nuño de Guzmán led the efforts to settle the region in the viceroyalty of Nueva Galicia, Juan de Tolosa received the charge of exploring the hinterlands after the Mixtón War. The existing tensions with the indigenous inhabitants, as well as the foreboding landscape, informed Tolosa's approach to settling Zacatecas. On 8 September 1546 Juan de Tolosa led a small contingent to a valley near a strange-looking mountain. The mountain appeared to have a spine, almost like that of a creature in mid-dive, submerging itself in a sea of rock. The Spanish soldiers remarked that it resembled part of the shriveled innards of a sheep, or a *bufa*, an ancient Basque word meaning "sheep's bladder." At the base of Cerro de la Bufa, the Spanish approached the local Zacatecos, in a nonthreatening manner, in an attempt to appease them. The Zacatecos responded in kind, according to local historians, by presenting the Spanish with several stones. Enveloped in a dull exterior, the stones revealed a high silver content, which only served to spur European interest.

The settlement of Zacatecas inspired the imagery on its royal colonial seal that associated mining with divinity, lending extraction a degree of holiness. After settling in the region, Juan de Tolosa supervised the growing population and the first mines while also following the orders of Cristóbal de Oñate in Guadalajara by building a church. When King Charles I and Viceroy Antonio de Mendoza recognized Zacatecas as part of New Spain in 1548, they granted the growing mining town an *escudo*, or royal seal in the shape of shield. On the escudo, the Virgin Mary holds the Christ Child while levitating under La Bufa mountain. At the bottom of the scene four men gaze up at the Madonna and the mountain. The figures of Juan de Tolosa, Baltasar de Bañuelos, Diego Ibarra, and Cristóbal de Oñate marvel at the divinity under the Bufa in the image, prompting the city's nickname, "City of the Four Conquistadors." With the Virgin Mary under the mountain, like a precious metal, the seal equated a search for silver with spiritual awakening, or rather silver as salvation. The Spanish endeavor to look inward and downward signified that the divine symbol on the earthly rock created a link between the precious metal and the divine. On the escudo, the phrase "Labor Omnia Vincit," or "work conquers all," struck an ominous tone, given the empire's voracious appetite for precious metals and the dangerous conditions of mining. The Spanish arrivals in the region sought silver and salvation, according to this royal shield. Moreover, the shield revealed how the Crown constructed its narrative of power in its new territory. By way of Christian imagery, mining served as a path to salvation to the benefit of both Crown and worker, as miners dug for silver and their souls.

The location and the mineral wealth of Zacatecas spawned a bloodline, both familial and metaphorical, that kept the Spanish Crown financially afloat for centuries. Juan de Tolosa succeeded in his quest for silver and received royal attention for being among the founders of the city. Along with Diego Ibarra, he received land from the Crown and established a mine north of the city called Real de Panuco. As a "reward" for bravery and noble achievements, he married Leonor Cortés Moctezuma, the daughter of the Mexica princess Isabel Moctezuma Xoyocotzin and the Spanish colonizer Hernán Cortés, which brought additional fortune. In Panuco, the couple had three children, including a daughter named after her baptized Aztec grandmother. This daughter, Isabel de Tolosa Cortés Moctezuma, married a son of Cristóbal de Oñate, Juan de Oñate, who eventually became an early settler in New Mexico.[20] The younger Oñate later extended the silver highway, the Camino Real de Tierra Adentro, into the U.S. Southwest through violent campaigns. The *camino* represented the origin story of the region, where the names Oñate and Tolosa, for example, carried cultural and political weight into the corners of the territory. Notably, many silver cities on the Camino Real shared a mining history similar to that of Zacatecas, inviting future comparative discussions.

The Three *M*s—Miners, Money, and Mercury

The establishment of the silver economy in the Americas incorporated European technology, Spanish investment, and indigenous labor to produce wealth that sustained the expansion of Spanish territory. Merchants, such as Bartolomé de Medina from Seville, imported amalgamation techniques, which eventually became standard in silver mining towns. In Pachuca, Hidalgo, Medina turned raw ore, or rock, into silver in 1554 by using mercury and salts.[21] The heavy use

2. The four Spanish conquistadors and the Virgin Mary on the colonial *escudo* (royal shield) of Zacatecas. Unknown artist, *Virgen de los Zacatecas o alegoría de la fundación de Zacatecas*, from the 1700s. Image from Instituto Nacional de Antropología e Historia, https://mediateca.inah.gob.mx/repositorio/islandora/object/pintura%3A2346.

of mercury in colonial mines raised questions of supply. At the time of Spanish settlement in Zacatecas, mercury came from Almadén in Spain, a well-known cinnabar mine supervised by a German banking family referred to as the Fugger House. Buoyed by a stream of labor, mercury, and investment, Zacatecas grew exponentially, from an outpost in the hinterlands of New Spain to a booming mining city. Its surroundings changed as well: cattle ranches moved into the grasslands, forests fell to provide fuel, and streams pooled to provide drink for humans, beasts, and mining.[22]

As one of the principal silver mining cities of the colonial era, Zacatecas boomed into a thriving city by way of the three *Ms*— miners, money, and mercury. Miners emerged as central to the extraction process in silver production, namely because of changes in New Spain's approach to labor. In 1550 Zacatecas moved to establish its indigenous inhabitants as *indios libres*, under the supervision of a judge, Oidor Martínez de la Marcha. Although economic reasons rather than humanitarian reasons lay behind the change, the *oidor* sought to provide an incentive for settlement and to lure skilled laborers who would benefit the mining community.[23] Meanwhile, wage laborers in the mines faced exploitation, as in the case of *tequío*. This practice allowed mine owners to pay for a set quantity of ore in exchange for a specific amount of money, granting them a network of laborers to extend beyond their property.[24] In addition, the viceroyalty ended its forced labor counterpart, the *repartimiento*, by the seventeenth century and started to rely on wage labor, although African slavery and debt peonage continued.[25] The indigenous population continued to grow in the region, as many saw an opportunity to escape the labor draft in other parts of the viceroyalty and to avoid paying tribute in their home communities.[26] As the community expanded, indigenous merchants arrived with new skills and products, laying the foundation for a market and artisan economy.[27]

Next, merchants and other investors also profited from the mining economy, providing the next *M*—money. New Spain investors contributed to and invested in mines while also pouring money into haciendas for ranching, crop agriculture, mining, or a mix of these. Some historians suggested that the alliance between miners and merchants spurred development in the Bajío region at the center of the country, a stone's throw from Zacatecas and other mining cities, such as Guanajuato.[28] For example, merchants in Mexico City earned far more than their counterparts in Cádiz, indicating they had capital to invest.[29] Investment in mining in the region signaled the growing power of the merchant class to develop economic interests in silver cities in central Mexico.

Lastly, miners required a third *M*, mercury, to produce silver, making it a crucial commodity with a demand that spanned continents and oceans. As Peter Bakewell has written, the viceroyalties in the Americas struggled to maintain a steady flow of the heavy metal to mining sites in New Spain and South America, often dependent on investments to facilitate the exchange.[30] Despite its vital role in production, mercury contributed to adverse health effects in workers. In South America, the *mita*, or forced labor draft, exposed thousands of mostly indigenous workers to toxic substances in the silver mines. *Mitayos*, or workers in this slave system, described the notorious mercury mine in Huancavelica as the "mine of death," while the *mita* itself represented a sure death in the seventeenth century.[31] Miners in Huancavelica experienced tremors, insomnia, rage, birth defects, and diminished fertility.[32] In areas of concentrated refining activity, women who traveled with their spouses to the work site experienced high rates of miscarriage, and, if they had infants, they saw their children die soon after the move to Potosí.[33]

In addition to facilitating mining activity, the three *M*s also spawned structures of power and ideas about nature that informed the ecology of extraction. The funds pouring into the city to finance and sustain the nascent mining industry created unequal access to wealth. Workers toiling in mines without major investors found themselves moving at a snail's pace through the rock. In contrast, mine owners with sufficient funds hired a larger number of men to follow a vein through the earth or provided them with additional tools, such as dynamite, in the hunt for silver. Meanwhile, some miners rejected working under a boss and instead struck out on their own. These *gambusinos*, or small-scale speculators, worked by themselves or in small groups, often skirting around property owners to mine lands they did not own. While miners negotiated and resisted where they worked and how, they also formulated ideas about nature through their daily labor. Mines emerged as a place for stories about nature.[34] Reading the veins, draining underground water, and giving the mine anthropomorphic qualities—all these activities illustrated a connection that gave meaning to nature and significance to labor. Miners wove folktales about underground activities and created mining legends as cautionary tales. Mine owners lent the caverns an air of superstition or myth with exotic mine names such as Mina Hercules or Mina El Porvenir. Sites of extraction emerged as places burdened with narratives inscribed in the cavernous rock like another sedimentary layer.

Mining and Amalgamation Methods

After the three *M*s had been secured, the different methods of turning raw ore into silver stirred debate among European engineers and local workers, pitting theory against practice. Mexican silver production relied largely on German amalgamation methods using Spanish mercury to enrich the coffers of the empire. In overseeing the vacillating zeniths and nadirs of silver production, Fausto Elhuyar supervised the Tribunal of Mining in New Spain in the late eighteenth century. In addition, he recruited German engineers and adopted metallurgical engineering methods for increasing productivity in New Spain's silver mines, thus cultivating European techniques in new landscapes. Because of his efforts, Elhuyar stirred significant discussion on engineering techniques in the 1780s with the new Born amalgamation method and the Nordenflict mission to South America. European engineers boasted, on more than one occasion, that these methods demonstrated the efficiency and quality control that the patio process never had.

The patio process quickly dominated early silver refining in Zacatecas and became the preferred method for turning raw ore into silver,

3. The patio amalgamation process as captured by Pietro (Pedro) Gualdi (1808–57) in his painting, titled *Patio de la Hacienda de Beneficio de la Mina de Proaño en Zacatecas*, 1840. Sotheby's sold this painting at auction under the title *Hacienda Nueva de Fresnillo con el Cerro de Proaño*, Zacatecas, Mexico. Image from Instituto Nacional de Antropología e Historia, México, https://mediateca.inah.gob.mx/repositorio/islandora/object/pintura%3A4068.

a transformation that revealed how the methods used in New Spain frustrated European engineers. As Saul Guerrero has observed, patio amalgamation remained consistent through the colonial era, even with silver smelting becoming increasingly common in the state of Zacatecas.[35] Despite efforts to introduce more efficient methods, Zacatecas silver workers preferred this process well into the twentieth century. The Italian painter Pietro Gualdi (1808–57) painted *Patio de la Hacienda de Beneficio de la Mina de Proaño en Zacatecas* (1840), which depicted the mining and refining of silver in the Cerro near Fresnillo, Zacatecas. The large *tableau* illustrated the steps of patio amalgamation. First, the mule train hauled the raw ore down from the hill to a large hacienda patio, where a mule-powered wheel crushed the rock into dust. Workers spread the pulverized rock into large circular *tortas*, roughly five to seven meters across, on open-air patios and began mixing salts into the ore powder.

Next, mules pulled rakes through the dusty ore to stir in copper pyrites, and the mixture was then left to rest. Days later, a specialist in mercury (an *azoguero*) added in the amalgamating metal, the quantity of which depended largely on the mixture's consistency. Over the course of days or weeks, depending on humidity and rain, the mixture quite literally "pulled" silver from the ore. Workers then rinsed the mixture in large pools before straining it through cloth, which drew out any remaining mercury, sloughing away any excess materials into a stream or river. A quick bake in the oven cooked out any remaining mercury. Finally, the refinery workers had a silvery clump called a *piña*, fittingly the size of a pineapple. The expansive display of *tortas* and pools in Gualdi's painting illustrated the impressive number of silver production sites in a single refining hacienda.[36]

Moreover, the painting displayed a larger context of work and resources. The use of organic actors, humans and animals, for the extraction of inorganic materials turned mining in New Spain into not only a social and economic process but also a chemical process on the molecular level. Humans and animals engaged with the process and did not simply serve as bystanders. Requiring constant monitoring, the silver ore mingled with mercury by way of carbon, salts, and a steady stirring as horses hitched to rakes pulled them through the mixture. The patio process generated bonds of a chemical nature as well as bonds between humans and animals. This harnessing of chemistry for the purpose of wealth relied on the empirical talents of *azogueros*, the power of horses, and a reliable climate. The ecology of extraction did not isolate any organism but rather depended on each organism's role in the process in order to transform rock into silver.

The other chemistry—of exploitation and colonization—expanded with the importation of new amalgamation techniques, and it concentrated knowledge of these methods into the hands of a few individuals not directly involved in the labor process. In the eighteenth century Fausto Elhuyar received instructions to study New Spain's mining industry in order to increase the production and quality of metals extracted. Friedrich Sonneschmid (1763–1824), an engineer and respected metallurgist, joined him with the goal of applying the Born technique. Educated in Vienna, the Hungarian scientist Ignaz von Born (1742–91) had received plaudits for his treatise on a new amalgamation method, which quickly gained a following in New Spain's mining circles. Hailed as an efficient counterpart to the capricious patio process, the method combined physics and chemistry to concentrate silver or gold with minimal use of mercury. The Marqués del Apartado and his brother Don José Fagoaga eagerly petitioned Elhuyar to test the Born process on his land in Sombrerete, Zacatecas.[37] Initial tests of the Born process in Europe revealed an increased efficiency of amalgamation—roughly eight to twelve hours and not days or weeks, as with the patio process. Moreover, the new method required less mercury, preserving the crucial metallurgical agent for other purposes. With the possibility of facilitating a quick turnaround in refining, Elhuyar and Sonneschmid began their amalgamation trials in September 1792.

With the Born method, Fagoaga's workers and the engineers followed a calculated procedure that used motion as well as the introduction of salts and mercury at precise moments during agitation of the mixture. The Born process required Sonneschmid to build large ore-roasting ovens. Miners and mule teams hitched to a wheel still needed to grind the ore down in order for "baking" to occur. For the heating, workers used a calcination process, heating the ore to high temperatures with limited exposure to oxygen, and then mixed in alkaline salt to produce a potentially combustible reaction with mercury, other salts, and copper pyrites.[38] The second step in the process took advantage of the potential combustion and required the construction of several barrels (roughly a dozen). Workers sealed the barrels and turned them on their sides to be rotated by horses or mules.[39] Each of the contraptions in Born's method had almost ten boilers, rotated by a sliding rake, which attached to a water wheel or horse-powered winch.[40]

Unlike the patio process, the Born process utilized a mechanized and highly calculated chemical reaction in the production of silver, which appealed to mine owners, scientists, and engineers. After careful stamping and grinding of the ore into a fine powder, workers added salts, repeating the grinding and sifting of the powder.[41] Next, mixing followed in a process called trituration, which involved assuring a uniformity of the crushed ore in order to distribute the salt evenly. A washing of the ore afterward assured the breakdown of residue compounds clinging to the valuable gold and silver. Workers then loaded the ore into large wooden barrels and began a lengthy process of rotating the barrels while heating them over a fire. Because of the intersection of physics (the rotation and agitation) as well as chemistry (the heating and alkalines), both motion and temperature needed to be consistent, requiring a constant source of heat as well as tireless muscle (provided by mules in the Sombrerete trial). During this stage workers added mercury, following Born's instructions, to assure even distribution of the mercury in the rotating cask. Through heat and motion, the mercury acted upon the ore as the precious metal emerged at the bottom of the circulating drum. A final heating produced silver.

The Born process failed in Sombrerete. Supplies of timber and wood had diminished from the region after two centuries of mining, which caused investors to balk. By the time Sonneschmid arrived, the vast amounts needed for both the barrels and sliding rake were not available.[42] A lack of wood sources also created inadequate and inconsistent heat in the boilers. Furthermore, the German carpenter accompanying Sonneschmid grew frustrated with the lack of technical skills among local workers, according to the historian Clement Motten, who noted that this did not imply lack of capacity but "merely a lack of training."[43] Perhaps more tellingly, workers simply had not worked extensively with lumber and woodcrafting. Their lack of experience hinted at the absence of forests as well as the long-entrenched preference for the patio process. Overall, Fausto Elhuyar and the German engineers hired to streamline silver amalgamation in New Spain blamed the native-born workers. Both cited the disorganized manner in which mining, refining, and oversight occurred in Zacatecas and its outskirts, characterizing those activities as "serpentine and irregular."[44] Despite Sonneschmid's best efforts, the Born process failed in New Spain.

While the preference for the patio system remained in place well into the twentieth century, the types of mines in Zacatecas changed according to the era. In the colonial period workers dug into a mountainside through an outcrop with a slight slope to it and then broke off into different branches of mines. In the nineteenth century, miners built drift mines, or horizontal entries into mountains, so that they could lay track, which facilitated the removal of the ore rocks. By the late nineteenth century, miners lowered themselves through any number of vertical shafts to access the mines that appeared like deep shelves around them.

Mining Codes and Ownership after Independence

In September 1810, Fr. Miguel Hidalgo launched the Wars of Independence with his Grito de Dolores, or Cry of Independence. The Grito referenced the land stolen from indigenous and native-born peoples and indirectly alluded to the concentration of wealth into a few hands. Father Hidalgo led a growing militia and rabble, which swept through Guanajuato's state capital, the mining city of Guanajuato. The following year, Hidalgo and his followers passed through Zacatecas while attempting to flee to the north. Throughout his campaign, he frequently emphasized the loss of lands to the Spanish. Fittingly, his argument resonated with the mining communities in central Mexico, and his movement continued even after his execution in 1811.

After independence in 1821, the nascent government established mining codes, which defined ownership as well as the limits of ownership on resources. Foreign ownership and the use of water eroded the initial legislation for protecting metals and water sources over the course of the nineteenth century. The newly formed congress encouraged silver production to proceed unregulated by granting unrestricted access to mercury in the country after 1824.[45] Mercury had been closely monitored throughout the colonial period, as it offered a way of measuring silver production. For the new republic, mercury availability allowed an influx of foreign investors in mining and refining. Two years later Lorenzo de Zavala, the president of the Senate, pushed for a *junta de minería* to supervise mining investment and bureaucracy while effectively facilitating the purchase of mines by foreign investors.[46] Finally, years later, the government decreed on 11 March 1842 that foreigners could receive permission to acquire and hold property in order to "augment the wealth and safety of the nation," according to Antonio López de Santa Anna, president of the republic.[47] Initially, foreign investors received the right to purchase mines only if they discovered metal ore deposits. By 12 July, foreign owners of mines had gained the same rights as citizens in purchasing property, regardless of a mine's condition or age.[48] The steady erosion of Mexican ownership had begun in the years immediately after independence and not during the Porfiriato, as historians of modern Mexico emphasize. With the freedom to purchase and sell their property, foreign investors in 1826 had access to mineral resources and the right to exploit them a full fifty years before the Porfiriato (1876–1910).

As legislators stripped restrictions against foreign ownership of land and mineral rights over the nineteenth century, mine owners also sought access to water sources in mines for use in the amalgamation process and for domestic use. During the excavation process, miners inevitably uncovered springs, pools, or even underground lakes fed by ancient aquifers. The Law of 11 April 1849 granted mine owners the rights to newly discovered underground water sources but retained their responsibility to indemnify neighboring mine owners if flooding or stream diversion inundated others' property.[49] Moreover, mine owners agreed to maintain drainage at the work site while providing workers a ventilated area.[50] City engineers purportedly visited each mine once a year to see that owners met all of the requirements, as outlined in the 31 July 1849 amendment to the law.[51]

The Mining Code of 1884 attempted to draw further foreign investment by modifying the *denuncio* period, or period for declaring ownership of mines, and lowering taxes on silver production. In reducing the amount of time for filing claims of ownership, mine owners had an opportunity to "amplify their belongings," as stated in the code's initial goals.[52] In these denuncios, or claims, potential buyers of mines declared to the city their intent to purchase by posting an announcement in newspapers, and if no one came forward to counter the claim, the claimant proceeded to complete the property transfer. Previously, buyers could claim an abandoned mine only after it had not been worked for at least ten years, per the Law of 11 April 1849.[53] By 1884, buyers had gained the right to purchase mines after they had been left idle for only four to six months (depending on the region) or for up to a year.[54] In addition, they sought mines deemed misused or badly maintained with regard to ventilation or drainage, making the yearly visits by city engineers all the more important.[55] Consequently, the mining code facilitated the purchase and claiming of mines by foreign interests.

While the code streamlined the process for buying land, domestic and foreign buyers still had to contend with the local mining council. Cities that had mines in their environs relied on mining councils to regulate and supervise local mining activity. Council members consisted of appointed representatives and judicial council members, who had legal expertise. At the state level, members of the Junta de Minería supervised the industry and reported to the governor while also communicating with the city mining council, water board (*abasto de agua*), and other council members.

In contrast to other mining cities, Zacatecas faced a distinct environmental challenge with regard to its water management. Its high-elevation location on an arid plateau made underground aquifers vital. Streams, lakes, and small rivers depended largely on natural springs or rain. In drought years or a short wet season, water did not flow in the riverbeds, leaving them a mere trickle before becoming muddy and stagnant. Farmers, city dwellers, and miners consequently relied on springs, wells, or nearby streams for water. City officials in the nineteenth century walked a careful balance in supervising the growing public health concern and in monitoring the water supply to both residents and the mining industry. In this precarious scenario, municipal government officials saw water and public health concerns overlap, producing a gray area where protective legislation and business interests clashed.

While legislation encouraged the purchase of and investment in land after independence, mining speculators faced local opposition over the use of water as farmers complained about the use of streams for mining activities. Mexican legislators enacted a series of mining laws over the course of the nineteenth century due to federal government interest in finding sources of income as well as increasing pressure from foreign governments to allow their citizens to invest in Mexico. The Ordenanza de Minería of 1823 permitted foreign ownership of existing mines.[56] Mexican investors and local markets encouraged the influx of investment after the Wars of Independence. Alienated from Spain, Mexicans scrambled to keep enterprises and investment viable while limiting access by potential foreign investors. In effect, they slowed the potential takeover by British or American speculators by creating competition with locals. Local investors still sought out the most competitive mines, yet they often competed with the general public for the right to use water. In Zacatecas, silver speculators and residents alike contended with the increasingly dire lack of water. Consequently, they squabbled by means of claims filed with the local mining council. Juan de Dios Melitón claimed as his property the Mina Santa Bárbara in the mining hacienda of Sagrada Familia on 21 June 1825.[57] He and his business partners began the obligatory sixty-day waiting period before commencing work. Pedro Ramírez raised an objection to the potential sale, citing the well and water wheel near the entrance of the mine, because he along with nearby neighbors drew water from these sites. Ramírez argued that the loss of water access not only alienated the hacienda community but also denied the general public access to their drinking water.[58] Melitón, frustrated by the snail-like bureaucratic process, wrote in September of his willingness to give the water away or fill receptacles provided by those who objected if only he could proceed with work in the mine.[59] In the end, the city's mining council delayed a decision on both claims and asked for further evaluation before issuing a ruling.

Melitón and his fellow investors represented the contentious atmosphere surrounding claims filed on mines in the region. With the 1823 ordinance facilitating foreign ownership of existing mines, locals scrambled to finalize their own ownership claims. The competition drove many to purchase work plans or to secure mines inherited from family through wills and testaments. Many sought the finality accompanying a deed if they worked the mine. However, Melitón and other investors revealed their intentions to speculate. They attempted to seek brief profit from the mines, as signaled when they offered to give the water to the community free of charge. Mining relied heavily on the accessibility of water. Therefore, Melitón might not have been planning a long-term investment but rather a quick turnaround, counting on eventual foreign buyers. In addition, Ramírez represented a community willing to counter the influential mining investors to secure access to water. Farmers typically resisted any other entity's encroachment on water sources, a struggle emphasized in subsequent chapters. Moreover, they also relied on the consistency of water sources to irrigate *ejidos*, or smaller lots devoted to food production, in addition to providing water for cattle. Melitón and Ramírez essentially illustrated the two sides to water management—the former wished to give away water if it meant continuing a mining investment and the latter pushed back against mining, the city's primary economic driver, if it meant not having access to water. These attitudes underscored every debate between the mining sector and the community regarding access.

Nonetheless, investors proceeded cautiously nationwide as political turmoil continued to rock the countryside. Insurgencies and invasions made investment risky to say the least. Agustín Iturbide served as emperor briefly (1822–23) after independence, only to have his reign rebuffed by a succession of military efforts led by Guadalupe Victoria and Antonio López de Santa Anna. Santa Anna and his eleven presidencies between 1833 and 1855 gave foreign investors reason to hesitate. Moreover, the Spanish attempted to regain the former colony in 1829 with attacks on cities along the Gulf coast, and the U.S.-Mexico War (1846–48) interrupted supply lines and financial resources. Due to external and internal turmoil, mining speculators proceeded cautiously in their investments and claims.

Meanwhile, secessionist militias in Zacatecas further destabilized the country and the mining industry in 1835, which added to the growing tension between the state capital and the president. Angered by Santa Anna's centralist demands and the forced reduction of state militias, Don Francisco García Salinas (1786–1841) outlined a plan of secession with the blessing of the state's congress on 14 February. Adding to the animosity, the remaining bitterness from Santa Anna's previous meddling in mining affairs lingered. Santa Anna had angered investors and locals in 1833 when he ordered the sale of the silver holdings in the city mint in order to pay for a conflict with the Spanish, a transaction that flooded the market and drove prices down.[60] Investors, already anxious from the discussion of further turmoil, grew even more wary when disaster struck in the state capital. Workers at a gunpowder factory outside the city accidentally detonated 360 barrels of explosives, killing more than 50 people on 20 February 1835. The explosion launched the victims' mutilated bodies and building materials hundreds of yards, further unnerving the population.[61] Santa Anna now had an additional reason to march into the city, as this explosion might be seen as a military threat to the rest of the country, despite the accidental nature of the disaster. Prepared to lead the army himself, the president assumed his military uniform with the intent of crushing the rebellion. The state's military failed to anticipate Santa Anna's plan of attack and pushed eastward. The general-president adroitly maneuvered his forces and placed his army between the city and the troops assigned to defend it. Consequently, he brutally quashed this rebellion and nearly destroyed the city in retaliation. Adding salt to the wound, he ordered his soldiers to send any silver in the city's mint to his personal hacienda, Manga de Clavo, in Veracruz, according to historian Will Fowler.[62]

Mining Codes and Ownership during the Porfiriato

With the flash of a pen, the Porfirian government nullified all previous mining laws and gathered all mining legislation under the
Mining Code of 1884. It passed a subsequent law in 1892 with the
intent to invite further foreign investment in the sector. Matías
Romero, during his time as ambassador to the United States (1859–
98), faced mounting pressure to simplify the mining codes and
facilitate foreign ownership of land and mineral rights.[63] In contrast
to the 1823 ordinance, legislators in 1884 allowed foreign specula-
tion of untapped mineral veins but insisted on the state granting
permission to investors first in order to maintain some degree of
domestic control. For investors, taxes emerged as a central issue. Lot
size determined the tax amount, but the city allowed individuals
to petition for tax reductions. Owners subsequently provided an
assessment by an evaluator to calculate reduced taxes.[64] Legislators
tried to lure even more foreign investors with a revised mining code
in 1892. With the changes to the new law, titleholders in good standing with regard to tax payments gained the right to freely exploit
their land without the need for any special concession from the
Secretaría de Fomento, Colonización, e Industira (the secretary of
development, colonization, and industry).[65] Furthermore, with full
title to the land, foreign investors retained rights to all new water
sources and silver veins discovered.[66] Thus, owners gained the rights
to all current and future profits.

Worker safety had long been a priority in mining ordinances in
the colonial and postindependence period, at least in writing. Title
IX in the Ordinance of 22 May 1783 emphasized that the lives of
the workers be "of the greatest importance" and emphasized ventilation.[67] Ventilation remained a structural feature of mine design
for safety and practicality. In digging the network of mines that
extended away from the entrance, miners relied on vertical shafts
(*tiros*) for ventilation, supplies, and an emergency exit. The reliability of these shafts offered some degree of security for miners.
In addition, owners had to keep water from accumulating around

workers' legs, a difficult task in a region with aquifers. Given the dangers of slipping and falling, workers also wished to avoid the underground water, as its cold temperature contributed to chills, aches and pains, and other ailments. These precautions outlined the first efforts to provide miners some degree of safety in the mines. As discussed later, *tiros* served as an access point to water when the city faced a dire drought.

Potential owners filing claims to existing or new mines experienced different levels of bureaucratic wrangling in their filings before and after the Mining Code of 1884, depending on their background. Juan Briseño filed a claim for a mine called Hercules in 1882. He detailed the mine's location, near the already established Mina Uriel in the north of city.[68] No one responded to his newspaper claim, and he then received the go-ahead. However, the archivist at the Oficina de Denuncios failed to find the file for the mine, a necessary procedure in the course of recording ownership and calculating taxes. Nonetheless, Briseño received ownership of the mine after the archivist settled the matter, and he proceeded with the purchase despite the initial confusion. Why did the ownership process proceed despite the hiccup? While he and the archivist might have shared a mutual acquaintance, Briseño had the advantage of being local and a Mexican national.

Indeed, investors perceived by city officials as being well connected, wealthy, or with foreign ties had a more difficult time before passage of the Mining Code of 1884. Carlos Birkbeck, the son of an U.S. businessman and his Mexican wife, claimed a mine in 1866. His father, Samuel Bradford Birkbeck, had traveled from Edwards County, Illinois, in 1838 and arrived in Zacatecas with the intention of investing his inheritance and participating in silver mining. He married Damiana Valdés and settled into the silver mining business.[69] In an effort to provide order to a rather chaotic process, he established a ranking system for workers in silver mines, according to David Macmillan and Brian Plomley. *Paleros*, or timber workers, kept the fires fed, *arreadores* drove the horses, and *capitanes* examined the ore for quality, as carefully outlined by Birkbeck.[70] Samuel soon experienced problems at the mint, or Casa de Moneda, although his diary did not reveal specifics.[71] Nonetheless, his actions and bitter relations with his business contacts may have influenced the decisions made against his son, Carlos. When Carlos submitted his claim, he quickly received a request for more money. He blamed the prejudice against him on a change in personnel, writing that *mala voluntad*, or "ill will," kept him from completing his tasks.[72] He further described his problem in a metaphor involving water. He argued that casual observations revealed water flowed down a mountain and not up. Therefore, the water at the bottom (himself) had little to do with the direction of flow at the top (the mining council). Carlos rescinded his claim and soon after followed his father to Queensland, Australia, where he died in 1883.[73]

The Birkbecks struggled with bias against outsiders, military campaigns, and a frequently unstable government before leaving for Australia. Patriarch Samuel Birkbeck wrote in his diary of being called "Spaniard" and "Jew" on his voyage from Veracruz to Mexico City.[74] Moreover, he experienced the anxiety of clashing military campaigns on his home turf and fears that the conflict would envelop his family. After the War of the Reforms (1857–61), the patriarch decided to relocate to the Land Down Under to avoid the forced conscription of his sons.[75] The Birkbecks illustrated the early presence of speculators who settled in Zacatecas and faced a stalwart bureaucracy while initially investing in mining. Nonetheless, the continued unrest in the country drove many to seek investment opportunities elsewhere.

For the most part, before the Mining Code of 1884, foreign investors received the cooperation of the local mining council in Zacatecas and attempted to convince the council of the problems regarding water. Grégoire Fermin, a Frenchman, claimed a mine in 1879 and easily received ownership of the land. He listed all the necessary information in his claim for Mina Nueva Potosí, noting in his petition its location relative to other mines and its abandoned state.[76] His claim proceeded without a hitch, and he soon received ownership. Meanwhile, the mining council in Zacatecas also worked

with major investors with foreign ties in order to keep their investments viable when they stumbled financially. Anthony "Antonio"
Kimball applied for a reduction in taxes for his part in Mina Que-
bradilla in April 1877.[77] While silver production remained steady
at 26.5 million pesos in the country that year, Kimball cited a drop
in local production and limited funds as his tax deadline loomed.[78]
Because mine owners paid taxes every three months over the course
of the year, the local mining council reduced Kimball's mining tax
to 200 pesos for the remaining eight months of the year.[79] Indeed,
they adjusted the fees knowing local businesses counted on foreign
investment in the region. However, in an October 1877 update
regarding the state of the mine, Kimball hinted at the overuse of
the steam-powered water pump, which allowed workers to clear a
mine of water in a shorter time. But where did the water go after
workers pumped it from the mine? While some mines pumped the
water into local streams, others provided local pools near mines for
locals to draw from, a mutually beneficial concession to the community. While Kimball did not specify, he alerted the city to the
opportunity for a water source in this same letter.[80] He recognized
the need to keep locals happy and cooperating with foreign mining
interests. A simple gesture, such as providing water, earned some
degree of tolerance.

After 1884, the new mining code complicated the claims process
by requiring those registering denuncios to provide a more detailed
record of existing mines. Fernando Calderón, a representative and
investor with the mining company San Pascual y Anexas, filed a
claim for La Plomosa in 1889 and identified Camilo Gallinar as the
former owner.[81] While he provided all of the necessary information,
Calderón found himself surrounded by a cloud of suspicion when
Gallinar arrived to argue that he did not own the mine and that
erroneous information had been given. Lic. Francisco Tenorio then
arrived to correct the original petition and claimed ownership of the
mine himself, arguing that the mining site described in Calderón's
denuncio actually referred to the ominously titled Mina El Porvenir.[82]
Tenorio slowed Calderón's claim with bureaucratic interference and

filed a brief railing against the prospector, the mining council, and mining code.[83] In his diatribe, he emphasized the need for *denunciantes* to provide the address of the rightful former owner to initiate the opportunity for counterclaim, as stated in Articles 61 and 62 of the Mining Code of 1884. Tenorio then informed the local mining council of the nonexistence of San Pascual y Anexas, Calderón's alleged company. In railing against the council, Tenorio hinted at an underlying corruption that willfully ignored the background of new investors in the name of profit. Furthermore, he insisted that there was no record of La Plomosa ever having existed. Finally, Tenorio argued his ownership again, stating that El Porvenir belonged to him, along with the dividing wall between it and the neighboring mine, La Valenciana.

Pascual López Velarde, the head of the mining council, finally intervened at the request of both claimants. He named Alberto Rueda as an assessor of the case and ordered the archive to provide background on the cited region. Rueda discovered twelve different claims to the same vein, with many overlapping in the specific area mentioned in the initial denuncio.[84] The proximity and cluster of mines sparked confusion in the archivist's office. While this bungled job explained Fernando Calderón's initial mistake, it also hinted at his immediate problems. Indeed, he remained a suspicious character because of his nonexistent company, which López Velarde reiterated. Furthermore, workers approached the council and notified its members of their anxiety over having worked in Calderón's "imaginary" company, San Pascual y Anexas. Despite his bumbling counterpart's headaches, Tenorio shared some of the blame for the debacle. As stipulated by the mining code, owners needed to work the mine, or pay employees to do so, in order to keep the mine viable and productive. Calderón filed the initial claim on 19 March 1889, and Tenorio countered six days later. López Velarde pointed out in his argument for the council that the mine appeared to have been worked recently and the workers on site did not respond to questions about whether they followed a regular schedule. The six-day period gave Tenorio enough time to send workers out and pretend to work the site, and López Velarde cited this as grounds to have a claim overturned.[85] Eventually, both men accepted the mining council's recommendation to call it a draw.

With the Mining Code of 1884, local mining councils demanded detailed information regarding the location, names of mines, and names of previous owners in order to correctly assign ownership while maintaining a degree of control in the rush to claim new sites. Enterprising individuals or mining companies, like the two parties mentioned above, faced a stonewalling bureaucracy when their denuncios did not contain the necessary information. In March 1891, Humberto Gómez Castellanos, along with Antonio Gómez Castellanos and Juan Goldman, filed a claim for Mina San Luis del Oro.[86] The Gómez Castellanos brothers came from Spain and joined Goldman, a German citizen, in investing in mines, but they quickly ran into trouble as they did not know who last owned the mine or the names of neighboring mines. The mining council tasked an already overwhelmed assessor, Pedro Espejo, to investigate. In the meantime, newspapers printed copies of the denuncio, and Jesús del Pueblo came forth. The mining council soon filed to dismiss the claim because of the counterclaims by the original owner, and the Gómez Castellanos/Goldman partnership failed. Moreover, Espejo used the opportunity to raise caution about accepting incomplete claims, especially from foreigners residing in the city.[87]

Despite the various pitfalls in filing a claim, more attentive applicants used the language of the Mining Code of 1884 to defend their interests. Agustín Buiza filed a formal denuncio for a mine, Cerro de San Andrés, with the Negociación Minera.[88] Unlike the Gómez Castellanos brothers or the parties in the Calderón/Tenorio debacle, Buiza took special care to write the claim in language that emphasized the city's gain. He described Mina Las Mercedes, its location with relation to other mines, and the general site in the western part of the city near refining haciendas. In addition, he detailed geographic features for the benefit of the assessor, describing how the stream San Clemente ran near the mine. Buiza noted that he wanted to start a refining hacienda to add value to the silver extracted from the mine. The hacienda already had a well, a small reservoir, and a water wheel to power mining and refining operations; the presence of the San Clemente stream was an added benefit. Nonetheless, Buiza argued that his hacienda required the stream to wash refined metals because his equipment frequently malfunctioned, leading to a considerable loss of metals in processing. He reminded the mining council of Article 95 in the Mining Code of 1884, which allowed mining and refining companies to use local streams in proximity to or on their mining sites. He insisted his company's use of the stream would not affect the city because he would not stop the flow, dam the stream, or alter its course as it made its way toward the populated area. Article 93 of the code gave local governments the right to dismiss any claim to streams, lakes, or springs if it threatened the water supply of the city. Regardless of its right to protect municipal water sources, the city did nothing and turned a blind eye to contamination generated by mining activity.

In short, denuncios served as a gatekeeping strategy to restrict access to mineral and water resources to parties deemed viable. The supervisory role of local mining councils soon gave way to a federal code that granted foreign companies greater access to mineral resources. Before the 1884 code, local mining councils had facilitated a way to monitor ownership of land and mines in order to assess production, local investment, and mining activity in general. Specifically, local officials oversaw the influence of foreign owners in extraction, keeping tabs on how much land they owned and how much wealth they accumulated in extracting Mexican ore. However, the supervising role of local officials fell to federal oversight on mining and water after 1884. With the government courting foreign investment, denuncios allowed foreign investors to identify mines with high turnover rates in ownership as well as mines with convenient water access.

Water: The Conduit for Public Health Crises

In the aftermath of the secessionist crisis in 1835, the global cholera pandemic struck the city of Zacatecas, forcing officials to begin protecting and managing water supplies.[89] As the scourge of its era, the disease *cholera morbus* and the body count left in its wake shaped public health efforts with regard to water management. As defined by examples in Europe and public health specialists, the idea of a "modern" city by the nineteenth century meant that it had to be clean, free of miasmatic odors, and open to circulating air, while water sources had to flow freely and be physically distant from the population.[90] In contrast, sickly citizens and filthy neighborhoods represented a menace to community health as a whole. The historian Charles Rosenberg has emphasized how cholera forced physicians to shift their focus from miasma theory to sanitation during the major global outbreaks in 1832 and 1866.[91] When John Snow, a London doctor, discovered water to be the conduit for cholera morbus (or specifically, its bacterium, *Vibrio cholerae*) in 1854, government officials stepped in to control community health, pushing cities headlong into modern water infrastructure.[92] As cholera shaped the community's approach to water with a public health focus, the Zacatecas mining industry slowed as residents monitored water sources and speculators kept their distance. The industry generated the traffic and brought outsiders into generally isolated communities, which led to the introduction of new illnesses in that preantibiotic era. Moreover, locals heightened their surveillance of water management and pushed city officials to fulfill their obligation of protecting the public's health. Indeed, after an outbreak in 1849, hospital workers in nearby Sauceda, Zacatecas, compiled for the state government a list of victims who died from August 1849 to July 1850. In this small town only twelve miles from the city of Zacatecas, with a population that fluctuated with the agricultural calendar and occasional mining booms, patients with cholera morbus suffered roughly a 60 percent mortality rate. Thirty-five men and thirty-four women died from the disease, as recorded at the local hospital, while thirty-eight men and fifty-four women survived.[93]

By 1853, Zacatecanos had faced a seasonal and persistent presence of cholera and remained unnerved, while mining speculators kept their distance. In November of that year the members of the local water board finally agreed to take preventive measures to lower the rate of the disease, voicing concern at the growing and frequent problem. Pedro Hernández, a city council member, issued an ominous statement that placed Zacatecas in the context of a worldwide epidemic. He described with increasing alarm a circular from London forwarded by the Junta de Sanidad, which placed the disease's origin in Persia. Hernández ended his statement with a list of three measures to prevent future outbreaks in Zacatecas, as suggested by the Junta de Sanidad. Therefore, to guard the populace from future outbreaks, the local water commission outlined a proposal to provide, "with security and abundance," water to the city of Zacatecas. Although Hernández did not clarify the methods, this suggestion meant to direct citizens to water sources on the outskirts of the city, especially springs that showed little contact with people or livestock. Moreover, he urged the commission to ban "great accumulations of putrid waters" as well as to prepare a budget. As worded, the recommendation sought to fault locals in the event they allowed water to pool and breed disease. In truth, it provided indirectly the first measures for sanitation and sewage management in the region. Although it seemed an unlikely prospect at the time, this inkling of a water and wastewater system quickly became a probability as cities pushed to create or modernize water management systems to protect the health of their populations. In addition, Hernández urged the city council to commit to addressing this pressing issue. Hernández and his colleagues vocalized the growing frustration with water management in the region, particularly in the face of a serious public health crisis.[94] However, forty years passed before the city installed a reliable water system to mirror the efforts in Mexico City. Historians have detailed Mexico City's measures to protect public health by improving the drainage and sewage systems, as doctors and legislators equated cleanliness and modernity with salubrious conditions during the Porfiriato.[95]

Cholera revealed a dynamic city ill prepared to face the existential crisis of deciding between providing water for its citizens versus kowtowing to its mining industry. Like Melitón and Ramírez in their fight over stream access, mining had an interest in water and resisted efforts to isolate water sources from industry. However, mining also served as the principal draw for the city, and with clean water an increasing priority, the challenges to both industry and water infrastructure lay ahead. Overall, these tensions arose with the fundamental question of whether there would be enough water for both. Bacteria could be passed between individuals as well as through water, facilitating the initial crisis with cholera. Moreover, mining speculators understood their ties to local water sources as ephemeral and utilitarian, as their long-term concerns did not include water. They did not have a vested interest in protecting this source. In contrast, locals monitored water, complained if the direction of flow changed, and used the water for what they viewed as long-term investments: livestock herds, agricultural fields, and domestic use. These two perceptions foreshadowed an inevitable clash.

On 10 March 1854, Hernández outlined a proposal in which willing local landowners dug wells on their land for public use if the city funded the project.[96] Recognizing the city's need for a ready source of clean water, the owners outlined several conditions. They conceded their land for public use only if the city paid an initial fee and covered the cost of drilling. The fee amount depended largely on the quality of the water drawn from the well. The owners received 3,000 pesos for potable water and 1,000 pesos if the water contained high amounts of sulfur or sediment. Likewise, if the well water quality or the levels dropped, the owners agreed to refund part of the money. In addition, the city also agreed to pay an overseer to monitor the machinery for drawing water. The proposal received quick approval on the condition that all parties clarified the terms of the agreement. While the city's sole condition appeared to settle the problem, municipal officials supplied rather slow-operating equipment. Seven years later, in April 1861, Juan Corristan offered to sell the city a steam-powered water pump to facilitate the drawing of water.[97] Although Felipe Parra, a city council member, approved Corristan's asking price, the date of sale indicated a snail-like bureaucratic response to acquiring technology that would provide water for the public. Mining speculators, meanwhile, dealt with their mines' difficult geographic location, wrestled for control over resources needed to operate the mine, and budgeted for water drilling equipment as well as high city fees and taxes.

After passage of the Mining Code of 1884, mining entrepreneurs flocked to Zacatecas for its proven reputation in silver production as local residents soon suffered health consequences due to the spike in mining. From the national capital, Porfirian legislators failed to account for the harmful effects of mine runoff on townspeople who accessed contaminated sources for cooking, cleaning, and drinking. The code granted mining corporations access to water sources but limited legal recourse for municipalities. Mexico City–based legislators imagined mining centers as isolated and distant from populations, but Zacatecas mines existed in and around the city, as did streams and springs. Consequently, water carried heavy metals used in mining into the farming plots and fountains of the residents. Just as the national legislation trickled down to local mining operations, so did the toxins residents consumed at their local wells and fountains.

While some mining sites on the outskirts of the city affected the quality of water flowing in, city engineer Luis Córdova issued a call for better public health measures in September 1885, which involved Arroyo de la Plata, a stream that flowed through the center.[98] The stream, he noted, contributed unhealthy miasmas to the list of toxic fumes already present in the center of the city. Locals believed miasmas contributed to the growth of disease, which reflected the commonly held view that persisted even after germ theory emerged in the late nineteenth century. Córdova suggested this common association between water and human health, one that saw flowing water as healthy and salubrious. Stagnant and still waters posed a threat by producing noisome smells, spawning dangerous ailments, and harboring waterborne illnesses. By providing basic services, the city could see its residents benefit from proper drains and sewer maintenance while avoiding a potential health crisis, he argued. In this case, Córdova endorsed municipal government intervention to keep the populace healthy. Despite his good intentions, reality revealed a lack of clarity on the relationship between mining and water. Because foreign enterprises accessed water near their mines and away from the public eye, as in the case of Buiza above, concerned individuals like Córdova did not grasp the enormity of the impact mining had on the community water supply. However, the number of residents suffering heavy metal poisoning in Zacatecas posed research challenges due to countless variables in the level and method of absorption, as well as the lack of self-reporting and hospital records.

In the meantime, Zacatecas locals took it upon themselves to identify the fetid pools before miasmas affected the community. They eventually cast judgment on their neighbors for not draining stagnant water and for adding to the miasmas with a different kind of watering hole. Zacatecas shop owners busied themselves with the morally questionable souls who wandered through respectable businesses downtown in the Calle de la Merced Nueva. The Mining Code of 1884 spawned another economy—small shops catering to the population of salesmen, miners, and families trailing the mining industry. The new arrivals inevitably clashed with locals' definitions of decency. Doctors, pharmacists, and naturopaths soon condemned *pulquerías* and bars as "pernicious" places that offended the health and decency of the population.[99] The concerned business owners reminded the city of its obligation to serve as "guarantor of the most precious guarantees" in the neighborhood, referring to health and safety. These business types denounced the taverns for enabling laziness, "stimulat[ing] the passions," and causing scandals among the population. Moreover, they reiterated the dangers to family and the public health, echoing Luis Córdova's argument regarding water. They registered their complaints with a focus on preventing problems by improving public morality and public health in an effort to highlight how lascivious enterprises spawned future epidemics. The patrons of taverns and *tocinerías* suffered from, as the authors of the complaint put it, *gases sulfo-amoniacales*, and perhaps more distressing, *mefitismo pútrido*, which a decomposing body produced, according to the anxious entrepreneurs. More nerve-wracking still, miasmas threatened not only the public's health but also the morality of unfortunate witnesses to the bacchanalian revelry, according to the offended authors. Pressured by this aggressive rhetoric, city officials relented and agreed to move the taverns to the outskirts of the city and to monitor the source of *escándalos*.[100] Like Córdova and his petition, citizens who decried the activities at these local establishments sought to control public health by restricting others' behavior. They attempted to curb behavior that threatened public health as they sought to wash away any undesirable pools of their population.

While mining remained a dominant industry, the shop owners highlighted the growing concern among the populace for public health and efforts to prevent large-scale epidemics. Residents still recalled the cholera epidemic in the region and wished to prevent a second outbreak. Moreover, they linked local consumers of alcohol to the larger question of morality as taverns menaced the health of the community. Like Córdova, the merchants sought intervention from the city to control, regulate, and enforce new restrictions on imbibing and scandalous behavior. In short, they desired moral order. Certain individuals likely to live near stagnant or dirty water or to visit *tabernas* with a wayward companion on their arm apparently presented a greater threat to public health than questionable mining practices. Despite these wishes for enforcement, the concerned citizens did not recognize the potentially toxic outcomes from the mining industry.

Conclusion: Blurring the Lines

From its volcanic history to water use in mining activities, the city of Zacatecas consistently erased the boundaries between the humans and nature. A geological history offers insight into the origin of silver, the principal reason Spaniards flocked to the region. With the metal as the primary draw, the European arrivals illustrated the social interest in an elemental component. Consequently, extraction and colonialism commenced based on the belief that mineral wealth enriched individuals while providing upward social mobility. In addition, the methods of extraction did not recognize borders when it came to the processing of ore. German financiers and engineers arrived in the city at the behest of Spanish interests, making Zacatecas a site of global investment. Techniques applied in mining and refining also originated in other countries or regions of Latin America. While workers often came from the region, the mine owners did not, as many foreign investors coveted silver and flocked to Zacatecas to make their fortunes. Furthermore, the interaction between human bodies and the environment illustrated a dynamic relationship unrelated to culture or alleged hierarchy. In effect, the environment influenced the health of humans, often spurring enactment of public health measures to correct the blurring of boundaries, as in the case of cholera. Finally, mining became central to the city's identity and to residents' daily life. As mining became more important to the city's economy, locals questioned the industry's water use, resulting in legal fights over water. Water emerged as the central resource to both life and silver mining in the region. In many cases, it served as a tangible link between the residents aboveground and the resources below.

2

The Home

Drought, Wells, and Bodies of Water

EVERY MONTH, THE MUNICIPAL ENGINEER IN SAN JUAN de la Isla, Zacatecas, received a questionnaire, and every month, he responded the same. Gov. Eduardo Pankhurst and his government issued regular inquiries about forest use, mining extraction, and news in communities surrounding the capital in an effort to quantify accessible resources. Yet this engineer simply wrote "No hay" in response to the same two questions from 1901 to 1903: "What type of mining and refining exists in the region?" and "What types of lumber exist in the region?"[1] The engineer's responses suggested a lasting impact of two events that had swept the region in the previous decades: the mining boom in the 1880s and the financial crisis of 1893. With the doors kicked open by the Mining Code of 1884, speculators and investors flooded into the region, betting on silver mining. However, the crisis quickly diminished hopes of overnight wealth as silver markets plunged. Adding to the troubles, drought set in. The combination of an economic downturn and a prolonged drought affected the management of resources in the city, illustrating the mutual dependency between industry and community.

This chapter is about control. Facing the crash of silver prices and a devastating drought, municipal officials sought to secure water, workers, and financial resources in order to assure the survival of the city and its industry. In controlling water, engineers attempted to limit the damage done by alternating drought and flooding. Periods of drought forced Zacatecanos to draw water from reservoirs one pail at a time only to be followed then by heavy rains that produced mudslides and flooded streets. The drastic changes in climate forced municipal officials to take the initial steps toward establishing a water distribution system while considering sanitation measures. Municipal officials also sought to demonstrate the modernizing of Zacatecas even as workers fled to other states in the aftermath of the financial crisis, which left the city devoid of local revenue. Meanwhile, as workers sought opportunities elsewhere, mining investors lacked capital after the crisis, which forced the city to contend with a lack of funds to complete the water distribution project. The efforts to establish control extended to installing new technology and implementing measures to protect meager natural resources, such as firewood and lakes. Overall, city officials attempted to control the three resources—water, workers, and money—that made Zacatecas a viable mining city in order to evince modernity during the Porfiriato.

Federal and municipal officials attempted to control resources by way of two prevailing currents in the era: positivism and public health. Auguste Comte (1798–1857) outlined the philosophy of positivism as knowledge gleaned from phenomena. Therefore, knowledge came from observation, yet empirical data existed as relative and anecdotal.[2] Positivist technocrats used biology and, more specifically, physiology to underscore difference and classification in Mexican society. They delved into phrenology in order to explain aberrations in social progress; in effect, the technocrats sought to separate the undesirable elements that slowed innovation and development. In practice, Comtian positivists argued that social progress evolved over time and under the right environmental stimuli, urging water management while restricting human behavior deemed degenerative.

In Mexico, politicians in the late nineteenth century applied positivist ideas to water management through federal oversight on water and through scientific observation. At the local level, engineers and landowners typically managed water sources, until 1888, when the federal government passed the Law on General Means of Communications, extending the government's oversight to rivers.[3]

Yet, as Alejandro Tortolero Villaseñor has argued, this law illustrated a shift from local to federal control, a sudden change in water management with consequences for how municipalities managed their water sources. Meanwhile, the national government implemented a water management system in Mexico City to separate potable water from effluvia. In designing this system, they used an empirical approach to underscore the danger of intermingling waters, a not uncommon sight in the aftermath of frequent flooding in the city. In alerting residents of the national capital to the menace of water that lingered, of water not controlled, politicians warned about the potential public health effects.

Globally, beliefs about water began changing with the introduction of new ideas and technology. Whereas at the beginning of the nineteenth century water was an open resource for communities to use, municipal officials had begun to regulate and monitor its use by the end of the century. After the cholera pandemic of the 1830s, cities invested in water infrastructure and even more so after the release of John Snow's 1854 study in London. While Snow's research helped establish a sewage system in the British capital, Mexican *científicos* looked to Paris. With a potable water system operational by 1874 thanks to the Réservoir de Montsouris, the French capital provided the urban model for Mexican francophiles such as Porfirio Díaz. In Mexico City, the Gran Canal del Desagüe and the draining of the remnant of Lake Texcoco offered ambitious parallels in engineering control over water while at the same time modeling public health initiatives to keep effluvia at bay.

Public health motivated engineers in the city of Zacatecas to design water distribution systems that best served the needs of the public. Faced with sporadic flooding rains and droughts, the distribution system illustrated a modern solution to a distressing issue in the context of the Porfiriato. The Zacatecas project sought to reflect the national focus on public health while it placed the city on a par with other urban centers equipped with modern systems that separated effluvia from that for distribution. While the project promoted a healthy community, it also mirrored the positivist trend as well as the influence of miasma theory on urban planning around the world. In this model, cities made public health a priority in water infrastructure by recognizing that water served as a conduit for disease, especially cholera. As a result, engineers and municipal officials emphasized a separation of "good" waters from "bad" waters. The clean "good" water hydrated human bodies and replenished family gardens in domestic use, while the "dirty" counterpart carried waste away, whether it be human, animal, or mining waste. Consequently, control of water meant implementing a system supervised by local governments and modeled in the national capital.

Through the framework of power, the ecology of extraction informed who accessed water and how, while at the same time distinguishing between water sources. In short, government officials at all levels obsessed over controlling nature, which emphasized a separation and sorting of resources as well as individuals. With a water distribution system, engineers and municipal officials distinguished between waters for domestic use and consumption versus effluvial waste from mining—a problematic scenario in a mining city. As the rhetoric of control and public health filtered down to locals, Zacatecas residents began to emphasize separation from and distance between those who reflected slovenly or immoral habits, even going so far as to report their neighbors. Many locals decided to move and distance themselves from the city after the economic crisis, while others sought to hold local officials to new standards.

This chapter examines how Zacatecanos sought to control natural and economic resources before and after the Mining Code of 1884. It defines resources in an inclusive manner, in not only environmental but also financial terms, such as capital. How Zacatecas locals viewed resources depended largely on the intended use, whether for domestic or economic purposes, which spawned a division in attitudes on how to manage them. By isolating the "undesirable" components of resources, municipal officials attempted to mirror and implement public health measures undertaken elsewhere, as well as to introduce water management to the mining city, with some success. This chapter begins with an examination of the alternating torrential rains and flooding followed by withering droughts, which exposed the challenges of installing a potable water system, a considerable struggle in a city surrounded by mining interests. Next, Zacatecas illustrates the consequences of long-term extractive industry, as both residents and companies scrounged for lumber as well as water sources. Nascent conservation efforts revealed a concern focused on the economic rather than the ecological, as lumber fueled fires used for beneficiation and smelting processes. Furthermore, the downturn in mining during the economic crisis of 1893 demonstrated how connected the region remained to the global silver market. Archival and notary sources have revealed that a number of shops shuttered their doors and nervous entrepreneurs begged for reductions in taxes. Finally, Zacatecanos pointed to their neighbors as a source of unsanitary conditions, suggesting that the rhetoric of public health influenced locals' opinions of others. Underscoring these examples, the theme of isolation or separation guided efforts to install a water distribution system and public health measures, signaling an attempt to impose order on an otherwise disorganized region.

The Context of Control

Legislation regarding water often went hand-in-hand with mining codes, which prompted the industry's attempt to wrest away some degree of control. In the colonial era, when the Crown or Church claimed ownership of land, water, minerals, and forests, Spaniards accessed water sources and pastures as part of the commons.[4] This un-limited use of natural resources allowed mining to grow in Zacatecas, while at the same time it granted residents access to the same wells and springs used by industry. The commons presented a double-edged sword—free, unlimited use as long as there was enough water for everyone. Consequently, industry and community came to an uneasy truce in Zacatecas as long as water sources satisfied both parties. After independence, the decentralization of authority culminated in extensive, unregulated resource use before a more concentrated approach resumed during the Porfiriato (1876–1910) and directed resources to specific industries. These "modernizing" industries included a wave of steam-powered technology as well as a new focus on water infrastructure, as evinced by the system of fountains in the national capital and the Gran Canal de Desagüe project. With this new infrastructure, resource use during the presidency of Porfirio Díaz initially reflected a positivistic approach, grounded in the ideals of improving health and society. In addition, advances and investments in the mining industry signaled further modernization and development, but in regions of extraction these efforts spawned approaches that contradicted efforts to bolster health and society. On one hand, municipalities faced pressure to model themselves after the national capital and implement water infrastructure to maintain a healthy populace. On the other hand, mining legislation allowed companies to access water sources with minimal hindrances and often without supervision. Zacatecas emerged as a site of this confluence of contradictory approaches.

Despite the growth and development of business and the mining industry, water management represented the social value of water. Scholars have previously identified water infrastructure as a reflection of how a city or community values the resource, yet environmental law professor Jamie Benidickson has argued that water could not be owned until someone put it to use, particularly after the introduction of sanitary systems.[5] In the context of Zacatecas, locals always employed water, whether through mining or domestic use, without regulation. Moreover, until the nineteenth century, the "tragedy of the commons" prevailed in the city, as unsupervised use allowed for wastefulness. Without checks on water use, the municipality conceded the resource to private interests, particularly after the Mining Code of 1884 and the economic boom in silver. Nonetheless, locals absorbed the Porfirian-era emphasis on public health and water and pressured the city to invest in water infrastructure.

In the late nineteenth century Zacatecas struggled with the consequences of mining as drought and a lack of water infrastructure set in, pushing the city into crisis. Without any trees or reliable water sources, the city increasingly relied on resources from other parts of the region. The city struggled to find a balance between industry and community as positivist models from the national capital drifted to state capitals. While models for infrastructure focused on Mexico City, the city of Zacatecas contended with larger challenges in the design and concept of water management while facing mounting pressure from economic interests. Specifically, because residents shared water with industrial interests, the municipal council encountered pressure from both deluged neighborhoods and parched farmers over mining's effects on water.

In order to implement resource management, a stable municipal government suggested and monitored programs to curb exploitation or overuse. However, stability proved difficult in Zacatecas, with its revolving-door municipal government. After independence, the Constitution of 1824 granted states the right to determine the political weight given to municipalities. Local politicians outlined provisions for education and basic services in addition to settling minor disputes and collecting tariffs on goods passing through the municipality. These political figures typically also constituted the municipal council, and from this cabal they elected a mayor. The mayor then supervised projects, like those involving water infrastructure, over the course of many months. The long-term supervision of these projects offered a degree of continuity as well as stability. By the time of the Porfiriato, the federal government sought to impose control over municipalities through the appointment of *jefes políticos*, which limited the sovereignty of local councils.[6] After the Constitution of 1857, liberals aligned themselves with municipal autonomy in an effort to balance the federalist influences at the state level. However, a crisis soon ensued among liberals, particularly after the rebellion of Jesús González Ortega (1822–81) against Pres. Benito Juárez in 1865. A loyal general during the French Intervention (1861–67), the Zacatecas military figure questioned the need for Juárez to remain in power during the crisis, especially since the Constitution of 1857 limited reelection.[7] Unimpressed by the revolt, Juárez ordered General González Ortega arrested in January 1867 during a visit to the city of Zacatecas.[8] While the general received a commutation of his prison sentence the following year, another political controversy continued to brew in the state capital. Trinidad García de la Cadena, a political ally and state powerhouse, became governor in September 1869, interjecting his interpretation of liberalism into the state and once again promoting municipal autonomy. The following year, he promoted the Plan Regenerador de San Luis, which continued the 1865 fight to depose Juárez and install none other than González Ortega. The plan also pushed for the reinstating of the Constitution of 1857 as well as state sovereignty. Juárez in turn invested heavily in quashing this rebellion with more than twenty thousand soldiers while appointing Gabriel García Elías as governor and removing Governor García de la Cadena. The humiliated governor fled the state and watched the new governor dismantle his goals and legacy. At the municipal level, García Elías appointed new jefes políticos and allowed them to choose new mayors. In addition, he granted them the right to change municipal structures as they saw fit. The Porfiriato saw increased influence of governors on local politics as Díaz consolidated power in the central government. While the mayors of Zacatecas remained on shaky footing, the governors of Zacatecas appeared to be comfortable in the seat of power. For example, Gen. Jesús Aréchiga served as interim or elected governor twenty-one different times from September 1880 to September 1900.[9] Even when not in power, he served as a shadow governor from 1884 to 1888, when his official role was as head of the federal forces in the state, even though Marcelino Morfín Chávez held the title of governor. Indeed, it appeared that the people of Zacatecas had failed to control their own government officials.

Mining and the Limits of Control

Mining investors, like bankers and miners in California, required not only financial capital but also the environmental resources of Zacatecas. Lt. W. W. Mather, a West Point professor of mineralogy and geology, composed a guide on mining and metallurgy in the nineteenth century for the intrepid U.S. investor of the era. Published in 1833, his detailed book on iron and silver production suggested how mining ventures needed water in addition to raw materials in order to thrive. Mather outlined the four factors needed to run a successful mining operation. First, he suggested testing the ore to determine quality before pursuing any significant investment.[10] Zacatecas, in contrast to Potosí in South America, consistently hauled ore of better quality from 1580 to 1750, despite producing less of it.[11] Speculators encountered low-grade ore veins on occasion, but generally Zacatecas and its Bajío counterpart, Guanajuato, produced good-quality ore. Second, Mather underscored the need for access to lead and mercury.[12] Miners and metallurgists often labored in remote areas that required regular shipments of these supplies as well as the raw materials. As a result, miners had to secure a reliable cart-and-horse delivery of these supplies and materials. Third, the lieutenant-professor underscored the importance of fuel to any venture's success.[13] However, he did not specify or recommend the best fuel for use in mining activities. Coal? Wood? In Zacatecas, nineteenth-century speculators contended with a dearth of wood for fuel, as four hundred years of mining had consumed any available fuel sources near the capital. Given the demand for fuel, farmers brought wood from villages and the mountains to sell in the city.[14] If necessary, miners relied on dried cattle dung to heat boilers.[15] Finally, water served a critical purpose in these operations, according to Mather. It not only carried away other effluvia from excavation sites but also provided hydration for the animals and workers at the mine. Having a sufficient amount proved difficult as drought settled into the region during the 1890s. Moreover, residents on the outskirts of the city flocked to springs near mines or in mines to collect their daily supply of water. Access to springs, such as the one pictured here, depended on securing permission from landowners or having convenient access. Investors also contended with the lack of reliable water supplies. Not all refining operations had underground sources of water, and not all mines had streams nearby to carry away the detritus of operations. With mining and water availability taking a downturn, Mather's advice went largely unheeded in a flailing market, leaving investors to play a game of chance.

Municipal government officials faced an increasingly perilous situ-

4. A spring fills a pool as a group relaxes near Sombrerete. Used with permission from Concurso Tiempo, memoria y plata 2009, Colección Luis Fernando Sánchez Hernández. Fototeca del Estado de Zacatecas "Pedro Valtierra."

ation as mining operations attempted to control bodies of water that, in turn, nourished human bodies. Enrique Carrillo, the Zacatecas city engineer, penned an anxious letter to the local mining council in October 1884.[16] He nervously warned of how a local company sought to work a mine near La Encantada, one of the city's principal water wells and springs. Fed by an aquifer, La Encantada well shared its name with a neighboring mine. Engineers like Carrillo typically trained at either a university or an *escuela de minas*, such as the notable Escuela Práctica de Minería (est. 1854) in nearby Fresnillo.[17] These institutions also produced engineers who found employment in municipalities with industrial operations. Trained to develop expertise in mining, Carrillo alerted the mining council to the sale of property near the critical well. The buyer was Benito Palacios, who purchased the land in March 1884 with the approval of a member of the city council, Jesús Nava.

On a daily basis, locals visited La Encantada well, or *tiro*, to fetch the water they needed and to participate in the social scene, mingling with other members of the community. Overlooking La Encantada well, Palacios and his workers mined the hill and eventually hit freshwater sources. Soon they were working to drain the flooded mine. Meanwhile, locals saw the water levels in their well drop, illustrating how the underground aquifer fed La Encantada. Palacios, cognizant of the danger of tapping the city's water supply, willingly withdrew from the site and sealed the mine. However, Carrillo, the engineer, pointed to the city's culpability in the matter: local mining council officials knew of the mining in the area but kept quiet and let excavation in the vicinity of La Encantada proceed. The public outcry, as well as Carrillo's warnings, forced the city to intervene and withdraw the site from future purchase at the recommendation of the engineer.[18] Nevertheless, Refugio Contreras came forward to purchase the abandoned site.[19] Carrillo, in his efforts to curtail the filing of further *denuncios* for the mine, circumvented the city and asked the state legislative body to prohibit mining around La Encantada. Since the mining council did not issue a petition to the state's congress and Carrillo's suggestion never gained momentum, La

Encantada continued to be a point of contention for local residents and mining companies.

Carrillo and his efforts regarding La Encantada well came at a tense time for the local mining council. In the nation's capital, Pres. Manuel González Flores signed the Mining Code of 1884 and cities scrambled to prepare for it to take effect on 1 January 1885. Municipalities attempted to protect their water sources or to reassure the public that they would continue to have access to wells, ponds, and reservoirs called *presas*. Mining investors felt a renewed sense of confidence in exploring for minerals and metals in the country with the passage of the new code, as they received mineral rights to previously unexcavated regions in addition to water rights. Carrillo also questioned why municipal officials wavered before intervening to overturn the mining claim for La Encantada, especially since it threatened the water supply and thus threatened public health. The stalwart mining council members faced a question of loyalties: be a roadblock on the way to wealth and progress or fulfill locals' wish to have access to water? Locals also valued the La Encantada well for other reasons. The tiro not only provided affordable water to the southern part of the city but also hosted a hub of communal activity. Gossip, business deals, flirtations, and other social interactions flitted around the well. The decreasing water levels muddied locals' opinions of the mining council and clouded community-building activity. Nonetheless, officials did little. Refugio Contreras and his workers did not proceed with their claim, avoiding further tension and conflict.

Mine operators on occasion offered to help contribute to the city's water supply. In June 1893, Pedro Gutiérrez notified the local *abasto de agua* of a self-replenishing spring in his mine; his communication demonstrated clear intent to sign a contract to sell water to the city. The spring's location suggested an ample water supply from a source seventy to eight meters deep.[20] Gutiérrez and his workers drained the water using a horse-powered hoist, or *malacate*, for hours but did not lower the water level by even a meter. His offer to sell water to the city came with free use of the hoist in addition to rotating the four horse positions with others in his forty-head herd. Despite his generous offer to contribute to the water supply, the city turned him down. Notably, the exchanges between the parties neglected to disclose a price for these services.

Miners also evinced concern for the general public with regard to water contamination during the course of mining operations, albeit more as a courtesy. In 1899, I. F. E. Cordary notified the local mining council of his intention to drain brackish waters from his six mines into *pluviales*, or rainwater collection sites providing fresh water for residents in the region.[21] Cordary did not indicate where the water came from or what compounds had been added during the mining process. Typically, miners and metallurgists worked in proximity to streams at their mining and refining sites, often using salts during the patio amalgamation process as well as for the flotation method of extracting metal from ores. This brackish runoff possibly also carried heavy metals used in amalgamation, such as lead, mercury, or zinc. The city offered no response, but Cordary reiterated his expectations that the briny water would simply wash away with minimal inconvenience. Moreover, by this time the city had a more reliable water source via fountains in the city, even though the well at La Encantada remained in use.

Both Carrillo and Gutiérrez demonstrated different cultural approaches in handling and managing water even as the city faced drought and dwindling reservoirs. In their estimation, water served an important function in daily mining operations, a point of view that ideologically separated water for mining from water for consumption. From 1890 to 1899, locals saw water availability diminish considerably due to severe drought and contested resource use among economic interests. Thus, municipal council members increased their vigilance in terms of water consumption and asked locals to draw water from La Encantada and nearby wells. Nonetheless, they remained hesitant to confront mining interests even as the drought settled in and exacerbated the situation. Carrillo wrote a letter of objection while Gutiérrez sought to ameliorate the situation by offering his services, albeit at a price. Cordary, however, disposed of briny *aguas saladas* near public drinking water supplies, warning the city only as a courtesy. Human consumption underscored these discussions, which presented mine water as separate and vital to the mining process. Cordary distinguished the effluvia from the public drinking water despite disposing of mining waste in cisterns used by locals. Gutiérrez presumably only proposed his idea to glean some profit. With locals removed from this discussion and treated as an unrelated third party, the essential link between a healthy community and good water quality received no attention. Humans and the community only entered the rhetorical fray with engineer Carrillo's argument, which underscored the threat to the community. Porfirian technocrats echoed these sentiments when they outlined the water projects in the national capital. They emphasized how regulating and monitoring water demonstrated orderliness in a city.[22] Water management exemplified Porfirian-era Mexico, whose capital city undertook drainage and sewage projects to control and limit the force of nature's inconvenient deluges.[23]

Limits of Control

Deluge

Residents and industry drank from the same metaphorical well, blurring the distance between humans and mining while raising the question of public health. Because city and industry could not be separated, locals had to adjust the traditional cultural weight assigned to cleanliness and a neat household. In Latin America the home typically illustrated honor and respectability in the domestic space. These expectations extended to servants of respectable families, since they too represented the private sphere in public spaces. Underscoring this perception, townspeople held wealthier and more elite members of society to a higher standard with regard to cleanliness in the home. Likewise, the working population adopted the same standards in an effort to mirror an honorable household and respectable family behavior. While practice appeared imperfect, the idea of domestic honor filtered down to influence social expectations.

Household members also attempted to model behavior by keeping an orderly home. In this cultural framework of high expectations, women did not go out without a chaperone, nor did they mingle with less desirable members of society; meanwhile, men behaved decently and not in a slovenly or drunken manner.

By the late nineteenth century, honor and respectability extended from the city center of Zacatecas, where the cathedral, government buildings, and central marketplace all lay within one block. While the description of honorable behaviors served as model and not reality, the ideas regarding respectability influenced the space of the city as well as the character of these spaces. The seat of respectability rested within the walls of the city's cathedral, as well as the nearby government buildings. Nuestra Señora de la Asunción began in 1729 as a small chapel and, with additions, grew over the next century to a cathedral. Its grand façade featured the Churrigueresque style, and in 1959 Pope John XXIII granted the building basilica status. The neighboring plaza held government offices extending from the cathedral's north side. On the south side, a large plaza once had fountains and stores, but they soon gave way to the Mercado Jesús González Ortega, a marketplace built in 1899 in the style of belle époque French markets. Thus, the well-to-do and those with honorable ambitions clung to the heart of the city, whether it be for the heart of Jesus or the heart of the republic, in order to glean honor and respectability through spatial association.

Yet, with the close relationship between the city and mining, the dust fell equally on everyone, along with mudslides and runoff. Residents of the city contended daily with the steep landscape surrounding the city center, as narrow alleys with cobblestone inclines reached outward from the colonial center in the late nineteenth century. Much of the traffic and social activity converged on what today is Avenida Hidalgo, near the cathedral and government buildings. Adding to the problem, the avenue curved through the city center at a slight slope, sending the mudslide from the hills west of Cerro de la Bufa down through the "respectable" part of the city. Because of the city's bowl-like shape, the detritus and effluvial waste from

5. The Mercado Jesús González Ortega on a busy market day. Library of Congress, Prints and Photographs Division, Frank and Frances Carpenter Collection, LC-USZ62-114768.

mines in the hills floated downhill and through the doorways of elites, as shown in a topographical city map from 1919. Mud, effluent from privies, refining materials, and other waste dirtied respectable households. Even in the most well-to-do section of the city, mining served as a constant reminder that the industry fueled municipal wealth, even at great cost.

While municipal officials claimed to prioritize water infrastructure in their rhetoric, they finally began introducing drainage projects at midcentury, but those projects soon faced interruptions, much to the chagrin of residents. By association, these projects underscored efforts to protect public health, while deluges added urgency. Public works initiated to provide potable water began in an attempt to control or limit the cascade of rainwater or mine waste from the mountains. They attempted to control water in a difficult setting: a city with steep, cobblestone-paved streets scaling the *cerros*. During the rainy season, the rugged topography frequently helped turn a wave from the hillsides and streets into a torrent of debris, filth, and mud. Tomás Lorck wrote to request that municipal officials

ZACATECAS

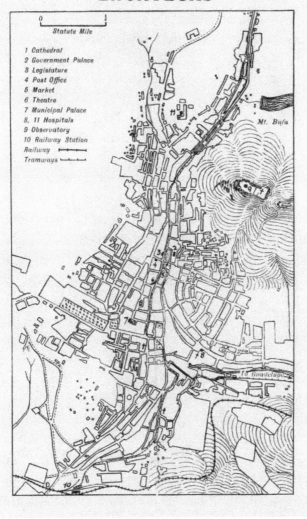

6. A city map of Zacatecas showing topographical features near the historic center.
From *Handbook of Mexico* (1919), Perry-Castañeda Map Collection. Courtesy of the
University of Texas Libraries, the University of Texas at Austin.

complete a half-hearted water infrastructure project on a neighboring street near his home in July 1884.[24] Municipal officials had
funded a drainage project in 1861 and hoped to create a network of
conduits channeling waste from smaller drain canals. The project
managed to rid some neighborhoods of wastewater, yet a principal drain near Lorck's house remained unfinished.[25] Lorck noted
how the drain remained uncovered, and when the other channels
fed into it, a waterfall formed, dropping into the channel below.
Consequently, a mist enveloped the drain and wafted into nearby
homes. The city, recognizing its past faults, urged the completion
of this drain the following month under the supervision of the city
engineer, Enrique Carrillo. Carrillo, who had cautioned the city
about mining near the drinking water source La Encantada earlier in
the year, now supervised this project's completion. The initial interruption of the project in July 1861 had stemmed from political and
national crises as well as upheaval in state politics. After beginning
this project in 1861, engineers had hastily halted it due to political
unrest in connection with the War of the Reform (1857–61) and the
French Intervention (1861–67). At the same time, Lic. Miguel Auza
handed the governorship to Jesús González Ortega in the midst of
the fight between conservatives and liberals in the region. Further
heightening tensions, cholera remained present in the city during
that year, hinting at a possibly rushed project.

María del Refugio Lamadrid de Mourell also alerted the city to
the frequent torrents flowing down her street after heavy rainfall in
November 1884. "A widow and a property owner," she enumerated
her property holdings lining San Roque, a street parallel to Avenida
Hidalgo and just west of the cathedral.[26] She wrote of how water
rushed down Cerro Grillo and into her neighborhood. The torrents
reached doorsteps and peeled the adobe from houses. According to
the widow, the city enabled these insalubrious conditions to persist
and brought illness to the neighborhood as well, not to mention
the possibility of damage to her property. The only directive issued
as a result of her complaint was for engineer Carrillo to monitor
the situation during the next rainfall.[27] Both Lorck and the widow

7. A man walking past the aqueduct along an unpaved road. The muddy streets indicate heavy rains, as do the walls of the houses on the left. Library of Congress, Prints and Photographs Division, Detroit Publishing Company Collection, LC-D 418-8336.

Lamadrid de Mourell witnessed extreme weather in 1884, with torrential rains and flash floods.

The U.S. photographer William Henry Jackson captured on film the evidence of recent rains. Wagon and cart tracks in the soil indicate a soggy trek, and mud-caked walls invited scornful glances and judgment about the character of those living in the dirty building. Ironically, as the aqueduct represented one straight, unwavering path of water, the street below revealed quite the opposite. Pedestrians and animals slogged through mud and runoff during rainy seasons while complaints flooded into municipal offices like the current flowing through the streets. Moreover, the encroachment of outside filth on the home violated social indicators of cleanliness. Locals tracked in the outside dirt, muddying not only floors but also the respectability of tenants.

Drought

In contrast to the flooding rains, drought offered an additional challenge that engineers failed to anticipate. While Mexico City modeled water infrastructure with its Gran Canal and fountains, smaller cities struggled to implement these changes. In Zacatecas, engineers failed to consider the longevity and severity of the drought even as the city counted on shrinking water sources. Whereas inundations underscored the need to control water, what measures could be taken to *capture* and *retain* water? Locals turned to springs or flooded mine shafts to draw their water as the city looked to its wells and reservoirs to find more suitable alternatives. In this case, the lack of control signified a lack of infrastructure to conserve water for times of exceptional need.

Wells and reservoirs represented this form of infrastructure and offered water ready for consumption in dire circumstances; they also offered the first ominous sign of prolonged drought. Engineer J. Rosa Aparicio contacted Jesús Aréchiga, the governor-general, regarding water levels on 30 April 1891. Aparicio warned that the water level in La Encantada well had dropped 25 cm, while La Reforma, another well, remained steady at a level of 3 m, 50 cm. Meanwhile, Presa Los Olivos and Presa García de la Cadena, two smaller reservoirs often used by locals as their water source, had dropped to, as the engineer put it, worrying levels. Presa San Bernabé held steady at 3 m, 25 cm and the Tenorio well at a solid 50 m. Despite those two bright spots, Aparicio warned the city that it lacked enough water to meet the needs of its residents. Two existing fountains remained in good state, he reported.[28] However, anxiety increased as the drought continued for the next two years.

By October 1891, municipal officials had seen the drought subside briefly enough to cause chaos. Waste from makeshift workshops in hillside homes as well as mountainside runoff sloughed into street drains, clogging channels. The city attempted to keep these sewers open and flowing. However, neighbors soon accused each other of contributing to the blockages. Tirso Arteaga pointed fingers at his neighbor, Señor Labat, who ran a match factory from his home. Labat allegedly dumped waste directly into the drain outside his home.[29] Consequently, the waste mingled with the water in the drain and filled the neighborhood with an acrid smell. Moreover, the drainage spout created a mist that condensed as malodorous water droplets on tile floors, windows, and walls.[30] Due to the heavy, persistent fog, tenants abandoned their tenements to the damp and left the area. Meanwhile, property owners rented out their houses rather than live in them. The municipality's response? The owner and tenant received only a warning. The indiscriminate disposal of waste and the unreliable climate further contributed to the city's water management woes. Wastewater represented water unfit for consumption and therefore not belonging near the populace, as the *vecinos*, or locals, living on Calle San Francisco insisted. Two years later, on 4 March 1893, neighbors on Calle San Francisco petitioned the city to fix their street.[31] The street, like that of the widow Lamadrid de Mourell, became a torrent of water during the rainy season. As the water rose to the doorsteps, the current sent debris into the drains, which made the flooding even worse. Nineteen neighbors beseeched the city to remedy the problem in the name of public health and safety. Understandably, residents dismissed the municipal government of Zacatecas as slow and unresponsive to needs in the community.

Adding to the disaster, Zacatecas saw silver mining, its lifeblood, disappear with the global collapse of silver prices, an economic calamity that further exacerbated clashes in local government. The Sherman Silver Purchase Act of 1890 encouraged U.S. and British investors to buy large-scale mining operations in northern Mexico. The act also allowed large purchases of silver to be converted into paper money. However, many participants in this exchange preferred gold, which they saw as the steadier and more stable metal. In combination with the Mining Code of 1884, speculators created a land grab in an effort to exploit the international silver market, thanks to the accessibility of Mexican mines. Within government circles, politicians contributed to the instability and inconsistency of water management in the city to a degree. The governorship changed hands often, from elected officials to interim governors to generals to local lawyers. The inconsistency caused delays in water management projects and often forced locals to take matters into their own hands, with persistent petitioning of municipal government. Zacatecas governors often interacted with local jefes políticos, which led to divisions in political relationships. Governor García de la Cadena (1823–86) unfortunately fell victim to this divisiveness.[32] An accomplished politician and mine owner, García de la Cadena maneuvered through the political minefield of the late nineteenth century, earning enemies in the process.

Pressured to leave his home state in September 1880 after his fourth turn as governor and after supporting an earlier rebellion against Pres. Benito Juárez, García de la Cadena lived in the national capital but continued to manage his mineral investments from afar. Governor-General Aréchiga viewed this as a seditious affront to his authority. (Notably, Aréchiga himself served as governor twenty-one times.) In the fall of 1886, García de la Cadena argued that he needed to travel to Zacatecas to visit his mining sites. Aréchiga ordered a small contingent to meet García de la Cadena at the San Tiburcio train station near the San Luis Potosí state line to halt his return to the state capital. Atenógenes Llamas, the local jefe político, joined this contingent. A confrontation ensued, and on 1 November 1886 Llamas shot the sixty-eight-year-old García de la Cadena six times, in full view of the public.

The instability of municipal and state leadership, as exemplified by the shooting at San Tiburcio, determined the success or failure of public works and was the cause of endless frustration. There were delays, half-completed projects, and volumes of locals' petitions to the municipal authorities. Moreover, this frequent confusion raised a question: if requests and municipal orders went missing, did funds disappear as well? Indeed, the only consistency suggested by the available archival sources, apart from the dire state of water, appeared to be engineers and the same residents beseeching the authorities for help, over and over again.

Population Woes

With drought looming and silver prices plummeting, municipal officials attempted to maintain the population in Zacatecas. Many

residents fled to other states as disasters loomed, and local businesses struggled to keep their doors open. Consequently, municipal officials lacked the tax revenue to install a water distribution
system, and the disappearing population diminished motivation
to develop such a system. It was local residents who had pressed for
the water management system, and without their urging it was up
to an increasingly unstable municipal government to muster the
will to build one.

There were several obvious reasons for the city's steady decline in
population between 1880 and 1910. When silver prices took a dive,
many miners scattered to agricultural properties throughout the
state, which remained largely rural with a majority of its population dedicated to haciendas, ranches, and community agriculture.[33]
In addition, many workers, particularly miners, migrated to other
silver cities in the state or to nearby states (such as Guanajuato).
In 1895, the General Census measured population as well as other
categories, such as occupation. In that initial census, the number
of miners in Zacatecas was 15,836, while the number of *peones de
campo* (farmhands) totaled 85,958 and *agricultores* (farmers) equaled
4,246 (fig. 1). Zacatecas had the highest number of miners in the
country that year. Next was Guanajuato, with 14,537 miners and
293,041 farmhands and, surprisingly, zero farmers identified for the
census. While the census data showed that all Zacatecas miners were
men, 706 women worked in mining in Guanajuato. Meanwhile,
207 men in Zacatecas worked as part of mining *administración*
and 100 labored in the beneficiation process, the method for concentrating ore of high quality. In contrast, Guanajuato had 456 in
beneficiating work and only 47 in administration. Other mining
states in central Mexico saw shifts in mining and agriculture during
a fifteen-year period (1895–1910), notably Durango, Hidalgo, and
San Luis Potosí.

These disparities suggest that more miners worked in Zacatecas
than in Guanajuato, which remained an agricultural state. In other
states with an active mining industry, such as Durango, Hidalgo,
and San Luis Potosí, the numbers of mine workers also decreased

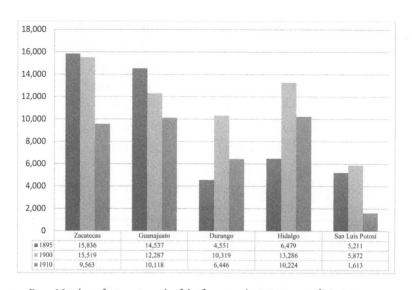

	Zacatecas	Guanajuato	Durango	Hidalgo	San Luis Potosí
▪ 1895	15,836	14,537	4,551	6,479	5,211
▪ 1900	15,519	12,287	10,319	13,286	5,872
▪ 1910	9,563	10,118	6,446	10,224	1,613

Fig. 1. Number of miners in each of the five central mining states of Mexico over a fifteen-year period. This figure is based on census data accessed online in August 2017 from Instituto Nacional de Estadística y Geografía, www.beta.inegi.org.mx. Sources: "Población según la ocupación principal," in *Censo General de 1895* (México DF: Instituto Nacional de Estadística y Geografía, online); "Población clasificada según el sistema Bertillon," in *Censo General de 1900* (México DF: Instituto Nacional de Estadística y Geografía, online); "Resumen general de población, según su ocupación principal," in *Censo de Población de los Estados Unidos Mexicanos 1910* (México DF: Instituto Nacional de Estadística y Geografía, online).

over that period. Where did mine workers go once mining collapsed after the silver crisis? Was agriculture a way out? With the loss of land tenure and foreign investors' significant presence in agricultural operations, miners in rural states decamped to farms, ranches, and haciendas to seek work. Only in Guanajuato did the number of *peones de campo* decrease over the period in question, although that figure increased slightly between 1900 and 1910 (fig. 2).

Regardless, the loss of miners to agriculture illustrated a devastating reduction in income for mining cities as a wave of residents migrated to the countryside. Did Guanajuato weather the forces concentrating land in foreign hands better than Zacatecas? How did the number of farm workers grow by more than 50,000 during the course of a decade in Durango? Despite these shifts in demograph-

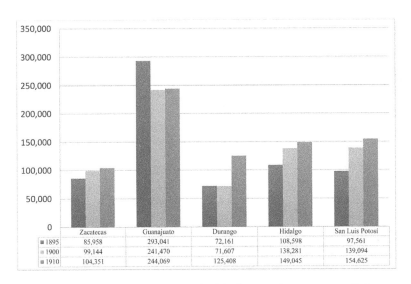

	Zacatecas	Guanajuato	Durango	Hidalgo	San Luis Potosí
■ 1895	85,958	293,041	72,161	108,598	97,561
■ 1900	99,144	241,470	71,607	138,281	139,094
■ 1910	104,351	244,069	125,408	149,045	154,625

Fig. 2. Number of *peones de campo* in each of the five central mining states of Mexico over a fifteen-year period. This figure is based on census data accessed online in August 2017 from Instituto Nacional de Estadística y Geografía, www.beta.inegi.org.mx. Sources: "Población según la ocupación principal," in *Censo General de 1895* (México DF: Instituto Nacional de Estadística y Geografía, online); "Población clasificada según el sistema Bertillon," in *Censo General de 1900* (México DF: Instituto Nacional de Estadística y Geografía, online); "Resumen general de población, según su ocupación principal," in *Censo de Población de los Estados Unidos Mexicanos 1910* (México DF: Instituto Nacional de Estadística y Geografía, online).

ics, the population of the state of Zacatecas grew from 452,278 in 1895 to 462,886 in 1900, and then to 477,556 in 1910.[34] The growth in state population signaled a shift away from mining and toward agricultural activity in the countryside.

However, if the shift was regional, how did the northern states fair in this pit-to-plow move? Notably, the four northern states of Sonora, Chihuahua, Coahuila, and Nuevo León all saw a rise in the number of miners over the same period (fig. 3). Why? U.S. mining corporations, such as the Guggenheim family–owned American Smelting and Refining Company, invested heavily in border states, drawing miners from floundering mining states across the country. In the 1895 General Census, the data collected included numbers of not only miners and administrators but also workers in *haciendas*

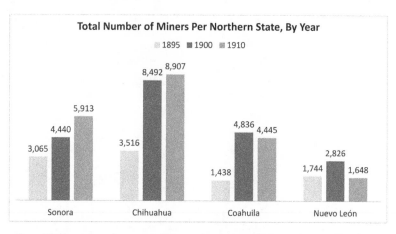

Fig. 3. Total number of miners in four northern states of Mexico, by year. This figure is based on census data accessed online in August 2017 from Instituto Nacional de Estadística y Geografía, www.beta.inegi.org.mx. Sources: "Población según la ocupación principal," in *Censo General de 1895* (México DF: Instituto Nacional de Estadística y Geografía, online); "Población clasificada según el sistema Bertillon," in *Censo General de 1900* (México DF: Instituto Nacional de Estadística y Geografía, online); "Resumen general de población, según su ocupación principal," in *Censo de Población de los Estados Unidos Mexicanos 1910* (México DF: Instituto Nacional de Estadística y Geografía, online).

de beneficio, or beneficiating estates.[35] Zacatecas had only about 100 workers in that sector of the industry; meanwhile, the central state of Hidalgo had 1,508 such workers, followed by Guanajuato with 456. In the north, Chihuahua led the way with 1,560 workers in *beneficio*, indicating a strength in refining rather than ore extraction.

The presence or absence of women in mining activity was another difference between central states and northern states. In the former, women had a negligible presence in the census statistics detailing participation in mining, especially in the 1895 census. Women's limited participation in mining suggests a hesitation on the part of male miners to allow them access to mines. Gendered constructions of mining, however, permeated the industry. Workers in mines tended to be men, yet they classified the mine in feminine rhetorical terms. Male miners employed gendered language in extraction—from the gendered noun (*la mina*) for their workplace to the gynocentric imagery of the mine as a womb, as Elizabeth Ferry shows.[36] They also prohibited women from entering the mine on the grounds of superstitions or cultural beliefs. Women did not enter the mine because the vein might become "jealous" or because the presence of women introduced bad luck, leading to cave-ins.[37] Nonetheless, women appeared in the census data devoted to mining for 1895, 1900, and 1910 in the central and northern states (table 1). Their numbers saw growth in some states in the last years of the nineteenth century while in others, such as Zacatecas, women never participated in mining, at least according to the census reports.

Table 1. Total number of women in mining per state, per year, according to census data

	1895	1900	1910[a]
Zacatecas	0	0	0
Guanajuato	706	103	0
Durango	0	0	0
Hidalgo	15 (9)*	22	0
San Luis Potosí	57 (56)*	121	0
Sonora	2	26	0
Chihuahua	14 (1)*	5	0
Coahuila	1	135	0
Nuevo León	92 (38)*	8	0

a. The 1910 census reported only one woman working in a mine in Querétaro.

Note: Numbers in parentheses and marked by asterisk (*) represent the number of women who worked in beneficiating. This number is included in the total number. Only the 1895 census distinguished between miners and those workers at beneficiating haciendas.

Sources: census data, Instituto Nacional de Estadística y Geografía, accessed August 2017, beta.inegi. org.mx, specifically: "Población según la ocupación principal," *Censo General de 1895*; "Población clasificada según el sistema Bertillon," *Censo General de 1900*; "Resumen general de población, según su ocupación principal," *Censo de Población de los Estados Unidos Mexicanos 1910*.

Between 1900 and 1910, women stepped away from mining work, for several possible reasons. The overall number of mining jobs shrank, as evidenced by the total number of miners in Zacatecas from 1895 to 1910 (see fig. 1). The collapse of silver prices throughout the country continued into the twentieth century, though the number of nonsilver mineral extraction corporations rose in number. In northern states, the growth in the number of miners indicated a boom in copper, lead, and other metals as a consequence of foreign investment. Private companies run by the Guggenheims and the Rockefellers, both of which owned growing stakes in various mining companies in the northern states, frequently determined whether miners' families would live in the region. Women often followed family members into the workplace regardless of mining companies' rules. If husbands or fathers worked in mines, women found positions sorting ore or working in beneficiating. When family members left the mines and returned to the countryside, women followed them, even if the numbers of farmhands did not accurately reflect their participation in agricultural camps. The presence of women, or the lack of women, in the census data raises questions. What made someone a miner? Was a miner solely the person who descended into the mine? In some cases, women participated in mining through sorting or crushing smaller rocks. In other cases, the personal bias of census takers possibly defined who constituted a miner.

Because of the peripatetic workforce, census data for Zacatecas varied. The state capital in 1910 saw a total population of 63,976, which included 31,451 in the urban center and 32,525 in communities surrounding the capital.[38] The 1910 population showed a significant drop from the 88,500 the state capital historian Elías Amador estimated in 1894.[39] Moreover, both estimates neglected the population of nearby Guadalupe, which identified as its own municipality and numbered 8,000 to 10,000 inhabitants. A largely agricultural and industrial center, Guadalupe had population numbers that vacillated considerably and often included its population with the state capital's total in unofficial estimates. Nonetheless, its numbers are included in the urban population number for 1910. Economically and socially, Zacatecas suffered a devastating population loss from the urban center between 1900 and 1910: 21 percent of the state capital's inhabitants.[40] Consequently, the state slipped into an economic depression with a largely rural population and a lack of infrastructure.

Engineering a Solution

In an effort to stop the backsliding trajectory of the city, engineers sought to control the only remedy they saw for the drought: a water distribution system. Water management prior to that time had largely stemmed from the positivist approach of separating "good" and "bad" water. While engineers struggled to find a suitable company to complete the contract, this project represented a shift in the Zacatecas approach to water: from one that saw water as utilitarian and part of the commons to one that protected the community to some degree. In addition, the water distribution system created an illusion of human control over water, with channels and fountains, even if the rains did not arrive.

Water management continued to falter after 1890, which added to the desperation of locals. Many locals took matters into their own hands and chided the municipal government for failing to address not a lack of water but flooding due to torrential rains. In 1893 a small coalition of neighbors, including Roque Llamas, Francisco Hernández, and Timoteo Herrera, among others, confronted the municipal assembly to express their frustration. They faced frequent inundations and cited numerous times that they had brought the issue to the city's attention, only to be ignored. Residents once again compelled the city to manage and to control the "bad" water that inundated their neighborhoods. While every resident had an opportunity to bring their complaints to the municipal government, certain citizens demanded a quicker response if they owned a business or lived closer to *el centro*. They insisted on the municipal government's role in limiting the infiltration of these insalubrious and torrential currents through respectable citizens' neighborhood. Their neighborhood, on the Calle de San Francisco and not far from the residence of the widow Lamadrid de Mourell, reflected the state of their homes, their health, and in turn, their morality.[41] They pointed to the lack of water infrastructure as the root of the menace. As with the Arteaga case, foul odors or moisture seeped into homes and brought the public filth very much into the private sphere, equalizing and dirtying all homes regardless of class. In addition, Zacatecas locals increasingly prioritized the availability of clean, "good" water to be consumed by the public. They had witnessed the devastation of cholera in earlier decades. Despite advances in germ theory in the 1880s, the public generally still cited miasmas as the cause for disease. Thus, they sought a more efficient network of channels to limit and control runoff that flowed into the city. By defining torrential rains, miasmas, and wastewater as threatening, locals classified what they did not control. Moreover, a distribution system of potable water granted some degree of containment and separation yet raised doubts with a drought on the horizon. Conversely, plentiful drinking water offered a picture of public health that preserved the salubrious, ordered state.

As the city sought to contain and to limit these torrents, municipal officials and the municipal water board attempted to engineer a distribution system to isolate potable water from the floodwaters. In the 1880s, landowners in the surrounding hills saw the municipality begin to encroach on water sources. In July 1886, Ignacio Bermiso, a landowner from the neighboring city of Guadalupe, denounced city engineers for installing without his permission a water filter at the small presa bordering his land.[42] In an attempt to secure water for the population, engineer Enrique Carrillo had intervened on private property. Bermiso cited an old claim to the water from early in 1882 in an effort to clarify ownership with the city. Now he argued that the city's water filter frequently clogged, causing the reservoir to rise over its banks.[43] In addition, the presa filled to the point that its waters joined those of a nearby presa, San Clemente. The resulting flood toppled houses and washed away adobe. Asking the municipal assembly to intervene in engineers' plans, Bermiso underscored how the flow menaced public health because the waters had commingled with mining waste. Bermiso did not receive a response to his petition; in contrast, Juan Pablo Martínez did. Martínez asked the city to lower the rent for wells on the slopes of the Cerro de la Bufa less than a month after Bermiso expressed his anger.[44] Officials with the local water board quickly approved the measure, indicating a plentiful supply of the resource from nearby presas.

In 1888, city officials and the water board presented a different approach to water management. Desperate to improve water access, the municipal government directed Miguel A. Rico to map the aquifer under the city streets, the goal being a pipeline between the aquifer and La Alameda plaza in the center of the city.[45] Farmers and cattle ranchers had written letters describing the pitiful state of their water resources. Farming and ranching activities still depended on access to rivers and streams, as well as springs that burst through the ground. In the city, however, engineers' attempt to tap the aquifer and pump water to a fountain at a more central location would serve the local public. Up to this time, locals had been forced to walk to presas for water or hire water carriers.

The worsening drought conditions in the region underscored the rural versus urban divide. Although rural inhabitants depended on water obtained directly from the source, urban officials attempted to engineer an industrial solution to water shortages. A pipeline and pump would not only bring water from the aquifer to a fountain in the city center; such a system would also provide less tangible benefits. It offered city officials a means of control over potable water, reducing the number of contacts that might pollute the resource. It also lent a degree of modernity to the city, reflecting the water infrastructure changes taking place in Mexico City. The earth beneath Zacatecas had been mined for silver ore, but with the crash of the silver market, the lack of rain, and the public need for safe drinking water, Zacatecas residents created an infrastructure to "mine" the earth for water.

Engineering Charlatans, Cheaters, and Hucksters

Desperation served as a beacon to swindlers and charlatans in Mexico, as many sought a quick fortune. Various individuals arrived in the city of Zacatecas claiming to be engineers but had little or no experience. Unsurprisingly, they demanded exorbitant fees and concessions to build a water distribution system while offering no timeline for its completion. Con artists sought official contracts with the city. Cheaters also interfered in the daily collection of water at wells and reservoirs. The dishonesty reflected a broader lack of accountability, which extended to the municipal officials. For example, locals such as Tomás Lorck, mentioned earlier, had personal experience with municipal officials who had not followed through on water infrastructure projects in previous decades or who half-heartedly agreed to complete them.

Enrique Carrillo, the city engineer, faced the task of hiring a company and crew adept enough to construct fountains, neighborhood drains, and pumps to bring water into the city. He screened and weeded through various companies, but deals repeatedly fell through due to money, problems with materials, or contract disputes. Finally, Luis Córdova recommended George "Jorge" Berliner, who in January 1889 offered his proposal to build the water distribution system.[46] Berliner, a self-proclaimed mining expert from the United States, had traveled to Zacatecas from San Francisco, California, in order to pursue new investments. He proposed to engineer and install a system to send 500,000 gallons a day to various fountains to serve 36,000 residents in the center of the city.[47] In addition, his system would steer storm water and sewage away from the city. The proposal came with a hefty fifty-year note of 833.33 pesos a year, not including maintenance fees. Municipal assembly members wisely rejected his offer, noting Berliner's lack of documented experience.[48] Berliner moved on to peddle his talents in other cities and spent the next six years traveling through the country. He ultimately departed Mexico in the most tragic way: in a box. Fascinated by the new steam-powered technology of the era, he wandered, against advice from companions, into the engine carriage of a train traveling between Veracruz and Puebla. He insisted on observing the steam engine at work.[49] While he gawked at the coals, steam, and gauges, the train derailed. After four days, he died of complications from the scalding burns that marked his body. His widow in San Francisco successfully sued Berliner's insurance company to recover life insurance from them and received a sizeable settlement.[50]

After the city declined Berliner's proposal, Luis and Guillermo Liebes lobbied for the water distribution contract a few months later, once again via Luis Córdova. The brothers offered a thirty-year note on a system to disperse five hundred thousand gallons a day, a comparable offer. Yet, they explicitly stated a guarantee: the company would always be Mexican, even if foreign members sat on their company's board.[51] In the wake of the Mining Code of 1884, city governments found enterprising foreign interests encroaching into municipal affairs. With this clause in the contract, the brothers Liebes presumably attempted to put city officials at ease. Moreover, foreign businesses had little interest in seeing these long-term city projects grow and develop over time. While this clause assuaged some city officials, the Liebes also included an eyebrow-raising clause in their contract: they desired from the city a guarantee that, should rebellion, acts of sedition, or political turmoil break out, the company would remain protected.[52] Did this inclusion hint at larger problems in the region? Zacatecas state government officials had attempted to secede in 1835, but tensions had calmed significantly since then. Had the Liebes brothers received xenophobic threats? While the motive for this clause remained unclear, other foreign businesses had not asked for such protection. More than likely, the political game of musical chairs surrounding the governorship, in addition to typhus epidemics, had unnerved many foreign interests. Nonetheless, engineer Carrillo and the Liebes brothers quibbled back and forth over the details of the contract, delaying the project for months.[53] Moreover, the Liebes brothers had not presented schematics for the project despite the negotiations, as one council member pointed out.[54] The brothers responded simply by noting that the presas had a steady supply, thus reducing the urgency for and the progress in planning for their project. In December 1889, Carrillo terminated the negotiations, despite Guillermo Liebes's individual efforts to petition for the project.[55]

Carrillo continued the search for engineers to install the city's water distribution system in 1891. Enrique Rougroy and José Fischweiler, two engineers from the state of México, had offered up a proposal the previous year.[56] They sent a letter to the city via local contact Jesús María Castañeda stating their excitement about the project while touting their credentials as European-trained "specialist engineers" and "specialists in hydraulic material" without specifying affiliation.[57] Their meandering and sycophantic communiqués to the assembly suggested a sluggish pace in the project's progress while the city continued its struggle to provide access to potable water even as a drought settled into the region. Despite earning the bid in November 1890, they had abandoned their masquerade as professional engineers by April 1891 and revealed themselves to be little more than hucksters. In his report for the week of 2 March 1891, J. Rosa Aparicio, the water supervisor, hinted at an impending disaster.[58] Three days later, the disaster seemed inevitable. As table 2 indicates, a dry spring had brought little rainfall, and the planting season was imminent.

Table 2. Water levels (meters) in local sources by date, 1891

Water sources	2 March	5 March	9 March	16 March	31 August
Tiro La Encantada	2.8	2.8	2.8	3.0	0.3
Tiro La Reforma	6.5	6.0	6.0	6.0	19.0
Presa San Bernabé	6.0	5.5	6.0	5.5	6.0
Presa El Tenorio	2.5	2.5	2.5	2.5	3.5
Presa García de la Cadena	n/a	n/a	n/a	n/a	5.5

Sources: March data from AHEZ, Jefatura Política de Zacatecas, Serie Correspondencia General, Subserie Abasto de Agua, Caja 1, Exp. n/a.; August data from AHEZ, Fondo Ayuntamiento, Serie Abasto de Agua, Caja 1, Exp. 91.

As the nearest and most popular source of water for household use, La Encantada proved particularly worrisome because its spring did not replace the water at the pace of the San Bernabé presa (table 2). While El Tenorio held steady, residents in the city center found it difficult to climb the rugged terrain to reach this northern spillway. Thus, Carrillo watched with growing alarm as water levels dropped at the spring-fed La Encantada well, and without rain to fill the aquifer feeding the springs, he welcomed the decision to finalize Rougroy and Fischweiler's contract on 6 March 1891. In a further act of desperation, Carrillo and the municipal government halted existing rental contracts on city wells. Juan Pablo Martínez, who had previously requested a reduction of his rent on city wells, already had plans to dig twenty to twenty-five new wells in order to reach the ancient aquifer deep under the city. Upon confirmation of the Rougroy and Fischweiler contract, Carrillo had placed those well access contracts on hold. Given the city's effort to protect all available water sources, local speculators using city wells faced increased pressure to find sources elsewhere.

Visitors to wells enjoyed an all too short respite. By late August, the water levels had bottomed out at La Encantada (table 2) but grew considerably at La Reforma well.[59] The disparity in water levels among the sites concerned engineers, as they wished to use gravity and pumps to draw water from these various sites to feed the public fountains in the city. Consequently, Carrillo terminated the contract with Rougroy and Fischweiler when they expressed their doubts on the project. Desperation seemed to grow by the day. Yripio Valdez took over from Rosa Aparicio and began to observe and record water levels in 1892. Specifically, he noted how technology affected water levels at various sites. He considered the importance of machinery to pump water out of the spring or presa. Up to then, locals had relied on the use of a horse-drawn wheel to feed a smaller pool. Despite accounting for the difference, Valdez's new measurements the following spring conveyed a gloomy picture (table 3). Nevertheless, he reassured locals and colleagues that wells, springs, *pilas*, and wall fountains remained in good condition.

Table 3. Water measurements by date (1892)

Bodies of water	30 April
Tiro La Encantada	n/a
Tiro La Reforma	1.12 meters
Tiro El Tenorio	dry
Presa San Bernabé	dry
Presa Los Olivos	dry
Presa García de la Cadena	dry

Source: AHEZ, Fondo Jefatura Política de Zacatecas, Serie Abasto de Agua, Caja 1, Exp. n/a.

By July and August, Valdez and Lorenzo Floressi, the new city engineer, had agreed to open another tiro, La Filarmónica, to the public. They posted the announcement and called for women and men to have access at different times of day. Women drew water from La Filarmónica well from 10:00 a.m. to 1:00 p.m. Men used the site from 2:00 p.m. to 6:00 p.m., while *aguadores*, or water carriers, used La Reforma as their source.[60] The separation of the sexes came from the engineer's desire to keep *escándalos* at bay and to reduce loitering. As the severity of the drought progressed, La Filarmónica visitors grew increasingly competitive. They quibbled over their places in line and complained when someone carried several containers. Floressi described how in one instance women took two or three containers with them and lined them up in the queue as if to suggest other women owned those containers.[61] They then quickly slipped back and forth between the water and their containers. Before anyone could complain, they had completed their water gathering for the next couple of days. Because the line grew over the course of the day, many women toward the end left with empty containers.

With the shrinking availability of water in the wells and reservoirs, municipal officials began limiting the number of people allowed to collect water there. As described above, some women took more than their daily ration and hoarded their ill-gotten surplus. These instances raised the question of community civility in the face of resource competition. A long period without water presented a choice between self-preservation and self-sacrifice for the community, and some individuals chose the former, steadfastly refusing to curb their water use during the drought. Mining companies had privatized water sources for their own use, but the presa signified the commons, a resource dedicated to the whole community. More than likely, Floressi failed to accurately account for the amount of water households used on a daily basis. He acknowledged this failure in a letter on 4 August 1893 in which he recognized that vegetable gardens, parched throats, and thirsty animals *all* required water in a drought.[62] Regardless of their specific needs, families faced an alarming lack of water. As table 3 shows, the presas had run dry a year earlier, and La Filarmónica alone was supplying water to the city.

Engineering Design and Control

In contrast to Mexico City, the project in Zacatecas experienced unique challenges due to the landscape as well as the labor problem in the region. Water infrastructure found an easy foothold in the national capital because of growing concerns over public health as well as seasonal flooding, which made the project a necessity. In Mexico City, engineers drew plans and schematics to drain the remnants of Lake Texcoco surrounding the city, emphasizing the common perception of standing water harboring public health threats. The project combined modern engineering and manual labor to build the large drainage canals that channeled water away from the national capital. The application came when engineers hired campesinos to serve as labor for this project. In effect, the drainage project changed the ecology of the region, not only reducing seasonal flooding but also damaging a fishing industry that had existed since pre-Columbian times.[63] While ambitious in its engineering schematics, the physical application of this design and concept for Mexico City's new water management system changed how households accessed water as well as the role of the government. In order to have a water line installed to a pump or faucet in their home, Mexico City residents filed a formal request with the Secretaría de Fomento, which supervised the installation of pumps and faucets in private homes in the late

1890s. The process involved petitioning the local office, noting how many gallons of water the household sought to use, and the preferred method of delivery. The petition went forward, and, if approved, the household paid a fee to have water connected.[64] Unfortunately, only the well-to-do had the means necessary, leaving the rest of Mexico City residents to rely on public wells or pumps.

Engineers in Zacatecas also grappled with concept, design, and application of water infrastructure yet experienced different results, in large part due to geography and mining. Initial concepts for a water distribution system varied as the charlatans and technology peddlers traveled through, bilking unwitting city officials along the way. City officials initially followed the inspiration of the national capital in developing a concept: installation of infrastructure for both water distribution and the evacuation of detritus. The design mirrored the efforts undertaken in the capital, which coupled aesthetics with function. However, Zacatecas faced obstacles in implementing such an expansive design in the difficult terrain of the city. The low rainfall and increasingly arid climate limited the amount of waste that could be washed away from the population. The bowl-like topography of the city's location limited everything from water pressure to fountain locations. Fountains had to be at the center of the city, or the lowest point, in order for there to be enough current and pressure through gravity to distribute the water.

In the name of modernity, politicians outlined a water distribution system that used water from wells and reservoirs to quench the thirst of a desperate city. In December 1893 members of the Jefatura Política signed a contract with engineers of Read and Campbell Limited. The British company already had a number of notable technological achievements, including its patent for a water-based, pressurized fire extinguisher. With the project in Zacatecas, the company's engineers brought their expertise with pipe systems as well.[65] Using the natural slope of the landscape and five pumps, the company designed a pump-fed network of channels from the different mines to a central collecting pool. Engineers installed pumps at the tiros for the mines La Encantada, La Reforma, and El Progreso to pull the water up before it began its downward flow, replacing the inefficient horse-drawn hoist.[66] They supervised the installation of five pumps as well as more than two thousand meters of four-inch iron pipe for the price of 23,502.00 pesos.[67] To fund the project, municipal leaders implemented new taxes and emphasized that unemployed miners had new job opportunities during its construction. Read and Campbell engineers projected output at each pump of at least ten thousand gallons a day, an amount sufficient to meet the demands of the population at the time. Nonetheless, funds soon dried up. Ramiro J. Elorduy, the jefe político, announced in April 1894 the need for public donations in order to complete the fountains at Plazas Tacuba and San Juan de Dios.[68] Elorduy, engineer Valdez, and Read and Campbell saw the project completed later that same year. Designed in a European style, the most elaborate fountains had ornamentation such as lanterns, obelisks, and shields. Others were more functional and allowed many people to gather water at once, as in the case of the Plaza Independencia fountain pictured. While the behemoth of Mexico City eventually swallowed its monuments of progress, to use Claudia Agostoni's phrase, many of these fountains still remain in Zacatecas.

In further contrast with Mexico City, the fountains in Zacatecas allowed residents to have equal access to water. While gravity and topography limited the placement of fountains, central plazas allowed for more people, from different parts of the city, to access them. Many residents had previously trudged out to wells in the foothills or traveled to La Encantada well in order to fill their *cántaros*, or clay jugs, for their daily needs. The open access to the water signaled the resource as part of the unregulated commons, for better or for worse. Residents accessed water at will, but they did not necessarily restrain themselves. With no limits in place, they consumed voraciously as they awaited the next drought or interruption. Nonetheless, the distribution systems of water in both Zacatecas and Mexico City illustrated the contrast between a visible and an invisible system. Alejandro Tortolero Villaseñor has noted that a visible system demonstrated and engaged with systems of

8. Zacatecanos gathered around a fountain to draw water during the Porfiriato. Library of Congress, Prints and Photographs Division, Detroit Publishing Company Collection, L C-D 4-3902.

containment on a daily basis. Walking by a canal or fountain, gazing over reservoirs, noting water pumps in the street—all of these actions brought the use and abuse of a resource to the forefront of public awareness of how individuals used water.

Facing both anxious locals and city officials attempting to curb hoarding, water carriers pushed to continue their services, despite the severe drought. John L. Stoddard, a U.S. travel writer, described how these couriers toted water on their backs, carrying it to customer homes. He noted the "number of water-venders in Zacatecas, whose little tanks (strapped on their shoulders after the fashion of Italian organ-grinders), contained the drinking water which they were carrying to the houses; for water here is precious, and has been sold sometimes as high as two cents a gallon."[69] Stoddard commented on not only the scarcity of water but also the informal economy that relied on it, particularly among the water carriers. When the fountains project remained incomplete and the drought settled in, the couriers found customers easily. Stoddard also commented on bathing practices in Zacatecas in racially tinged discourse, suggesting that to "none of the natives was a bath either a reminiscence or an aspiration."[70] At a windswept 8,000 feet in elevation and with poor medical infrastructure, a bath during this era tempted fate with a cold or chill. Stoddard clearly referenced ideas of cleanliness and concepts of hygiene, undoubtedly imported with Eurocentric haughtiness. Despite this criticism, there were in fact public baths throughout the city of Zacatecas. While they did not offer the most hygienic facilities, as described in a subsequent chapter, they grew in number after the successful completion of the Read and Campbell water project.

Elorduy and Valdez celebrated the success of the project only briefly, as challenges with new technology limited correct implementation. Engineers found the quality of water poor and inconsistent, which proved problematic because the water went directly to consumers. In June 1893, Valdez tasked A. Romo Vega with conducting tests at three potential sources of drinking water.[71] Specifically, he requested a test on a water sample labeled "No. 4" in order to compare it with samples from La Nevada and San Martín wells. The latter two proved to be "harder" water for drinking, implying greater concentrations of calcium and magnesium. Romo Vega tested only the chemical composition of the water, while Lorenzo Villaseñor, the city engineer, attempted to measure not only the chemistry but also the taste and smell of samples taken in February 1894. He wrote of one sample that it had no smell and no gas taste and was otherwise free of particulates.[72] Upon closer examination of the samples, he cautioned against the frequent intake of high calcium and magnesium sulfates of hard water among the population, arguing that long-term exposure affected human health.

Municipal employees bungled the initial implementation of the water distribution system due to inexperience or impatience. Pascual López Velarde contacted Elorduy in May 1894 after an employee sabotaged the fountain water. In a fit of impatience, the municipal engineer had opened the floodgates wider to fill the network of channels feeding the fountains. Unfortunately, the channel proved too small for the torrent of water and much of the reservoir poured down the hill.[73] Elorduy subsequently terminated the employee who had acted on his frustrations generated by the new system, which required maintenance, supervision, and upkeep. While employees ran short on patience, the project stumbled considerably early on because its technology assumed the availability of resources that could not be guaranteed. For example, in order for the fountains to function, the reservoirs needed to be full, which did not happen during drought conditions. When the drought peaked in 1896, the water levels in the presas dropped, which caused low water pressure for the fountains. Without a steady stream of fresh water, the fountains quickly became what the national capital had warned against—stagnant, unhealthy pools. In addition, farmers and ranchers watched crestfallen as clear skies failed to bring the spring showers needed for the planting season.

With renewed desperation, municipal officials entertained outlandish solutions to combat the lack of water. For example, municipal official Lorenzo Villaseñor asked local businesses to donate to the city's scheme to arrange for a sixteen-car rail shipment of water, or fifteen thousand "liquid pounds," every day for five months or until the seasonal rains returned.[74] This ludicrous plan underscored the exploitive nature of desperate schemes being considered in the region and failed to provide a serious, long-term remedy to address a growing problem. In February 1896, neither the municipality nor the office of the governor, Jesús Aréchiga, proposed finding a consistent water source. Rainfall continued to determine the availability of water during this period, even as streams, such Arroyo de la Plata, slowed to a trickle. Villaseñor and his railcar proposal raised alarming questions. Where did this water come from? Whose idea was it? The Villaseñor proposal never clarified. It did, however, raise ethical issues. The municipal leader effectively suggested moving water from one location to another, thus taking a resource from one community and bringing it to another. While unrealistic, the planned daily transport of water erased any official pretense of protecting the provenance of resources and their communities of origin. Indeed, if farmers lost streams to mining companies or to other municipalities, then communities inevitably lost access, whether they be Zacatecas or a far-flung *pueblo* on a river. Extraction exacerbated inequality of access, even in this unrealistic and hypothetical scenario. But the ideology that resources were for the taking persisted.[75]

In pushing for water infrastructure, Elorduy and other municipal officials attempted to echo the public health concerns of Porfirio Díaz's government. Public health signified a stable, modern society, and having water infrastructure illustrated this commitment in the Valley of Mexico. Porfirio Díaz invested in new technology and infrastructure in order to channel water away from the city while providing safe, potable water for (some of) its citizens. Hundreds of workers excavated and dug the Gran Canal del Desagüe in Mexico City in order to carry the waste of the metropolis out to the countryside and eventually, the Gulf of Mexico.[76] After years of work, they completed the project in 1910. By widening the divide between potable water and wastewater, the capital prevented the contamination of drinking water with illness-causing bacteria. In the social sphere, politicians and the technocrats reinforced the divide between the haves (who had access to clean water) and the have-nots (who did not). Household plumbing came at a hefty price, and many continued to rely on fountains or well pumps for water. To further underscore the inequality, residents in the capital saw an increased privatization of the water supply, especially between 1880 and 1930. Private companies sought to sell not only water but also water controls, such as drainage and sewage.[77] In the late nineteenth century, to further cement federal control over water access, technocrats recommended that the president order the draining of some of the last traces of Lake Texcoco, once the site of the pre-Columbian center of Tenochtitlan, the ancient Mexica city.[78]

9. One of the few green spots in the city back during this period, the Alameda offered
shade for locals who faced a treeless landscape in the surrounding hills. Library of
Congress, Prints and Photographs Division, Detroit Publishing Company
Collection, LC-D 418-8335.

Controlling Resources

Trees

In January 1897, municipal officials in Zacatecas also sought to recover and restore the landscape with a series of programs dedicated to remedying environmental problems as well as unemployment. With the support of Gov. Lic. Pedro Navarrete, they asked mining companies, refining haciendas, and ranches to plant trees in an effort to prevent erosion, to rehabilitate the lack of forests, and to replace trees lost to drought.[79] Donaciano Hurtado, the jefe político, supervised and pushed for this effort yet saw it fade. Politicians failed to hold mining and agricultural enterprises accountable for planting trees, as this initiative came at the same time as welcome rains. Whenever rainfall increased or held steady, the impetus to plant declined. The delay continued until 1906, when Gov. Eduardo Pankhurst backed and supported the planting of trees in agricultural and industrial settings in order to combat drought and to beautify the landscape.[80] Planting trees for the sake of aesthetics came as something new as four hundred years of mining had decimated area forests. As a result, farmers and hacienda workers struggled daily to collect enough firewood to feed hearth fires and refineries. Botanically, few choices remained other than short shrubs and trees, such as the *gatuño* tree (genus *Mimosa*), which served as kindling. Overall, this conservation project, as well as Hurtado's planting program, quickly collapsed. Locals found some respite from the treeless landscape in Alameda Park, one of the few green spots in the city as pictured.

Money

Business owners faced shortages in the 1890s of not only firewood and water but customers as well. Zacatecanos watched helplessly as the drought compounded the economic crisis sweeping through silver mining and the nation's economy. Suddenly, Mexican silver mines contended with Chinese brokers buying an increasing amount of silver while U.S. purchasers of silver watched as their banks dissolved.[81] Entrepreneurs saw businesses crumble in Zacatecas as mining, the primary draw to the city, collapsed. Unemployed miners had little need for *ferreterías* (hardware shops), boardinghouses, or even *pulquerías*. Without a population to feed, farmers and ranchers also experienced the silver collapse. Cattle ranchers saw the demand for beef tumble, which raised questions of public health as slaughterhouses struggled to keep up with a heavy cull. Because the slaughterhouses and butcher shops stood in the center of town, ranchers herded their cattle into the city. José María Sandoval requested permission in October 1893 from the city government to slaughter three hundred steers in order to prevent any more financial losses before winter.[82] Without customers, he faced a loss of investment if he continued to graze cattle through drought and cold. A few weeks later, Sandoval asked for permission to slaughter an additional five hundred head at his home at 30 Calle de la Victoria near downtown. He easily received permission from the city, as the drought had devastated grain for winter fodder and threatened the remaining cattle stock.[83] In addition, other business owners filed a flurry of notes in the fall of 1895 notifying the municipality of their closure due to lack of funds or customers.[84] In their desperation, some asked for an intervention by the municipality in order to manage their costs or rents. For example, Sacramento Palacios and other miners requested a decrease in their monthly payments for their mining licenses. Palacios received a lowering of his taxes on his refining hacienda, San Juan de Dios, from ninety-one to fifty-two pesos, as well as reduction in the cost of his mining license, which fell from forty to thirty pesos a month.[85] For the service industry, traveling miners and people conducting business had previously served as the principal clientele. Now restaurant owners faced empty dining halls and hoteliers shuttered their doors. Verónica L. de Apestegui ran Hotel El Comercio, an ironic name in the midst of a financial crisis. The French transplant asked in 1896 and again in March 1897 that the monthly business license tax be reduced, as the number of guests had dwindled dramatically.[86] From the numerous petitions to reduce taxes, municipal officials presumably preferred to negotiate fees, quotas, and license taxes to suit specific entrepreneurs, rather than apply a blanket reduction.

Cattle

Farmers and ranchers, in addition to absorbing extra labor from the silver collapse, also relied on Zacatecas to sell and distribute their products. In particular, haciendas in the late nineteenth century continued to have a stake in the survival of the city. Likewise, Zacatecas residents relied on nearby estates surrounding the city. Workers at haciendas in this region labored seasonally in estate agricultural production and in mining, if a mine existed on the property. Most haciendas relied on a mixed economy, investing heavily in both mining and cattle. When the silver crash affected Zacatecas, jefes políticos proclaimed without evidence that the salvation of the city had been agriculture. If anything, the collapse highlighted the divide between landowners and workers, particularly during this era of economic strife. Trinidad García, a mine owner and jefe político in nearby Fresnillo, later commented on how mining never served as "agriculture's Cinderella."[87] The industry consumed too much from surrounding farms to be the saving grace of farmlands during economic collapse. Wood, grease, leather, hay, and fuel drove

extraction, from mining to hauling.[88] With these intertwined economies, agriculture lost as much as the city did when mining collapsed,
even as it absorbed miners and made them *peones de campo*.

While the slaughter of cattle conjured public health concerns for
city officials as previously mentioned, cattle also served as a divisive
issue for both agriculture and mining interests. The introduction
of cattle quickly filled the backcountry of Zacatecas in the colonial
period, creating problems early on for the Crown. Wandering, un-
fenced herds invaded maize crops on indigenous *ejidos* before moving
into the grasslands of the north.[89] Mining also informed the success
or failure of cattle, as the industry required the animals for food,
hides, and grease. Drought, especially the prolonged drought of
1891–93, affected both the city and agriculture the same way. Cuauhtémoc Esparza Sánchez has compiled data on the fluctuations
in livestock numbers not only for cattle but also other ungulates
(such as goats, sheep, pigs, and horses) during this drought and into
the twentieth century. In 1875, these beasts numbered 3,282,000,
rising to 3,788,000 in 1892, and then 4,250,000 in 1894.[90] Many of
these animals belonged to the haciendas surrounding the city, which
makes the following statistic all the more staggering: in 1902, the
combined total for all of these animals was 1,578,160. The drop in the
number of animals paralleled the drop in the global price of silver,
as well as the effects of the devastating drought. The public health
consequences of this drought will be discussed in chapter 4. In this
fairy tale of well-fed *peones* and fair rations, cattle became both Fairy
Godmother and Wicked Stepmother to agriculture and mining.

Conclusion: Unmanageable Resources

As municipal officials attempted to control torrents of water that
periodically ran through the city, they also sought to manage the
resources of water, wood, and labor that flooded the state capital.
In controlling nature, they evinced the hubris of seeming to dom-
inate nature through mining, even as water proved unmanageable.
Meanwhile, these officials echoed the Porfirian-era beliefs on public
health, orderliness, and cleanliness in their quest to implement a

water distribution system. After several false starts and an increasingly severe drought, they achieved their goal despite falling water levels and an economic crisis. Resource management emerged as a priority when parched crops, cattle, and residents threatened livelihoods. Residents saw their financial resources dwindle as the crisis swept through the country and affected commerce, leading to business closures and little investment. City officials managed resources in a manner befitting Porfirian goals, and while they encountered considerable setbacks, they attempted to control water and supervise the use of lumber. As the twentieth century loomed, they sought to implement order and progress on an increasingly unruly resource: the people of Zacatecas.

3

The City

The Mine and the Body

TRINIDAD GARCÍA, THE FRESNILLO *JEFE POLÍTICO* AND
mine owner, recalled an 1866 story in which a miner suffered a phantasmagorical experience in the depths of the Beleña mine. Toiling
in the damp space for hours, the worker left his fellow miners and
went in search of a place to relieve himself. He disappeared into the
labyrinthine darkness and soon became lost. Twenty-two days later,
he remained lost and hungry in the belly of the mountain with only
a box of matches. Quite suddenly, he heard a voice in the darkness
that reassured him, calming his worries. When he lit a match to
see who spoke to him, the hollow eye sockets of a skull gazed back
at him.[1] While the tale borrowed heavily from legends and ghost
stories, the yarn illustrated how mines captured the imagination and
presented them as a place where anything could happen. Meanwhile,
reality offered incidents no less horrific, including violent crime,
traumatic injuries, and catastrophic contagions that spurred public
health campaigns.

While the previous chapter featured water as a central concern
because of its role as a conduit for toxins or disease, this discussion
focuses on bodies and the surveillance of bodies by municipal officials in the name of public health. As the Porfiriato sacrificed individual privacy for the sake of the collective's well-being, municipal
officials set their sights on identifying threats to public health. For
example, prostitutes in Mexico City received medical examinations
and attended lectures on hygiene. While male "visitors" to brothels
did not face repercussions, sex workers carried the responsibility of

containing their own infections in the name of the public's well-being and not solely their own personal health. In prisons in central Mexico, the criminologist Carlos Roumagnac subjected countless prisoners to personal questions and pseudoscientific studies to explain violent actions that menaced both the community and the narrative of the Pax Porfiriana. In Zacatecas, municipal officials practiced selective surveillance, offering social programs for specific sectors of the population while largely ignoring the overwhelming threat posed by mining companies. This selectivity permitted extractive industries to continue their activities and remain unhindered by public health measures the municipality promoted to protect the community at large. By looking the other way, municipal officials allowed locals to suffer exposure to invisible contaminants from mining operations through consumption or absorption. As this threat to health bioaccumulated in nature over time, it did not prompt any programs to protect public health. In contrast, other public health threats spurred quick attention and action because of their visibility. Moreover, the cases described here evinced a scientific and methodical approach to tackling individual cases of injuries and ailments—except for those that involved mining. Because of the historical presence of silver mining in the region, the industry influenced the Zacatecas government and its approach to the topic of bodies, especially when municipal officials weighed what they labeled as dangerous. In silver mining, workers faced the daily threat of traumatic injuries and tragic accidents, which heightened the danger of their labor. Consequently, miners and workers demonstrated the effects of the industry on their limbs and bones, giving historical extraction very visible consequences.

In discussing the topic of bodies, this chapter examines how external forces act on the body via crime, epidemics, industrial trauma, or legal restraints during an era of growing public health concerns. It begins with a consideration of mines as liminal spaces, or locations too distant for surveillance and too close to isolate from human avarice, backlashes, and grudges. While exchanges between workers may have ended casually or politely, some ended in bloodshed. Men coming to blows in common squabbles and murders near mines on the city's outskirts suggested an area of liminality, one far for authorities to intervene. Evidence of violence on the human body created a visible reminder of the vulnerability of health when exposed to external forces. Likewise, the violence also extended to accidents and injuries in the mine. Workers experienced devastating and violent trauma in mines, which left municipal officials scrambling to uncover how these casualties happened. While often dismissed as the price paid for extraction, workers' injuries in the nineteenth century eventually led to the medico-legal jargon of regulations involving occupational hazards in the twentieth century.

In the late nineteenth and early twentieth centuries, advances in medical and biological sciences increasingly informed how municipal officials viewed bodies in criminal investigations and programs targeting social groups or public health threats. With scientific evidence to identify culprits (both human and microscopic), investigators provided courts with evidence to build more thorough cases against the accused. In criminal investigations, the emerging field of forensic science allowed physicians and police to identify the cause of death and whether foul play should be considered. Resources in locations such as Zacatecas remained scarce, but autopsies did take place after suspicious deaths. Investigators methodically collected details from the body, surroundings, and witnesses while piecing together the actions that produced a violent scene. For some mining accidents, municipalities deferred to criminal investigators to eliminate intent and foul play while giving a nod to the increasing interest of insurance companies in workplace accidents. In the public health arena, both state and municipal officials had particular interest in animal bodies, since they served as indicators of how well officials managed their cities' operations. For example, wandering street dogs signified disorder and a lack of territorial control over public spaces. With the work of Louis Pasteur and the growing awareness of disease transmission, government officials in Mexico attempted to curb hydrophobia (or rabies in animals), a disease common in the rural areas of the country. Although those suffering from hydrophobia hardly "fear" water, as the name implied, drought and the arrival of a rabid animal in the region spurred fear of the disease. Municipal officials sought to limit its spread by introducing the opportunity for mass vaccination among farmers and city residents alike. Moreover, animal bodies also served as a barometer of the dire environmental consequences faced by humans, as in the case of drought. Municipal officials made use of scientific advancement in vaccines and disease pathology to monitor the population of the city, particularly with regard to personal vices. Physicians as well as city officials observed sites frequented by the locals and noted the interactions that took place. In Zacatecas, just as the water distribution project brought some degree of control over the quality of water in domestic use, the understanding of microbes and viruses forced municipal officials to examine and corral would-be vectors of disease. Alleged carriers of diseases included women who did not meet the patriarchal expectations of their conduct in Porfirian Mexico. As a result, municipal officials extended surveillance to women and their interactions with men during illicit affairs. City fathers and physicians also made use of new scientific knowledge by pushing for the professionalization of doctors and establishing medical institutions in the city. With the construction and funding of a hospital, Gov. Eduardo Pankhurst provided a physical entity for dispensing public health remedies while investing heavily in a vaccine program against rabies.

Recognition of medical science and its uses buoyed a structure of power in Zacatecas that allowed for surveillance of individuals while turning a blind eye to the mining industry—the biggest threat to the health of Zacatecanos. While proposed preventive measures against rabies and venereal disease drew financial support from the state government, governors and municipal officials continued to ignore the menace of contamination from the ever-present patio amalgamation system. Public health programs demonstrated how cohesively institutions work (ideally) in a society, with a cycle of communication among hospitals, municipal councils, and doctors all focused on keeping disease under control. Yet, these institutions are not foolproof. The mining industry in Zacatecas fed the creeping threat of heavy metals in water, soil, and food along with their accumulation in the human body. Other external forces also affected the body, including violent crimes and industrial trauma. In crime, the human body became a site of harm, intended or unintended, onto which a person enacts malevolence. Likewise, miners faced daily dangers in their work, and when physical trauma did occur, investigators labeled such accidents a by-product of mining, thus reducing humans and their bodies to economic parlance. Investigators worked methodically to find the cause of mining disasters but placed blame on the victims themselves rather than shoddy working conditions. Despite the surveillance and monitoring of individual bodies, municipal officials failed to isolate the mining industry and prevent it from harming the population.

Liminal Bodies, Liminal Ideas

Mines surrounded the city of Zacatecas and offered a liminal space between order and disorder. In these spaces, individuals entered a space designated as transitional and between two environments.[2] In this liminal space, workers toiled for foreign investors, who wished to escape the watchful eye of the governing and mining councils. Workers and supervisors saw few attempts to enforce water regulations far from the municipality, so mines escaped scrutiny. The sites existed near enough to Zacatecas, however, to be formally subject to its laws and the expectations of the community, albeit inconsistently. Foreign investors applied for *denuncios* and filed claims for land in mines surrounding the municipality. Those efforts complied with the Mining Code of the 1884, which necessitated filing with the local mining council. Regardless of the mines' distance from the city, municipal authorities knew the presence of foreign enterprise in the hills. While their gaze did not control actions, they hoped their laws would keep order through suggestion. Miners and workers labored in a space on the border between order and lawlessness, making mining sites transitional.

While some mines existed in the city, other mining sites were located far enough away to escape intervention. Anger, frustration, misunderstandings, and misdirected action snowballed into violence on occasion. Antagonism grew over perceived slights, jealousies, and other workplace tensions. In addition, mine laborers participated in the liminal space of law and order as well as human psychology. Mines offered a physical removal from the population, thus encouraging the melding of psychology, the body, and nature through extraction. Regardless of the time of day, these industrial sites sank workers into darkness. Deprived of the light of day, these workers allowed their imagination to run wild, projecting demons, ghosts, and even *calaveras* (skulls) in the darkness.

Mines represented popular motifs in mythology and early Christian history. In Greek mythology, Orpheus ventured into the underworld in a valiant effort to bring his love, Eurydice, back to life. A gaping cavern served as their point of transition between the subterranean sphere of Pluto and the earthly realm. After beseeching the gods with his elegiac lyre, Orpheus saw his wife emerge from the ghostly surroundings. The gods granted her passage to the earthly world on the condition that Orpheus did not glance back at her until they emerged from the subterranean realm into the sun-filled world. As their boat passed from the shadows to the light, Orpheus impatiently and thoughtlessly looked behind him at Eurydice. The gods whisked her back to the underworld as punishment, magnifying the cavernous gap as a transitional point for life and death.[3] Early Christian hermits also used caves as sites of spiritual transition. Saint Macarius, Saint Jerome, and Saint Paul the Hermit all took mines, caves, or caverns as their homes in search of spiritual growth, as the subterranean calm offered solitude for personal reflection and spiritual contemplation. Moreover, meditations in the hollows of the earth offered a point of transition—one not part of the earthly sphere or the darkness but rather between the human confines of spirituality and the Christian higher power. Trinidad García signaled an understanding of these motifs in nineteenth-century Mexico when he related the 1866 event of a man lost in a mine. In the darkness, the neophyte hallucinated dragons coming for him and made a renewed commitment to his faith, with the mine serving as a space of change.[4] The darkness had, in effect, led him to the light.

In addition, mines illustrated a transformative, liminal location. Liminality, according to the anthropologist Victor Turner, implies a shift in psychology and philosophy once the individual has passed through to the other side.[5] Workers likewise experienced a transformation as they went into the belly of a mountain. They entered as men on one side of the liminal space and later emerged as miners after having performed the physical tasks of extraction. Mines inhabited the social, legal, and cultural gray areas in the distance, far removed from municipal order. In their physical structure as gateways, mines connected the sunlit land with subterranean, culturally imbued darkness. This transition represented a shift sufficient to encourage many workers to identify themselves as "miners" in the censuses of 1895, 1900, and 1910. These tallies lent identity via occupation to many former farmhands who sought to make a living by extracting silver from the mountains. Elizabeth Ferry has suggested that miners in twentieth-century Guanajuato identified strongly with their occupation because of patrilineal inheritance and patrimony. Many miners inherited their position from their fathers, who had also labored in the mines, while others viewed the long history of mining in the city as part of the cultural patrimony of extraction.[6]

Various scholars have explored the cultural significance of underground space. Lewis Mumford has suggested that mining opened an inorganic, inedible world, one that separated miners from the organic, sun-filled world above.[7] Rosalind Williams examines the characterization of this binary and echoes Carolyn Merchant's lament on the loss of the organic world to mechanization.[8] These scholars have described the cultural significance of mining as it transitioned from a site of human labor to an industry dependent on steam-powered technology. In addition, the loss of human jobs to technology underscored a larger emphasis on patrimony—one that hinted at pride in a particular city or region because of its historical ties to extraction. Nonetheless, this romanticized view ignored the damage mining inflicted on the human body and the environment. Nothing romantic existed about lung diseases or bone-crushing trauma or water too toxic to drink. At the same time, mines became inorganic spaces because of their concentration of inorganic elements and because they also presented to the naked eye an environment that lacked life.

Despite liminality and cultural interpretation, the mine remained attached to the world above through sun-filled shafts and water. Miners constructed vertical shafts, or *tiros*, in order to provide access to the mine below and to ventilate the underground space. As supply points, these tiros proved invaluable, particularly when the mines extended in other directions. Over time, miners created an underground network of tunnels that extended downward, upward, and in all directions, in layer upon layer. In older mines, the network extended deeper and in various directions, which turned the mine into a maze. At the bottom, water filled the lower levels, giving miners and locals access to underground water, as with the well of La Encantada. Local residents or mine workers accessed these water sources through the tiros, blurring the line between the mine and the local community. Water thus became the link between the underground space and the land above. Residents too far from the spring-fed well of La Encantada relied on tiros for their water supply. At great physical expense, they drew water using pulleys, often sharing the mechanism with mine workers. Furthermore, the source of this water extended beyond the underground space of the mine, as aquifers fed streams and other reservoirs around the city. While mines pockmarked the municipality of Zacatecas and its surroundings, water circulated underground, connecting different mines with different bodies of water.

Miners also ventured far from the mine and only seasonally engaged in extraction. Miners and other mine workers often worked for different employers throughout the year. Some preferred seasonal work in the mines, splitting their time between collecting the harvest and pursuing ranching activities. Others simply moved on to other mines that needed workers, as observed by Trinidad

García, a mine owner. García noted that workers often abandoned a mine or moved on when production slowed.[9] Still others lived and worked in exploitive mixed-economy haciendas that included mining, agriculture, and cattle. Miners represented an itinerant labor force that traveled to wherever work became available. In most cases, local miners found sufficient work in the state of Zacatecas, but increasingly they traveled to rural mines or subsidized their income with work as farmhands, particularly in the early twentieth century. While traveling allowed them to find work, it marked them as unskilled labor, neglecting skills such as the ability to read veins. In particular, labor pushed the focus from production to the economic output of the human body.

In the underground, miners took part in a workscape unlike any other. Thomas G. Andrews explained a workscape as being "on the most basic level . . . a place shaped by the interplay of human labor and natural processes. Workscapes straddle material realities, the ways in which people have tried to perceive and direct the course of shifting realities, and the identities people have created out of these material and perceptual building blocks."[10] By definition, workscapes served as liminal spaces, always in the dynamic process of exchange. Likewise, mine workers existed at points of transition and survived only at the whims of tectonics and physics. As they maneuvered through the hillsides, they dodged drops, poorly supported beams, and the ever-present danger of collapse as they hammered or drilled their daily quota of ore.

Violence in Mines

Crime viewed through an environmental lens offers insight into the social boundaries of legal intervention on the outskirts of Zacatecas. Extraction sites often proved to be far from governing authorities while still close enough to the city to draw financial interests and workers. Bosses of mines, wells, or other industrial works counted on the distance and isolation of the sites to avoid government scrutiny. At the same time, the voracious appetite of industry stirred competition among workers and other groups to hit the vein and find the bonanza. The competition spilled into the surrounding environment. Business owners, engineers, metallurgists, miners, merchants, and peddlers—all competed for silver, for space, for water. The sites of excavation drew these disparate groups and pitted interests in business, property rights, and water concerns against each other. While grudges and resentments stemmed from these interactions, workers had reason for anger. Digging and excavating underground elevated body temperatures as well as temperaments, piling on additional stresses to the daily burdens of life in the mines. Moreover, overbearing *jefes* (often foreign-born) added to the growing anger and contributed to explosive criminal cases.

While violence did not necessarily occur at a higher rate in mining than in other industries, miners interacted in a distinct environment. Antonio Silva, a worker at Mina San Tiburcio, accused Martín Salar and the ironically named Tranquilino Rodríguez of injuring him.[11] On the night of 26 February 1883, Salar and Rodríguez beat Silva, injured his forehead, and threw him down the mine shaft outside Vetagrande. Salar and Rodríguez lashed out against Silva's persistent requests for repayment of a small loan and the return of a mining tool. The night security guard heard the commotion and pulled the semiconscious Silva from the flooded shaft. In the isolation of the mine, the accused had reacted violently to the persistent Silva. However, the narrative eventually shifted. Silva changed his story as he recalled that the incident had happened at one in the afternoon on a Sunday and not at night.[12] Did the injury to his head cloud his memory or did he hope to add to the drama of the case by placing it in the darkness of the mine area? Witnesses initially did not come forward until Viviana Sánchez and José P. Soto approached authorities.[13] They stated that they had seen Rodríguez at a local cantina at the time of the incident. Martín Salar emerged as a credible witness and not a participant in the crime, as initially thought. Salar recalled that he had walked by the mine on his way to the town of Vetagrande and saw a small crowd surrounding the shaft opening. When he approached the gawkers and inquired as to what held their attention, he saw someone thrashing about in the water. He quickly ran up to a man approaching on a horse, who happened to be Rodríguez, and asked for his rope in order to help pull the man from the water.[14] Rodríguez said no to the request, leaving Salar to scramble to the municipal government offices for help. In the end, municipal judges convicted Rodríguez, though sentencing him to less than a month in the municipal jail.

While municipal officials eventually resolved the Rodríguez case, some criminals repeatedly took advantage of the mines' isolation. In an outlying mining area, a serial murderer took the life of a miner, leaving behind a body bearing the signs of violent trauma. Gerardo Ramos left his work near Mina Marte (the Mars mine) at the end of the day and soon after began drinking on the evening of 15 May 1882.[15] As his coworkers departed, Ramos sat on a rock on the side of the road that led to the city and talked with his friends as they passed him on their way home. The next morning, Esteban Buzola found Ramos dead in the same location. Buzola stated that he thought that the deceased had fallen face down while in a haze of inebriation, but he discovered that something worse had happened when he turned the body over.[16] Someone had bashed Ramos's head with a rock. In addition, two witnesses, Concepción Suárez and Bernardino Huerta, claimed that as they walked nearby they had witnessed two men struggling in the darkness.[17] Days passed before municipal authorities identified any suspects. Finally, on 29 May, through an anonymous tip, they arrested Abraham Murvato, a local who lived near the mine. Murvato later revealed that he had also murdered brothers Joaquín and Arturo Sandoval, as well as Juan Fernández, thus following a trend of criminal behavior he had originally begun at age fourteen. Murvato confessed to the murder of Ramos, admitting that he knew him.[18] Like the Silva and Rodríguez case, this incident took place at night, after workers had gone home. The culprit acted under the cover of darkness and away from any eyewitnesses. As pictured, the remoteness of some mines did not offer many opportunities to call for help. The vague, transitional area where workers spent so much of their time—and where they could meet an untimely death— exemplified the transformative space of Victor Turner's definition.

10. Mines between Guadalupe and Zacatecas, circa 1890. Library of Congress, Prints and Photographs Division, Detroit Publishing Company Collection, L C-D 43-1579.

Violence on the Body

Other workers suffered a violent death not at the hands of angry debtors or serial killers but rather as a consequence of a wrong step, miscalculated leap, or unfortunate explosion in the mine. Deaths caused either by accident or poor design underscored the violence of the mining industry toward the human body. Mine owner Trinidad García witnessed the physical exertion of miners and how they changed the environment. In their profession, they seemed "wary of life" because of the constant dangers they faced in the mines, which made some prone to indulge in excesses, García suggested.[19]

In the chaotic legal and investigative rhetoric used by insurance companies and mine owners, miners suffered injury as a result of their own recklessness, particularly if the bodies evinced signs of violence and especially if family members filed a lawsuit against the mining company. In one case, engineer Don Manuel Icaza accompanied Enrique Würst, the German administrator of a section of the famous El Bote mine, to inspect the division between two mines within the sprawling El Bote site, according to witness Luis Canales.[20] Two wooden beams separated Mina San Rafael from Mina Clérigos deep inside the mountain, signaling to municipal and mining officials the property dividing line. Icaza, the engineer, ignored Würst and his colleagues' warnings and walked on the planks to test their sturdiness. He climbed the planks, which quickly gave way, and he fell thirty meters, suffering a cranial fracture that caused his death in the depth and darkness of the mine. His failure to heed the warnings, according to an official, led to his death. Responsibility appeared to be liminal in mines as well, where walls and planks less than a meter wide signaled the divisions between properties in the mountain. Consequently, two municipal officials, Francisco Zarate and Luis Córdova, initiated an investigation to see which mining company should pay damages for the death of Icaza or to determine if his death involved foul play.[21] Lawyers and mining company representatives argued that the fall had happened in a space that belonged to no one. Furthermore, Würst and colleagues had warned Icaza not to venture onto the wooden planks, as the bolts did not have a solid hold on the wood or the mine walls. Eventually, judges cleared everyone involved in the case, citing Icaza's own poor judgment as the cause of his death.

Workers also sometimes suffered gruesome accidents due to machinery and new technology. Félix Hernández worked in Mina El Diamante, part of the profitable Negociación Vetagrande company, nearly eight miles from the center of Zacatecas.[22] Investors from Europe and the United States relied on the steady production of silver from the site, whose easily mined walls allowed for the construction of several branches off the main mine. Around 2:00 p.m., Hernández, while drilling in Mina El Diamante, placed dynamite in holes bored through the rock in order to expose new rock and mining ground.[23] He then quickly exited the mine in order to let the lit fuse reach the charges. Growing impatient for the blast, he went to relight the fuse, thinking it had gone out. As he turned the corner of the tunnel, the explosion went off and he received the full force of the blast. The blast wave also drove a borer bit into Hernández's chest. Coworkers quickly notified his cousin Pascual Hernández, a miner at the site, who ran to the scene and dragged Félix from the mine. He died soon after. Miners often experienced physical traumas due to the increased use of steam engines, dynamite, and machinery introduced by foreign investors. Distance often compounded the injuries, as most happened far from hospitals and medical care. Coworkers of Félix Hernández made a valiant effort to take him to the hospital but did not arrive into Zacatecas from Vetagrande until 8:30 that night, more than six hours after the explosion.

The distance from the hospital did little for the irreversible trauma suffered by Hernández; it served as a death sentence. Severed arteries, mechanical trauma, and falls served as ever-present threats in the mines, but workers received medical attention for serious injuries only if they were near the city. Critical distance included underground distance. Miners often ventured into the belly of a mountain where older mines had been dug, excavated, and abandoned many times over. In the rush after passage of the Mining Code of 1884, novice miners from farms or villages entered old tunnels with weak walls or rotting beams. Compounding the threat, the new technology that began arriving from England, the United States, and Germany in the late nineteenth century forced inexperienced handlers to manage unfamiliar steam-powered equipment, like hoists or pulverizers. Many did not know how to work machinery or set dynamite and received little if any training. Working new technology, recognizing weak beams, knowing how to handle dynamite—these skills required practice and a steep learning curve that many investors and novice miners simply could not afford.

Berardo Carreón and Francisco Hernández both experienced horrific injuries that raised legal questions in the aftermath of an accident on 31 October 1891. The young men suffered physical trauma during a cave-in inside Mina Los Tahures, located near Sauceda, a small town ten miles from the state capital.[24] Carreón bore the brunt of the rocks and died of his injuries, as the autopsy report detailed.

The rocks crushed his midsection, broke ribs on his left side, and smashed his left leg. While the injuries did not kill him instantly, he died from the blood loss, per the examiner's description.[25] Hernández escaped with a broken leg and shattered pelvis. As with Icaza, Félix Hernández, and now Carreón, municipal authorities called for an investigation to determine who, if anyone, should be held responsible for the deaths of these workers. After interviewing all witnesses, municipal officials received the permission of Eufemia Jaramillo, the young widow of Carreón, to inter the body of her husband.

Accidents in the mines appeared so gruesome and violent that lawyers filed the cases in the criminal records alongside accusations of murders and burglary. The Criminal Code of 1855, Article 253, required that all municipalities investigate accidents for foul play and murder. Likewise, lawyers and archivists printed in large letters on the cover page of the legal binder, "Who is at fault for the death of Berardo Carreón?" Lawyers attempted to establish an *averiguación*, or investigation, by asking if someone should be held responsible. Witnesses gave depositions regarding the events that led up to the mechanical or accidental trauma. Who accompanied the victim? Did anyone warn the victim? Did anyone harbor malice toward the victim? If no one actively committed a crime, lawyers considered the company culpable unless released by witnesses or family members, who might suggest that the accident was a tragedy and not the result of negligence. Oftentimes, family members recognized in their depositions how the mechanics and physics of beams or machinery inadvertently caused the death of their sons or husbands, thereby releasing the company of any negligence.

Technological Trauma

The arrival of industrial technology in mining created an inevitable uneasiness among workers in Zacatecas, who preferred tried-and-true methods. Scholars have posited that the shift from hand tools to machinery in mining and agriculture fueled modern capitalism.[26] Initially, humans manipulated tools to maximize output and created an extension of themselves, according to Lewis Mumford channeling Karl Marx.[27] The introduction of machinery or new technology complicated the success of mining in the late nineteenth century in a global context. For example, drills powered by steam technology drove miners deeper into the earth. Invented in England in the 1870s, mining drills, such as the Ingersoll rock drill, facilitated a faster carving out of the walls of the mine.[28] In California, miners and spectators flocked to the hillsides with steam-powered equipment to join in hydraulic mining. Miners pointed a hose that released high-pressure water toward the hillside, which eroded the earth and exposed any coveted metal.[29] For the most part, Zacatecas miners rejected the new technology from Britain or the United States. While some parts of Mexico, particularly Guanajuato or Taxco, might have opted for these modern tools, Zacatecas did not.[30] The examples from England and California suggested a facile incorporation of the drills and other technology. However, these sites differed considerably from central Mexico. In the United Kingdom, mining and especially coal extraction had long been pursued, in well-established mining villages. Miners used tools, drills, and other apparatuses, which they continued to use into the twentieth century. Meanwhile, in the U.S. West, miners arrived in California at roughly the same time as hydraulic technology, facilitating an easy transition.

In contrast, miners in Zacatecas adapted slowly to technology, largely because of the itinerant workforce and the option to mine independently. Miners changed mining sites frequently, which created a peripatetic workforce too mobile to learn technology skills. The growing mining economies in states such as Guanajuato and Chihuahua continuously drew miners away from Zacatecas as they followed mining booms around the country. As previously noted, many Zacatecanos worked in mines only seasonally, heading to ranches or haciendas when mining slowed.[31] Still other miners preferred to work by themselves. *Gambusinos*, or speculators, mined independently from larger companies and typically engaged in small-scale operations. Because workers had various options in where they found employment as miners, they delayed or ignored technology changes, particularly in mechanization, as other opportunities took them from one site to another. The preference for hand tools among workers made humans an extension of the hammers and picks themselves until steam-powered technology intervened. Powered by the caloric energy in the body, as Thomas Andrews has emphasized, these tools built a connection between the organic human form and the inorganic walls of the mine.[32] Subsequently, through this exerted energy, workers changed the landscape above and below the ground.

When miners in Zacatecas did employ steam-powered technology, they did so haphazardly. Their lack of practice showed when mining and refining changes arrived in the late nineteenth century to make the industry more efficient but failed in the stubborn state of Zacatecas. Moreover, workers needed access to new mechanized equipment to learn how to use it but lacked the "knowledge or know-how, ideology, and values" to fully implement the new technology.[33] With apparatuses from the United States and Europe filtering in, workers experienced an exchange between the other countries and Mexico. Hesitation to adopt new machines in certain sectors of industry did not mean that workers lacked the capacity to understand the technology but that they lacked proper training in using the machines.[34] In addition, technology during this era changed rapidly over a short period of time. The rapid industrialization of the country, coupled with the introduction of foreign technology from England or the United States, affected workers' ability to learn the imported methods of extraction while keeping up with mining technology in the region.

Chemistry of Consequences

With the technological acceleration in late nineteenth century, supervisors pushed workers to maximize output as steam-powered machines increased productivity. While industries tested steam-powered technology on mining communities, investors encouraged better science for efficiency and quality. For example, the patio amalgamation system had long relied on large amounts of mercury to draw the silver out of crushed ore. It was a system that proved to be expensive, inefficient, and dangerous, as rain simply washed the mercury and other heavy metals away from the open-air *tortas*, sending toxic runoff into streams and riverbeds.

The advent of two new amalgamation methods in the 1890s offered the promise of greater efficiency with materials and a less costly process of silver refining: cyanide solution and the flotation method. Cyanide process (*cianuración*) signaled the transition away from the large-scale patio process as production shifted to smaller operations after the collapse of the silver market and the abandonment of silver mines. In the early twentieth century, the cyanide method arrived with the MacArthur-Forrest process, which had been developed in Glasgow in 1884 to extract gold from ores; however, enterprising chemists experimented with applying the technique to silver, with limited success.[35] The nefarious compound resulting from this technique came in the form of cyanide (CN^-). Deleterious to nerve endings, the toxic element slipped into the bloodstream through absorption or consumption, much like water, with even small doses causing stomach pain. The cyanide process required considerable amounts of cyanide in order to function as an alternative to the patio process. Furthermore, the process became a known threat to human health and was eventually banned in certain provinces in Argentina, as well as Colorado and Wisconsin in the United States.

Despite the acclaim, the cyanide process developed for gold did not easily transfer to the amalgamation of silver, which limited implementation of the method in Zacatecas. This new process required additional labor, as silver ores needed to be ground to a finer degree and mixed with more potent cyanide mixtures and salts in the agitation vat. Workers then added sand to kill the "sliming" effect of finely ground ore.[36] Despite adaptation of the method for silver and gold in other states, the state of Zacatecas remained "untouched" by the cyanide process, as Edward Beatty puts it, as late as 1907. Even in the 1920s, workers adamantly held on to the patio system, much to the chagrin of foreign investors.[37] The skepticism about new methods largely underscored the tried-and-true practicality of the age-old method used by Zacatecas workers. In addition, because of the silver quality in the region, other methods did not perform well. While experiments and tests had been conducted in different regions with different samplings of silver, engineers introducing new amalgamation methods underestimated the resources in the region as well as the character of silver ore found there. Combined with workers' doubts and unanticipated setbacks in silver production, the cyanide process came and went with little fanfare in Zacatecas.

The flotation method offered yet another path to silver production, made possible through advances in industrial chemistry. Like the cyanide and the patio processes, flotation combined the pulverized silver ore with several compounds. Specifically, it involved adding zinc sulfide to the mixture, which separated the metallic silver from the ore. At the same time, it released toxic fumes into the air over the bubbling cauldron of chemicals, concentrating heavy metals in workers' lungs and allowing them to enter the bloodstream.[38] The workers knew how to handle the mixture and how it helped their process, but did they recognize the dangers associated with their work? Understanding the dangers of these mixtures to human health required a chemist's background as well as insight into how molecules passed through the pores of their skin or from the lungs into their bloodstream.

The lack of training in these techniques suggested a haphazard handling of these toxic materials. Inevitably, the workers came into contact with these mixtures, either directly through the skin or through inhalation of toxic fumes. Workers and the ill effects they suffered as a result of the conditions or materials encountered in their work had been a topic of discussion in the medical community since the time of Bernardino Ramazzini (1633–1714). Ramazzini explored the ties between work occupations and disease, expounding on the effects of extraction on "mine-diggers" in a chapter of his classic work *A treatise of the diseases of tradesmen*.[39] Quite possibly, doctors or engineers simply assumed that workers used sensible techniques without formal training or workers were incentivized to produce results quickly, leading to cutting corners or a rushed process. In all likelihood, miners changed jobs all too frequently in an economically unstable era, making historical analysis of the long-term effects of these techniques a challenge. A darker consideration might be that engineers or technicians possibly withheld information on how new amalgamation techniques affected human health. When company supervisors imposed new technology on workers, the company owners benefited when those workers simply followed instructions and asked few questions, particularly about the toxic nature of their labor. With human health given so little consideration, the soil and water of mining sites absorbed the spilled or discarded waste of each day's operations. As Antonio Avalos-Lozano and Miguel Aguilar Robledo write, workers in the colonial period remained convinced that the chemicals used in the patio process did not harm them despite evidence to the contrary in their animals.[40] In the modern period, mining companies locked horns with locals over contamination, as discussed in chapter 4.

Public Health Threats

Mercury

Because the terrain of the Zacatecas region drew runoff away from sites of patio amalgamation, municipal officials faced a mounting public health crisis as heavy metals accumulated in the environment. Spilling down from the surrounding hills, rivulets of mercury and other metals went into waterways during rainstorms, via the wind, or through other modes of erosion. Streams, rivers, lakes, and agricultural fields absorbed toxic metals, eventually carrying them through the food chain as humans consumed grains grown on polluted *milpas*, or cornfields, or cattle grazed on contaminated pastures.

While mercury played a significant role in the inorganic chemical process for producing silver, it contributed to the accumulation of heavy metals in Zacatecas and proved deleterious to long-term human health. The pervasive use of mercury in the patio process and the unmonitored runoff into streams allowed for this toxin to accumulate in the soils, waterways, and animals over time. Over centuries of patio amalgamation, the toxic metal so entrenched itself in the ecology of Zacatecas that it inevitably reached the human population through direct contact or consumption of contaminated animals and plants. By ingesting mercury-tainted food or water, the human organism absorbed the metal and continued to hold it for days or weeks, allowing the metal to wreak havoc on internal organs. *Azogueros*, or the experts in applying the mercury mixture to the fickle patio process, did not always measure the amount of mercury used in processing; instead they determined the amount of crushed ore on hand to be turned into silver. Whereas silver production and mercury always seemed to be measured in the account books of haciendas specializing in amalgamation, the amount of mercury washed away into the surroundings remained unmeasured. The ecology of extraction involved not only how much earth the miners moved in the search for silver but also what compounds they put into the earth. How much mercury was lost in the soil and waters of Zacatecas over the course of the nineteenth century? How can these effects be measured? These are questions weighed in chapter 4; this chapter addresses the public health concerns associated with the compounds used to produce silver in Zacatecas. Specifically, I address two questions: Did mercury poisoning manifest itself in behavioral symptoms? If so, how do these symptoms emerge in the historical record?

A variety of factors determine how and to what degree mercury affects the human body. To determine a person's level of exposure and the degree of danger the toxin poses, several questions must be answered. Was the person exposed to ethylmercury or methylmercury? Was the mercury concentrated or diluted? For how long was the human exposed? How was contact made? Through touch? Ingestion? Inhalation? Although any number of factors affected the toxic impact of mercury, some Zacatecanos presented behavioral changes that raised the likelihood of exposure. Those exposed to the heavy metal in high doses suffered from a staggering gait, gastrointestinal disturbances, kidney pain and failure, anxiety, irritability, insomnia, wrist drop, tooth decay or loss, and psychological disorders.

According to the Centers for Disease Control, the body expelled mercury naturally after about two months, again often depending on the variables listed above.[41]

Notwithstanding all of the factors above, the phenomenon of bioaccumulation makes a historical study of mercury all the more complicated because of the inconsistency of mercury amounts in different sources. Bioaccumulation occurs when an organism absorbs a heavy metal faster than the body can expel it. Moreover, heavy metals become more concentrated at each level of the food chain. For example, marine species take in lead and mercury in coastal regions through pollution and the natural food chain. Smaller fish in polluted waters consume or absorb the heavy metals while feeding. They fall prey to larger fish that not only ingest the mercury from the fish consumed but also swim through polluted waters themselves. Then, in the next step on the food chain, perhaps a dolphin eats the medium-sized fish and thus ingests the mercury from it as well as the smaller fish it had consumed. Furthermore, mercury accumulates in the fatty reserves of organisms, making it even more difficult to eliminate. As a result, predators at the top of the food chain often contain the largest amount of mercury. Most notably, marine mammals (or cetaceans, such as dolphins and whales) hold the highest amount of lead and mercury, and despite limits on whaling, they continue to be consumed as food in some parts of Asia. While Zacatecas is landlocked and far from any ocean, the topic of bioaccumulation of heavy metals informs current studies on soil and water in the region.

With the variety of ailments signaling mercury poisoning, it would be difficult to pinpoint a single cause behind so many symptoms without considering the patient's residence, daily activities, food consumption, and employment, among other factors. Outward symptoms, however, alerted family members and the community to the patient's medical needs. In some cases, these outbursts or behavioral issues alerted the authorities. Violent outbursts typified mercury poisoning in some patients, which led to municipal officials categorizing would-be patients as criminals. Methodologically, the undetected and unmonitored poisonings of the era often left no evidence or only a few scattered clues in criminal records describing behavior.

The criminalization of behavior emerged in the Porfiriato as part of an attempt to curb what the *científicos* deemed irregular or abnormal acts. The criminologist Carlos Roumagnac studied thousands of prison inmates to gain an understanding of the personal circumstances that had led them to a life of crime. To the criminologist, the inmates largely came from the poor, uneducated masses, which explained, in his pseudoscientific view, their "degeneracy."[42] Roumagnac believed that people living in poverty had a genetic predisposition to alcoholism, violence, and behavioral problems, a biased argument that he supported with family histories and pseudosciences like craniometry. Meanwhile, patients filled the halls of La Castañeda Manicomio after its construction in 1910.[43] This asylum saw a range of patients—from those with behavioral issues to those with microcephaly. According to the widespread official views in the era, violent acts and outbursts only signaled a larger social problem that needed to be isolated from the rest of society.

In a representative case described below, municipal officials criminalized the behavior of a Zacatecas man who lashed out violently and displayed erratic behavior. Did he have contact with mercury? Yes. However, he did not come into contact with it through exposure in mines or in waterways but rather through a commonly used treatment for syphilis. In 1890, Margarito Bernal raised red flags when he behaved in an uncharacteristic manner. Adelaida, his wife, noted that he frequently suffered from *ataques de locura* (attacks of madness). She described these episodes as frequent outbursts that sent him into violent fits in which he harmed himself and others.[44] In the most recent episode, neighbors walking near the Alameda in the state capital had heard a woman calling for help. Adelaida yelled for assistance as Margarito attacked her, injuring her face, hands, and torso in the process.[45] Friends testified that he did not appear inebriated, as he rarely consumed alcohol.[46] Officials noted an indeterminate cause for his behavior in the criminal documents.

However, there were suggestions that his "madness" came from his syphilis, a condition for which he had sought treatment. In this era, syphilitic patients often received mercury as a treatment, which offered a remedy for their illness despite the inherent risks involved in using it. The Bernal family agreed that Margarito suffered these attacks before engaging in illicit affairs with both men and women, but his irritability had become increasingly violent. Without a proper analysis of Bernal's interactions with mercury, his behavior only raised more questions, which cast doubt on mercury causing his behavior. Nonetheless, how mercury affected public health in mining towns in the nineteenth century foreshadowed a growing environmental health problem in the twentieth century. Sites such as New Almaden, California; Asbestos, Quebec; Huancavelica, Peru; and Ducktown, near the Georgia-Tennessee state line in the United States, illustrated the lingering effects of toxic metals on public health in former extraction sites.

Rabies

Municipal officials also applied public health measures to curb animal-borne diseases, an indicator of how well programs targeted roving vectors of disease. The rush to contain the potential pathogens from animals in the late nineteenth and early twentieth centuries underscored the advances in medicine during this period. It also demonstrated how medicine perceived threats from even the most domesticated of animals. In medicine, germ theory and a growing comprehension of viruses targeted specific creatures in an effort to limit contact with human populations. At the same time, ideas of modern infrastructure moved abattoirs away from town centers and water sources, further limiting the threat from animal products and waste. In addition, municipal officials moved to combat zoonotic diseases because of the cultural fear of seeing domesticated animals transformed into wild beasts. Of all the viruses, rabies prompted the most fear in municipal officials, farmers, and citizens alike. The disease hastened a dramatic change in the character of a loyal, domesticated dog, as it turned from loving to vicious. In cattle, the virus caused a gentle milk-producing cow to suddenly stagger and stumble toward hallucinations. Wild animals affected by rabies attacked without fear and without fleeing.

Armed with an education from Guadalajara and positivist ideas from Mexico City, Eduardo Pankhurst served as governor from 1904 to 1908 and sought to curb the incidence of rabies in his home state of Zacatecas. In the surrounding rural areas, domesticated animals suffered exposure from their counterparts while occasionally tangling with wild cousins. The spread of the disease coincided with drought and remained endemic in the region because of the rampant stray dog population. In addition, rabies proved costly to cattle ranchers, as the zoonotic disease targeted mammals of all sizes. With an economic and social motive, Pankhurst requested vaccines from Mexico City to start a vaccination program in the city and on farms.

Pankhurst had reasons to be encouraged, as advances in science coupled with a national emphasis on public health supported the introduction of vaccination programs. Louis Pasteur (1822–95) had developed a rabies vaccine in 1885. Despite initial hesitation, he tested his vaccine on a young boy who had suffered a dog bite. Pasteur's vaccine famously introduced a dead form of the virus into an organism's system, which allowed the body's natural defenses to attack it. Subsequently, the body distributed natural antibodies against the disease and future infections. To create the vaccine, Pasteur and his students allegedly wrestled rabid dogs in an effort to extract saliva from the animals' chomping jaws.[47] With the virus isolated and defunct, the vaccine proceeded to a set of tests and trials using rabbits. Finally, the French scientist succeeded by administering the vaccine to Joseph Meister, the first human to receive the rabies vaccine. With the vaccine soon available for wider use, Pankhurst administration officials began vaccination campaigns in order to curb the spread of the disease in their region.

The rabies virus has a long history in medicine and culture. It belongs to a family of RNA viruses (that is, those with RNA as genetic material) called Rhabdoviridae and more specifically, the *Lyssavirus* genus. Frequently described as having a bullet shape, lyssaviruses often thrive in bat populations, and because of easy mutation in RNA viruses, the rabies lyssavirus emerges as the most common and most prevalent in mammals. From the initial puncture wound of an animal bite, the virus then travels to the central nervous system, then moves on to other organs, such as the salivary glands. After this diffusion throughout the body, the host serves as a reservoir for the virus. From infection to the first appearance of symptoms, the host incubates the virus for roughly one to three months. Initial symptoms range from the nondescript (malaise) to the minor (a headache or slight fever), then quickly give way to hyperexcitability, insomnia, confusion, abnormal behavior, and hydrophobia, all of which signal inflammation of the brain. The final phase of the disease begins with paralysis of the infected limb. The paralysis then spreads, leading to death. On a global scale, the disease claims roughly fifty-five thousand lives every year, mostly in developing nations.[48] In the pre-antibiotic era, victims of animal bites faced the added threat of sepsis, also commonly known as blood poisoning, making any animal bite a life-threatening event.

Government vaccination programs applied modern science to solve problems perceived as backward. With this type of program, nature remained controlled, while humans remained healthy and did not need to fear minor animal bites. Like the visibility of occupational trauma, the bite of an animal lurched society back into an era of human versus creature, survival versus mortality. A ferocious creature stirred human fears of uncontrolled nature, creating a primordial need for self-preservation in humans.[49] The image of a rabid beast did indeed render nightmares: a salivating, staggering, and lunging animal baring its teeth at any moving object. Moreover, the visibility of an attack by a perhaps rabid animal and a gaping wound shocked bystanders into action. In many cases, a mob descended on an animal that had bitten a human to beat the creature to death. In Zacatecas, Governor Pankhurst sought not only to eliminate the spread of the disease but also demonstrate the larger control of nature in line with the policies of the Porfiriato.

Pankhurst and his team encountered difficult weather conditions that encouraged the spread of rabies, a setback in an otherwise solid program. At the beginning of his term, the governor saw the state plunge into a decade-long drought just as it was recovering from the previous one. The lack of rain left farms bare and cattle ranches desperate to keep their animals alive. As the drought grew worse, domestic animals began to die and the situation grew even more dire. Drought only exacerbated the threat of rabies, as wild animals often traveled down from the hills to seek water, making contact between wild and domestic species more probable. Moreover, the collapse of the agricultural sector reduced the number of animals in the region because many ranchers had no option but to cull their remaining livestock. Nonetheless, Pankhurst ordered the rabies vaccination program to proceed in an effort to minimize the spread of the disease.

The vaccination program began in September 1907 under the direction of a small council focused on bettering public health.[50] Governor Pankhurst and municipal officials ordered that the injection of the rabies vaccination should be free to those who needed it, as determined by the public health council's director, Ignacio Castro.[51] Nevertheless, some locals still had to pay for the vaccinations. Owners of dogs and cattle received the vaccination for a fee ranging from five to fifteen centavos per animal, based on the judgment of the council.[52] Municipal officials and newspapers announced the opening of clinics and began a rousing publicity campaign to push locals to bring their animals. The Hospital Civil contributed a majority of the staff and materials needed for the antirabies clinics around the city, while some employees staffed the rural clinics.[53] Vaccine administrators must have anticipated an intense push to receive the vaccines, as they stipulated that people needed to register and would be called in order.[54] Nonetheless, vaccination culture remained in its nascent stages, and few took advantage of the opportunity to have their animals inoculated.

Why the sudden government interest in locals' struggles against hydrophobia? Enveloped in the awareness of public health, the vaccination program in Zacatecas attempted to implement policies gleaned from the urban centers of Mexico City and Paris in order to evince modernity. As a signifier of disorder and chaos, the proliferation of the disease indicated a local government's poor grasp of the health problems facing the population. Engineers resolved water issues. Doctors tackled communicable diseases among the population. However, with animal vectors of rabies coming into frequent contact with townspeople, the charge fell on local governments to limit the spread of the disease, especially one as virulent as rabies. Because of municipalities' responsibility to prevent the spread of disease, proponents of the vaccine grasped at modernity as defined by science and medicine at the dawn of the early twentieth century.

While vaccinations of animals highlighted efforts to protect domesticated creatures, this campaign also targeted human patients recovering from animal bites. The vaccine program initially targeted domestic animals but municipal officials also offered the vaccine to humans soon after the clinics opened. They issued the open call to locals to receive the vaccine as a preventive measure, especially those who worked with animals or had come into contact with undomesticated species. Likewise, the city also offered the vaccine to those who suffered from any animal bite as a precaution and who had not yet shown symptoms of the disease in its advanced stages. Because of the relatively facile transmission of the disease from animals to humans, a rabies vaccine became a cause for elation among doctors and politicians alike. Moreover, the vaccination subdued the appearance of a barbarous, untamed nature at least temporarily. To prevent this turn to the darker side of nature, the vaccine protected the domestic animals and secured the well-being of the community.

As a necessary precaution, human patients also received the inoculation in order to prevent the development of rabies after being bitten by an animal. In Zacatecas, forty-nine men and twenty-one women received the vaccine after a bite. Meanwhile, thirty-eight of those vaccinated ($n = 70$) represented the younger portion of the population (from newborn to age twenty).[55] Those who received the inoculation displayed bite injuries primarily on their arms, and only twelve of those victims received treatment in the hospital.[56]

Of the seventy cases in which persons bitten received vaccination, twenty-one animals did indeed suffer from rabies, while almost half the cases were bites from animals only *suspected* of having rabies.[57] Although donkeys, horses, foxes, and cats frequently became infected, sixty-three of the vaccinated patients accused dogs of being the diseased culprit.[58]

Even after the vaccination program, Zacatecas locals continued to encounter rabid animals on occasion. However, with the sudden death of Governor Pankhurst in 1908, patients then needed to petition an antirabies council in order to receive the vaccine. For example, María Martínez, daughter of Ángela Alvarado, encountered a dog on the way home from school in April 1913. When the young girl went to pet the dog, it lunged at her and bit her. Her adolescent brother suffered a bite as well in an attempt to pull his little sister away from the rabid dog.[59] Their mother beseeched the local government of Sauceda to give her children the antirabies vaccine. The antirabies council agreed but received a surprise when only María and Ángela arrived for the vaccine.[60] The archival file did not mention the older brother or his outcome. As for the dog, neighbors killed the animal in the streets soon after it bit Martínez.[61] Onlookers had spotted the telltale signs of an unsteady gait and the infamous "foaming at the mouth" on the dog that had bitten the young girl. This case occurred in an era of military chaos and troops passing through the area, but the Martínez family still managed to receive prompt medical attention.

Cattle

As part of the sanitation and hygiene effort in cities, governments exercised oversight and regulations to limit human contact with animal waste and cattle effluvia in the state capital. Previously, butchers had processed cattle in the center of the city, with the waste and smell hovering for days in the summer. When the wretched smell lingered in the air, medical doctors and municipal officials alike fretted about miasmas wafting through neighborhoods. Miasmas, believed to be invisible sources of disease, sparked concerns in the

Pankhurst administration even though germ theory had gained traction with the public. The construction of new abattoirs outside the city illustrated the moment when miasma and germ theory overlapped in rhetoric as well as goals in the implementation of measures to protect public health. With slaughterhouses on the outskirts, city leaders eliminated the threat of the smell and contact with the germ-filled waste from processing.

Pankhurst and his government, however, faced an uphill battle in a ranching state where the number of cattle processed served as an indicator on the health of the local economy. If the rains faltered and drought set in, ranchers culled a significant number of animals in anticipation of a die-off from the heat. If the economy tumbled, they slaughtered more than the usual number in order to avoid the drop in meat prices that followed the recession. Unlike Mexico City, where Porfirian officials faced opposition from private meat industrialists, Zacatecas ranchers relied on a public slaughterhouse located in the city, roughly three blocks from the cathedral. As a result, the waste sat and festered in the city, creating a nauseating brew of noisome vapors. Because of the stench, abattoir workers petitioned municipal officials for permission to slaughter some of their cattle before bringing the herds into town. Nonetheless, city leaders faced a daunting task of supervising public health when the slaughter of hundreds of head of cattle took place in or near populations. The stench along with the ubiquitous "miasmas" saturated the air as entrails, blood, and manure seeped into streets and drains. Despite the economic and climate factors driving the slaughter during Pankhurst's era, health inspectors in the city had long shared their concern about the proximity of such unsanitary and harmful effluvia. In October and November 1898, health inspector Francisco Ponce led an examination of the city's slaughterhouses. His review revealed unhygienic conditions, with meat and feces mingling on the floor, dirty water being used to wash the meat, and the disposal of entrails directly into streams.[62] Ponce initiated the inspection after a series of undefined illnesses led to the cremation of roughly sixty pigs in July and August 1898, with more the following year.[63]

In order to displace the central abattoir, Pankhurst recognized the need to construct a new building, since the city's only two slaughterhouses (one for bovines and the other for swine) suffered from unhealthy conditions and poor work supervision.[64] In Mexico City, the *científicos* imposed new changes on the meat processing industry, which provided Pankhurst with a model for the *rastros*, or slaughterhouses, in Zacatecas.[65] The governor supervised the signing of a 200,000-peso contract with the Zirión Sarabia Company to construct the new slaughterhouse. Ranchers and municipal officials welcomed the new facility as the number of animals slaughtered reached an astounding one hundred thousand in the four-year period from 1903 to 1907.[66] Moreover, the region entered a period of drought during the first decade of the twentieth century. It wilted cornstalks in the fields and killed grazing animals by the thousands.[67] In this desperate situation, the drought foreshadowed the growing frustration among farmers, ranchers, miners, and laborers in the region, just as the Mexican Revolution loomed on the horizon.

Bodies as Medical Subjects

Pankhurst also invested in the medical infrastructure of the city. Under his administration, a hospital was constructed in a central location, thus emphasizing the growing importance of public health to his administration. Since independence, the national legislature had pushed to professionalize the role of physicians through education and certification to challenge superstitions as well as traditional remedies for treating illness. By the end of the nineteenth century, Mexico City had a medical school and a curriculum oriented toward positivist ideas about diagnosing patients. This model had filtered down to medical schools around the country by the 1890s, when many cities established educational institutions to address local patient populations. Regional medical schools soon enrolled students but struggled to secure solid funding. In 1884, the volume *La Escuela de Medicina* included mention of the Facultad de Medicina in Zacatecas, a medical school opened in 1870 but closed before the turn of the century.[68] Nonetheless, medical schools and hospitals became a salient feature of the Porfiriato and of the Pankhurst administration. These institutions reflected a three-pronged effort to promote public health in municipalities around the country: surveillance, containment, and remedying. Medical professionals monitored patients during intake and alerted the authorities if they detected a contagion dangerous to the rest of the community. In addition, they limited the spread of disease by isolating a carrier of an infection or virus in a sanitarium. Then, they either healed such patients (if possible) before sending them on their way or made recommendations to the local government to limit the spread of contagion. Without the infrastructure to maintain public health, Pankhurst and his administration faced an interminable cycle of infection.

Beginning in 1904, the Pankhurst administration committed funds for the renovation of the city's hospital in an effort to bolster its ability to respond to public health crises in the region. Increased funding allowed for an expansion in the number of beds available and the hiring of new employees in the existing hospital. Since opening in the early seventeenth century as a convent hospital, Hospital San José had closed for extended periods of time due to poor facilities or a lack of funding. Pankhurst and his government funded new beds, supplies, and construction for the growing public health infrastructure.[69] Moreover, the hospital staff participated in the antirabies campaign, donating time and some supplies in the effort to eradicate rabies and rabid animals in the region.

Bodies of Women

A search for municipal documents on cultural activities revealed misplaced files that showed another facet of Zacatecas society. Under a series labeled "Diversions," two files on prostitution revealed activities not covered above. Written by individuals who wished to remain anonymous, one letter detailed the exploits of a nearby house and ended with this ominous note: "We do not know how to write or how to sign," which suggested a hired scribe had penned the letter. The anonymous citizens complained in January 1892 of the women in a nearby house on the Callejón de Puentecillos. In their letter, they blamed the women for corrupting the neighborhood's moral standing. They named the women as María Refugio Flores, Manuela Rivas, Eleuteria Amaro, María Reyes Zamora, María Luz Mendez, Victoria Trejo, Guillermina and María Arellano, and Petra Castillo.[70] The homeowner, Antonio Dávila, had previously owned a house on Callejón San Agustín before the operations of that "house of tolerance" moved to Callejón Pedro Nolasco and eventually to their current house on the Puentecillos alley. The authors argued that the houses of tolerance damaged the reputations and honor of those living in the vicinity of a house of ill repute. While Mexico City officials relocated activities deemed vice to tolerance zones, smaller cities had limited space. With limited housing, neighbors had little choice but to acknowledge, if not tolerate, houses of tolerance.[71] Moreover, the complainants cited the small amount of monthly taxes paid by the house (ten reales a month). They argued that the women should pay more. In addition, they stated that the presence of the house threatened the morality of all, especially since the women walked the streets and flagrantly displayed their state of being *empeoradas*, or worsened.[72]

The expectations for women largely reflected those outlined by historical monographs written about this era. However, they faced local challenges in Zacatecas that made their lives separate and distinct from what women in other regions around the country faced. First, many women worked in the late nineteenth century, shaping family dynamics of the era. In a devoutly Catholic region, Zacatecas women faced the challenges of fitting into a role while at the same time contributing to a working household. These expectations did not come solely from the Church. The Registro Civil of 1859 characterized women as the submissive partners in marriage, which limited their legal options in the city.[73] Moreover, Genaro García, the beloved state governor and mayor of Zacatecas, famously declared women to be unequal because of their dependence on men for everything.[74] In addition, city officials and legal experts viewed women as minors, per the Código Civil of 1884, Article 596, which blocked women from leaving their paternal home without permission.[75]

In the name of public health, municipal officials insisted on a degree of surveillance over the population, particularly over women. Municipal officials sought to keep tabs on the spread of venereal diseases in the general population and especially in men who visited sex workers. The 1872 Reglamento followed European practices of the era that required sex workers to register and to undergo occasional "inspections" to identify diseases such as syphilis or gonorrhea.[76] When they identified a sex worker in need of medical attention, municipal officials isolated that person during treatment and kept statistics on how often that person faced infection.

With this level of supervision, municipal officials monitored the most private of activities of individuals. Worse still, women carried the blame for the transmission of disease in the medical establishment's opinion, which encouraged physicians to list women in municipal registers. Furthermore, municipal officials argued that physical ailments contributed to social ills. Therefore, bodies became a focal point for control of the moral downfalls brought about by vice. The mingling of the sexes in unmonitored and unsponsored social events attracted the attention of Zacatecas officials. Indeed, these officials and the police who reported on such activities became the greatest gossips when they detailed the private parties where dancing occurred. In particular, the reports in April 1888 illustrated a concerted effort to curb private diversions in private homes. Gendarmes reported to city officials that a series of private parties had taken place during 10–14 April in various neighborhoods. On 14 April, for example, the *gendarme nocturne* described a dance in Calle de San Pedro at the home of Emilio Vargas Vásquez. Justo Vásquez, presumably a relative, hosted a dance near the principal intersection of San Rafael in house number 21. While these reports highlighted the efforts to keep a close watch on the happenings in Zacatecas, the participants in these dances demonstrated restraint in keeping social activities in the home. Moreover, the gendarmes served as the eyes and ears of municipal officials, illustrating Porfirian omnipresence even on the peripheries of Mexican society.

Bodies of Outsiders

Because mining demanded a considerable workforce, foreign workers came to Zacatecas and some died during their visit. Their deaths inevitably raised a number of questions, including whether they had suffered violence. Anthony M. Kimball, born in Mexico to a Mexican mother and a father from New Hampshire, served as vice-consul in the city's U.S. consulate and noted with disdain the number of undesirable characters who arrived to work on the burgeoning railroads or in the mines. He complained to John C. Davis, a U.S. assistant secretary, about their intolerable rowdiness and penchant for disturbing the peace. These "workmen [and] adventurous roughs" all claimed U.S. citizenship despite having no proof thereof, he stated.[77] Moreover, many foreign laborers invited police attention by engaging in brawling, gambling, and drinking, according to Kimball.[78] In their troubles, the workers often sent for Vice-Consul Kimball at all hours of the day and night in order to negotiate with the Mexican authorities. They expected and demanded to be let out of jail without a trial or legal repercussions. Mexican police and judges, for their part, worked with Kimball despite the offensive behavior exhibited by the foreigners.[79] Nonetheless, these workers exhausted Kimball's patience, and he tendered his resignation after fifteen years due to the less than decorous behavior of these men.

Zacatecas locals resented the presence of foreign laborers despite a willingness to tolerate inebriated brawlers, as Kimball mentioned. Did Mexicans hold a grudge against employers for preferring the skills of foreign nationals over their own? Did they dislike the use of Mexican land for American enterprise? Mexican workers suffered egregious violence in response to their union activities at foreign-owned businesses, examples being the Cananea massacre (1906) and Río Blanco textile strike (1907). However, Mexican workers also performed acts of sabotage against foreign workers decades before the revolution.[80] In Zacatecas, Kimball related a tragic tale in his quarterly communiqués. On 29 April 1884 nineteen railroad workers boarded a construction train in the nearby city of Calera.

As they traveled, the train struck a rail that had been laid across the track in an act of sabotage. The ensuing crash and derailment killed English and Irish workers, while severely injuring eleven others. Kimball hinted that "private revenge" and "bad feelings towards Americans" by the people of Calera had led to the malicious act.[81]

Conclusion: Surveillance and Supervision

Zacatecas attempted to implement public health measures that reflected advances in science at the turn of the twentieth century. Municipal officials ushered in a new era of public health concern, as they attempted to supervise the daily activities of locals to curtail behavior deemed dangerous. In order to understand the vices and diseases ailing Mexicans, municipal officials monitored the habits that threatened the health of Zacatecanos. For a mining city in a largely rural state, bodies indicated threats specific to how they used the land. Workers suffered mining accidents and mercury poisoning, providing a shocking illustration of how the body interacted with the ecology of extraction either through direct contact or through physical absorption. While crime warranted investigation, the creeping villains of mercury and other heavy metals escaped prosecution. The examples described in this chapter demonstrated a growing scientific understanding of how the body lived and withstood the barrage of toxins, physical assaults, and viruses encountered in day-to-day life. Yet, for municipal officials in the late nineteenth century, surveillance for the sake of public health focused on aberrant practices for the sake of the collective, except when the collective involved the mining industry. Whereas sex work drew castigation, the unmonitored dumping of mercury into local waterways did not, and mining firms avoided punishment in large part because of the economic importance of the industry and its lingering colonial legacy.

11. A diverse group enjoying a day in the countryside near a natural spring in Tlaltenango, Zacatecas. Used with permission from Concurso Tiempo, memoria y plata 2009, Colección Bernardo del Hoyo Calzada. Fototeca del Estado de Zacatecas "Pedro Valtierra."

4

The Body as Land

Water, Mining, and the Revolution

The mining industry . . . is a fount of finite richness. The countries
that live by mining, if they do nothing to prepare for the future
with other industries of a renewable character such as agriculture
or manufacturing, are fatally condemned to economic decadence
and even death.

—Pamphlet on drainage and sanitation in Zacatecas, 31 July 1902

J. M. G. DE MENDOZA WROTE AN ANXIOUS LETTER TO
the Secretaría de Agricultura y Fomento, or the Secretariat of Agriculture and Development, in March 1944 to complain about an
unsettling alliance. *Ejidatarios*, or communal land users, of San
Marcos, Durango; Santiago, Zacatecas; and Miguel Auza, Zacatecas,
had formed the Comisariados Ejidales, a council of communal land
leaders.[1] Ejidatarios and other rural farmers formed this group to
negotiate with the government at the state and federal level as mining
companies encroached on communal landholdings, an alarming scenario for everyone.[2] The *ejido* leaders accused the mining companies
of mishandling shared water sources, which served both mines and
farms. Federal officials fretted over the gray area in the legislation,
which allowed ordinary farmers to petition mining companies to
use underground water. In July 1944, Joaquín Franco urged the
Departamento Agrario (Agrarian Office) to send engineers to the
site in order to determine provenance and ownership of the water.
Despite the urgency behind the message, engineers dragged their feet
and failed to respond until 1949, leaving the ejidatarios to scramble

for irrigation sources. Using supplicant language, Benigno Ontiveros wrote as representative of the council of ejidos to Pres. Miguel
Alemán (1946–52) and requested permission to use in the meantime
the natural spring on nearby communal lands called Ojocaliente. To
speed up the process, Ontiveros asked that an engineering survey
be conducted quickly, as the council feared the economic fallout
they faced because of Alemán's stalling.[3]

The above case tangles with the three principal themes of this
chapter: water, government supervision of that resource, and isolation. The water discussed here refers to water in mines (or rather,
the underground water from aquifers) and in streams that flowed
near mines. Ejidatarios petitioned mine operators and local governments to access these sources because of the arid landscape or
because of the easy access to water near mines in the vicinity of
the ejido. In both cases, the dry streambeds and the pockmarked
terrain illustrated the mining history of Zacatecas. In addition, the
state had a long history of redirecting waterways and speculative
excavation. While ejidatarios requested access to the water at the
bottom of mines, the petitions also revealed a growing desperation
on the communal landholders' part. Even though the revolution had
promised land reform, a significant number of Zacatecas farmers
faced land and water insecurity. In an effort to ease that desperation, municipal officials deferred to the federal government to
grant permissions regarding water sources. The government then
determined if the water fell under the category of "national property," thus assuming for itself the role of keeper and hoarder of water.
However, government officials hesitated to intervene in local water
disputes, particularly when a mining company became involved.
Consequently, engineers once again assessed the provenance of
water and to whom it belonged—the mining company, the ejidos,
or the national government. Even with an engineering assessment
that declared the resource a national property, officials responded
slowly if at all. This lead-footed response extended from the number
of water laws being passed during this era at the national level to
the specific circumstances of each petition.

With Zacatecas located in the geographic periphery in relation to the national capital, many ejidatarios struggled in far more remote corners of the state and faced the same challenges as the state capital, but with more desperation and urgency. The city of Zacatecas, surrounded by a largely arid desert, had even more remote neighbors to the north, nestled near the state lines of Coahuila and Durango, and to the south in the rugged sierra. Farmers in isolated parts of the state also shaped the narrative on water disputes. In the ecology of extraction, they demanded to know why the government chose to interfere with or ignore a petition for access to water.

On the eve of the Mexican Revolution, foreigners and an elite class owned most of Mexico's land while the rural poor faced pervasive landlessness when their ejidos were privatized. The revolution's conflicts began with work stoppages and a violent strike in the mines of Cananea, Sonora, in 1906 and the textile factories of Río Blanco, Veracruz, in 1907. It exploded in 1910 when Francisco Madero, the Anti-Reelectionist Party's presidential candidate, denounced the skewed results of the election, which had given Porfirio Díaz yet another term in office. In his Plan de San Luis Potosí (1910), Madero declared the election illegal and then fled to the United States. After a brief period of fighting in the country, Díaz too left the country, fleeing to Europe in May 1911, and Madero became president in November. When Madero failed to tackle the issue of landlessness, Emiliano Zapata issued his Plan de Ayala that same November, which reignited fighting. In their revolutionary call-to-arms, the Zapatistas emphasized agrarian reform and rejected the monopoly of "lands, forests, and waters."[4] Despite calls for the expropriation of water sources from hacienda owners' lands, the project of agrarian reform largely emphasized land, not water.

While scholars cite the Plan de Ayala as containing the core tenets of the revolutionary ideology, they have also revealed a more complicated narrative on the question of land reform. Domingo Diez, an anthropologist, offered a "hydraulic thesis" to the Mexican Revolution in the context of Morelos sugar plantations, suggesting that the concentration of waterways on hacienda lands had sparked the Zapatistas' ire. In contrast, historians emphasized the "agrarian thesis," or a reaction to pervasive landlessness with calls for land redistribution, as the reason why the conflict began in the first place.[5] Alejandro Tortolero Villaseñor, through Diez's lens, suggested that land reform presented a problem in the state of Morelos: without access to water, farmers could not cultivate enough sugarcane to survive economically.[6] In short, how could land reform succeed without water for crops? With the liquid resource limited to a privileged few, Diez argued that the agrarian question was easily subject to "agrarian feudalism," denoting a hierarchy in access to resources.

In the state of Zacatecas, both before and after the Constitution of 1917, farmers encountered similar challenges in gaining access to water, mostly because the mining industry controlled access. Geographically, the farmers of Zacatecas struggled to grow crops on both the arid altiplano in the northern half of the state and the mountains in the southern half. When planting season arrived, they irrigated crops using water from local streams or springs. When these were not available, they drew water from mines, which fell under federal jurisdiction after the Constitution of 1917 and subsequent laws. Without the political will to settle these arguments over water rights, farmers encountered a hurdle, as noted by Diez: "The social problem, that is, the agrarian, in which the intervening principal elements of the population are composed—its race, its idiosyncrasy, its crop (or culture), and its industry—to which we must add the political, because given its nature it takes advantage of circumstances in order to accomplish its own goals."[7] Diez imagined agrarians as radicals in racialized discourse, but he neglected to consider government as the problem rather than the circumstances in which agrarians found themselves—without access to water and without "ecological autonomy" as described by John Tutino. That is, "a family or community that produces most of the essentials of survival on land or other resources it controls—or uses in open access."[8] When farmers petitioned for use of water sources, particularly during drought or in areas of water scarcity, these fights dragged for months if not years, leaving fields dry. When the mining companies relented and allowed a community or a pueblo to use the water, they did not guarantee the purity of water.

While water remains a central focus here, this chapter also weighs the absence of water, which further politicizes its use by mines and farmers. What happens when waterways run dry? When the mining companies block ejidos' access to water? When mining pollutes the last viable stream? When it simply does not rain for months? In the absence of water the federal government served as the arbiter of access, grantor of use, and mediator of disputes. Conflict studies scholars have previously demonstrated an increase in violence during times of water stress, or periods without consistent water availability. However, their results varied when they saw cooperation and more violent acts in wetter years in various locations, in contrast to previous work.[9] Nonetheless, in Mexico, the water disputes discussed here extended well into the 1940s, when revolutionary politics allowed farmers to air their grievances and request an engineer to map out source provenance. Yet, Diez's "hydraulic thesis" raised questions as to whether farmers would turn to violence as the decades after the military conflict turned the center of the country into a potential powder keg.

This chapter assesses the success and failure of water legislation in protecting resources for farmers near Zacatecas mines, under-scoring the limitations of revolutionary promises and emphasizing the desperation that accompanied climate-triggered health crises. A reading of the petitions for water access revealed a largely hesi-tant government and a growing restlessness among ejidatarios and ranchers. The petitioners seeking access to water in mines lived far from the state capital and depended largely on agriculture or mining to make a living. In isolation, these two backbones of the Zacatecas economy created a chimera of legal confusion over waterways and underground aquifers. With the resource essential to the survival of both economic sectors, federal officials and engineers faced difficult decisions and angry ejidatarios. Furthermore, when mining did utilize waterways, locals complained of the contamination, gen-erating environmental memory in the legal record. In essence, the legal arguments over water illustrated the ecology of extraction that poisoned agrarian communities and killed animals that drank the water while government officials exercised their power by simply doing nothing.

In what follows, I examine how tensions emerged from legislation to protect water. In an effort to protect the resource, legislators contributed to the struggles of farmers and ejidatarios in the state of Zacatecas, which in the aftermath of revolution had politicians publicly championing land reform while privately hoarding water. I do so by first exploring the absence of water and its link to public health in a discussion of typhus and diphtheria—two epidemics that spawned preventive measures across the country. Then, I move into the revolutionary period (1910–46) to show how water legislation promised protection for the vital resource despite the growing industrial dependence on waterways in mining states such as Zacatecas. My aim with this chapter is to underscore the continuities between the Porfiriato and the revolutionary period, specifically with regard to water and public health. I argue here that Zacatecas, a state on the periphery, saw little material change since it remained a site of extraction, as it had since the colonial period. One significant difference between the two periods is emphasized in the stories of farming communities. Stories of polluted waterways, laments over dead animals, memories of long-gone trees—these all emerged as part of the record of the revolution in the state, and all demonstrated the ecology of extraction.

Microscopic Foes

On the eve of revolution, Zacatecanos faced a twofold attack from a decade-long drought and multiple epidemics. With the extended drought, disease continued to plague Zacatecas, illustrating the link between climate and contagions despite government efforts to intervene. Vectors such as fleas multiplied exponentially as they fled from drought-stricken cattle ranches to human populations. Cattle-producing areas faced an even greater danger from fleas and lice as these insects transmitted typhus to human populations. The insect-borne illness swept through urban and rural populations in the early twentieth century as doctors marked a shift from miasma theory to one that considered disease to be spread by bacteria, parasites, and viruses. While the global debate on the origins of disease reached Mexico at this time, the poor and rural people fell to the ferocity of the epidemics, which illustrated the lack of public health infrastructure to meet their needs. With only a few hospitals and ill-equipped doctors, the state government failed a significant part of the population even as Mexico City touted its public health programs.

Typhus in history coincides with wars, famine, and natural disasters as well as their aftermath. The disease arises from a particular microbe genus called *Rickettsia*. A type of bacteria with some features of a virus, the microorganism that spawns epidemic typhus flows in the blood of rats, mice, and humans. It stows away in the bellies of insect vectors after they have feasted on these infected mammals, and it then goes on to seek new hosts. Variations in the *Rickettsia* strain depend largely on the vector. Mites from mice introduce scrub typhus in humans; endemic typhus comes from the rat flea; and ticks carry Rocky Mountain spotted fever.[10] Most commonly, humans contract typhus from lice (*Phthiraptera anoplura*) infected with *Rickettsia prowazekii*, named after codiscoverer and victim Stanislaus Prowazek (1875–1915). When a louse bites an infected person, the insect ingests the microorganism from the person's bloodstream. Upon finding a new host, the louse bites its new victim, causing the person to scratch, leading to irritation and small openings in the skin. The louse then defecates live typhus into the open wound, spreading the disease into the bloodstream.[11] Disease caused by *Rickettsia prowazekii* reaches epidemic status as the infected host carries lice into large, overcrowded population centers.[12] At the outset, the bitten victim presents with severe flu-like symptoms, including a high temperature, weakness in the limbs, achy joints, and headache. Soon, the infected person demonstrates a rash on the torso, which then spreads to the limbs. The patient eventually develops a headache that signals the onset of meningoencephalitis, or the inflammation of the meninges, the lining between the skull and brain.[13] A quick death mercifully follows.

In previous decades, municipal officials saw typhus sweep through the city following an extended drought. Francisco Árbol y Bonilla wrote to the Junta de Sanidad de Zacatecas (Health Council of Zacatecas) in 1852 begging for an investigation into the epidemic of typhus that had swept through the city the previous year.[14] Árbol y Bonilla cited the start of the epidemic in Europe but wanted to know how local conditions had spurred the outbreak. He also noted that farmers and ranchers had suffered losses in cattle, goats, and sheep because of the lack of rain. Árbol y Bonilla posited that the economic loss of herds and the lack of crops drove the rural population to the city, which set in motion the epidemic.[15] The scene repeated itself in 1892 as another drought swept through the region and once again brought a wave of typhus. In the same file containing Árbol y Bonilla's letter, a report from the Junta de Sanidad in the city to the national capital details the efforts of municipal leaders to provide aid to patients with various stages of typhus. The masses arrived in the state capital to seek relief but found crowded streets and only a few charitable efforts to help them. Adding to the misery, patients at the *hospicio* near the Ciudadela found a throng of people in stifling rooms, which heightened the epidemic. The elderly and the young suffered the most, with a 50 percent mortality rate. These victims died from *padecimiento nerviosa*, or "nervous suffering," signaling the onset of meningoencephalitis.[16]

Whereas most cases of illness arising from environmental conditions underscore the presence of toxic materials from industrial works, the link between health and climate is considerable. The history of natural changes in climate patterns coincides with shifts in health, according to the epidemiologist Anthony McMichael.[17] McMichael asserts that climate amplifies or contributes directly to disease by encouraging the reproduction of disease vectors that thrive in the heat, such as fleas.[18] From the dawn of agriculture to the medieval bubonic plague, climate has exacerbated the conditions in which humans thrive, wilt, or simply disappear, as in the case of the

12. Dry streambeds in Zacatecas. La Bufa looms over the city in the background.
Library of Congress, Prints and Photographs Division, Detroit Publishing
Company Collection, L C-D 418-9073.

ancient Mayan cities.[19] While fleas have parasitically lived among
human populations for thousands of years, the insects have hinted
at things to come, with typhus outbreaks in Texas as recently as
2017.[20] Moreover, for the grand time line of Mexican history, typhus
seems to be a constant. Since 1655, there have been twenty-two
outbreaks of typhus recorded in historical materials, such as diaries,
letters, doctors' notes, and other sources. To analyze the timing of
these outbreaks, researchers used dendrochronology, studying more
than fourteen hundred tree ring samples to establish the years in
which drought had swept through central Mexico.[21] They found that
the epidemics of typhus coincided with the drought data gathered
from the tree rings, suggesting a correlation between fleas and the
extremely arid conditions.

In 1892, the tanners of Zacatecas disposed of putrid animal waste
and chemicals in the city's waterways, which compounded problems
arising from an ongoing drought and the fight for the water distri-

bution system. Municipal official Atenógenes Llamas posted a flyer in October that asked people to stop dumping animal skins into the central waterway of the city, the Arroyo de la Plata, or Stream of Silver. Llamas sounded the alarm about noisome waste going into the stream because the channel served as a water-collecting site for several families nearby.[22] As pictured, houses crowded waterways in Zacatecas, which exposed many residents to the smells from muddy stream beds. Because of the persistent drought, the tanning waste festered in stagnant pools as the current in the stream dwindled to a trickle. To make matters worse, local business owners added to the rotting miasma with the waste of slaughterhouses, butcher shops, and soap factories.

In order to stop the contagion and its vectors, Llamas echoed the theme of cleanliness, particularly in the home. He reiterated his condemnations of the slovenly habits of locals and reminded residents that they congregated with the uncouth whenever they attended festivals, mass, or other events. He admonished the irresponsible behaviors of locals who menaced the community at large. In an effort to fight the fleas, Llamas encouraged residents to have their homes cleaned, inspected, and fumigated with sulfuric acid as well as sprayed with carbolic solution. Finally, he ordered a halt to all funerals and wakes in order to contain the disease.

The recommendations Llamas described reveal the struggle in public health between scientific reason and long-entrenched Catholic devotion to rituals. Llamas underscored the effects of miasmas wafting from the stream into populated areas and warned against these invisible "airs" affecting the health of the population. Despite the growing belief in germ theory, ideas regarding miasmas lingered and shaped life in Zacatecas—from the location of houses to the steady stream of complaints sent to municipal offices. Germ theory remained largely entrenched in medical terminology and not accessible to the wider population. As a result, most Mexicans not familiar with the scientific advances of the era defaulted to the miasma theory, which remained part of the popular mythology. Even as the epidemic and stench pervaded the city, locals continued to attend wakes, pray novenas, and crowd funerals to pay respects to the deceased even though these practices gave the disease ample opportunity to spread. By limiting these displays of cultural ritual, Llamas and the municipal government revived the tensions between the Catholic Church and the government, a conflict that had persisted since the War of Reforms (1857–61). Nonetheless, locals capitulated and agreed to shortened, open-air masses with limited gatherings. As Llamas offered his solutions, engineers at the time worked to supplant Arroyo de la Plata as a water source by opening reservoirs, such as reservoir La Filarmónica, for public use and by constructing the fountain system.[23]

In November 1892, typhus patients continued to come forward, prompting the city to launch a concerted public health campaign that resulted in municipal officials entering private homes. José M. Echeverría, the mayor, and Pedro Espejo, the principal engineer, initiated a campaign of assistance for the city's population with a three-pronged approach to tackling the epidemic: medical assistance, an inspection troop, and a home inspection group.[24] In offering assistance, they targeted poor residents who could not afford medicines and disinfectants or manage to access clean water, especially in neighborhoods affected by the disease. If residents did not know how to identify the suitable conditions for typhus, Echeverría and Espejo offered an inspecting force to examine their dwelling and their symptoms. They divided the city into eight sectors for inspections headed by different engineers who dispensed disinfectants as well as the gospel of cleanliness and proper hygiene, or the "perfect and constant state of cleanliness," which signified proper ventilation, tidy rooms, and access to water for washing.[25]

With municipal officials involved in public health inspection, Zacatecanos added to the paranoia by lobbing accusations at their neighbors. M. F. Ocampo wrote to city officials in May 1905 to gossip on the affairs of the Arrellana and Matabedejuno families. He discussed four infected members in the first family and then a single case of disease in the latter, charging all family members with being complicit in the conspiracy to threaten public health.[26]

Specifically, he noted that the families interacted with local circus workers and lived near the public baths, which made them especially subject to scrutiny. Ocampo blamed the start of a localized epidemic on "the stash of dirty clothes and the lack of proper nutrition to the sick . . . in the handling and care of a stable of cows, and the dirty sewer in the Mesón de Vivac."[27] In his accusations, Ocampo emphasized the city's responsibility for containing the epidemic from the start and offered a suggestion: temporary closure of public toilets, the inspection of homes, and the cleaning of the stable in the alley, as well as a better sewer for the neighborhood. This nuanced argument counted on government officials to enforce their own recommendations. While municipal officials circulated pamphlets on cleanliness, they did not monitor the application or enforcement of these suggestions and left neighbors to serve as the supervisors of public health. Moreover, the petitioner pleaded for a preventive approach to disease in general. As with the rabies campaign, municipal officials sought to eradicate potential threats before they began. However, the onus of responsibility fell largely on the public rather than on the city government. Consequently, municipal recommendations came off as shrugged suggestions. As a result of Ocampo's letter, municipal officials closed the toilets for scrubbing and banned circus functions. A clean-up program attempted to rid the area of damp and dirty streets by encouraging the sweeping of the streets as well as the cleaning of stables.

While typhus occurred in seasonal waves, diphtheria left an indelible mark on families across the region as it grew to pandemic status in the mid-nineteenth century. The disease stems from a rod-shaped bacterium called *Corynebacterium diphtheriae*, which is bulbous at one or both ends.[28] The three strains of the bacterium include *gravis*, *intermidius*, and *mitis*. The *mitis* strain provides immunity if survived but does prove fatal in children.[29] The disease spreads effectively by entering the lungs through inhaled respiratory droplets. The bacterium then incubates in the lungs and produces a toxin carried through the system. The toxin then spurs symptoms that, like those of typhus, resemble a severe influenza, with moderate fever, malaise, sore throat, and cough. While typhus incapacitates its victims with meningoencephalitis, diphtheria strangles its sufferers. As the disease progresses, the upper respiratory tract produces mucous membranes as a response to the disease. As they grow thicker, the soft tissue in the mouth, nose, and trachea swell, making breathing increasingly difficult. The disease kills by asphyxiation.[30] Patients also die of secondary effects in the heart as the toxin damages nerves and muscles in the cardiac system. Only immunization limits the spread of the disease to other persons.[31] Doctors in the nineteenth century referred to diphtheria as *morbus suffocans* or *la garrotilla* after the twisting *garrote* torture device that strangled those condemned by the Spanish Inquisition.[32]

Zacatecanos soon pushed municipal officials to limit or contain disease as much as possible, inspiring local physicians to offer their own assessment of the city's failings. Physicians such as Dr. Rosalío Torres emphasized the role of the government in handling threats to the health of the community and in following through on recommendations. To prove his point, he drew comparisons between Mexico and countries he labeled as *países cultos*, or learned countries. Torres maligned municipal officials in 1898 for their stalling and criticized the federal government for not moving as fast as governments in other countries, particularly in regions outside Mexico City. He wrote in a report to the Junta de Sanidad in August 1898,

> Conserve health, preventing illness, make epidemics less terrible, lower mortality, better the races and preserve the strengths of man while increasing the population and the public wealth, even if there is not a hygienist present, at least they attempt to increase the duration of life of man on this planet, perhaps in a few words the beautiful ideal that follows science. Just as the cleanliness of a person, the care in how they dress, the courtesy in their manners, the beauty in their language, and the harmony in their thinking turn man learned and civilized, likewise the healing of cities in the buildings of the law.[33]

While this doctor outlined the goals of Porfirian *científicos* in the first sentence, he reflected the embedded racism and classism of the era, once again labeling the rural poor as the backward element in the country despite the misery facing the countryside and the regions with predominantly indigenous populations. Indigenous communities suffered from not only a loss of land and ongoing debt peonage but also from a lack of economic and social opportunities due to institutionalized racism. Notably, Torres attempted to exempt the "cultured and civilized" members of society from responsibility for disease, pointing to the government as a central guard against such perceived backwardness.

Moreover, Torres warned about the specific physiology of diphtheria and underscored the environmental factors that encouraged the disease to spread among the poor. The bacillus, discovered by the German scientist Edwin Klebs in 1883 and grown in a laboratory by Friedrich Löffler in 1884, caused diphtheria to sweep through the state the year that Torres wrote his letter. Poor children had been disproportionately affected, he argued, which hinted of a worse year to come. While preventive measures slowed and stopped the disease before it unfolded into a larger tragedy, diphtheria concentrated in poorer populations because of the lack of medical care as well as the living conditions. Notably, he added that the canals, streams, and sewers needed to be cleaned while homes should be orderly and neat, once again linking cleanliness and health. As with Ocampo and his critique of neighbors, the boundary between private lives and public facilities blurred during epidemics.

A Continuity of Maladies

Historians increasingly dispute the argument that the Porfiriato and the Mexican Revolution created a rupture in Mexican history. In this work, the two periods share an uninterrupted thread in the management of threats to public health and the poor supervision of environmental health concerns. The public health crises continued, and they illustrate a failure on the part of national leadership to enforce preventive measures, despite the calculating and blustering rhetoric in both eras. This section tracks four continuities in public health between the two periods for the state of Zacatecas.

First, the political influence of Zacatecas quickly faded in the early twentieth century, as financial resources and workers shifted away from the city. After the premature death of Eduardo Pankhurst in 1908, municipal officials watched projects go unfinished as a two-fold tragedy enveloped the city: a prolonged drought and a wave of typhus. In addition, city authorities hesitated to move forward with projects, either from hesitation due to a lack of leadership or a lack of funds to implement restrictions during the scourge of fleas. Because of the chaos, the population rapidly declined. Alan Knight has written that the growing urban centers provided a potent landscape for politicization, as did regions with *ranchero* agriculture.[34] Workers left Zacatecas in droves, with many moving to boomtowns in 1895–1910 or relocating to urban centers such as Guadalajara or Mexico City. Meanwhile, many other workers went to *rancherías* in the region or worked at haciendas. Consequently, municipal officials had little motivation to work toward a solution to the ongoing crises. After all, a shrinking population meant a shrinking epidemic.

After the 1910 upheaval, a series of generals replaced municipal officials in Zacatecas, who neglected to curb the spread of the disease from the region and into Mexico City. When armies swept through the region, soldiers quickly dispatched cattle or goats for their meals, which prevented fleas from finding animal hosts; the insects instead began infesting the soldiers. During the military phase of the conflict, the disease launched its most memorable and savage assault as it swept into urban centers. While it had become endemic in regions like Zacatecas, typhus did not reach Mexico City until 1915. By September of that year, six hundred patients had overwhelmed the Hospital General, with several being turned away, according to historian Martha Eugenia Rodríguez.[35] The fight continued into 1918, when drought allowed a small pocket of typhus to live long enough to again grow into an epidemic.

Second, the maladies continued in part because the political chaos brought about by the conflict only mirrored the already tumultuous political life of Zacatecas. With the beginnings of the Mexican Revolution in 1910, factions cut a large scar through the countryside.

In the Plan de San Luis Potosí, Francisco I. Madero called for the end of the presidency of Porfirio Díaz and new elections. Madero had initially enjoyed the support of different factions around the country, including that led by Emiliano Zapata, but these alliances soon fell apart. From 1900 to 1910 Zacatecas had five different governors and the government changed hands twenty-two times between elected and interim governors.[36] Nonetheless, nominal public health programs squeaked by during this time, like the rabies vaccinations as well as the end of slaughtering cattle near the city center. When typhus and diphtheria swept through the region, the epidemics exposed the weakness of political inconsistency. Political chaos in local government perhaps served as the most consistent thing about the Porfiriato. Knight has underscored how Porfirio Díaz culled any rebellious aspect from the political hierarchy in states in order to maintain his power.[37] Loyalty to Díaz over loyalty to citizens characterized the era, in the historian's estimation.

After 1910, political instability continued in the city and exacerbated existing public health crises while armies swept through the country. Two generals, a lawyer, and a doctor served as governors of Zacatecas from 1910 to 1920 a total of fourteen different times.[38] At one point Gen. Pánfilo Natera was serving as governor intermittently because he had resumed his duties as part of the Division of the North. The political flux of the era eliminated much of the success of public health programs.

A third continuity in public health extends to the theme of isolation. During the Porfiriato, physicians and public health boards recommended exiling and isolating the sick from the rest of society while creating factions of the healthy and the unhealthy, the rich and the poor, indigenous and mestizo—a divisive dichotomy that illustrated the Porfirian approach to governance and society. Before 1910, medical researchers seeking to explain the origin of disease did not necessarily see miasma theory and germ theory as conflicting but perhaps in dialogue. Doctors used both theories to express how they understood the origin of disease. However, when it came to solutions, the scientists separated into factions. Isolation and quarantine offered a remedy to wall off infection and contain panic from spreading before 1910. Here, I outline two examples: typhus in Zacatecas and in La Castañeda, a care facility in Mexico City. During the 1892–93 epidemic of the flea-borne illness in Zacatecas, Dr. Luis Mora Castillo of the Junta de Sanidad proposed housing 100 to 150 typhus patients in a hospital high above the city, on Cerro de la Bufa. In isolating the patients and tending to them in a hospital setting, he hoped some of them might recover. The Junta de Sanidad dismissed the suggestion, instead outlining measures on how to stop the spread of the disease by limiting social functions. Similarly, isolation became the prescription for psychological disorders in Mexico City. Díaz ordered the construction of an asylum, La Castañeda, on the outskirts of the metropolis in order to contain, in his view, the unstable sectors of society. Patients with developmental disorders, birth defects, or simply anxiety arrived at the hospital for supervision, care, and treatment.[39] By rejecting the perceived "backward" part of society, Porfirian-era doctors isolated and segregated them to limit interaction with society at large under the guise of benevolence.

After 1910, medical doctors continued to marginalize certain sectors of the population and face challenges from local belief systems. As previously mentioned, indigenous people and the poor often suffered due to a lack of medical infrastructure, such as hospitals and clinics. Isolation proved deadly to marginalized communities. Politicians cited geography, the lack of doctors, recalcitrance on the part of indigenous communities, and the great distance of mountain villages from urban centers as reasons for not providing medical care. Without access to care, many died from accidents or poorly monitored illnesses. Consequently, indigenous peoples suffered from neglect—sometimes spiteful and almost always deadly after 1910. Other groups pursued a separate approach to medicine, far from the professionalization of medicine and medical science. While curanderos remained part of the indigenous tradition, many people hesitated to rely on medical doctors trained in professional schools. As a whole, doctors, healers, científicos, and would-be patients alike remained split on how to approach public health in terms of both ideology and application.

The fourth public health continuity between the Porfiriato and the revolutionary period includes mining and its associated industries. As discussed in previous chapters, farmers and ranchers questioned mining companies' use of water sources before and after the Mining Code of 1884. The code allowed foreign parties to purchase mining rights on Mexican soil, including mines that existed near farms and streams. These early clashes only set the stage for the larger battles over water rights in Zacatecas that once again pitted farmers against miners. However, the farmers and the miners had by then been absorbed by larger entities: the farmers sold their land and relocated, while the miners now served multinational conglomerates. As this chapter later explores, how populations in the vicinity of these large mines responded to the consumption and contamination of water illustrated a continuity from the Porfiriato regarding industrial access to waterways.

In one of the most notable breaks between the two eras, villagers recognized that mining effluvia made them ill. While most observers in late nineteenth century pointed to miasmas as the source of disease, *campesinos* after the 1940s blamed mining companies for water contamination that made them and their animals sick. Subsequently, they understood the association of dirty water with dying animals and what happened when a human consumed contaminated water. Consequently, the definition of "health" changed from one involving superstition to one that emphasized the exchange between the environment and the body.

The Impending Battle

Armies swept into Zacatecas and affected the safety of the city and properties. By 1912, U.S. and British investors had become worried about their investments in the country. U.S. secretary of state Philander C. Knox sent a telegram tactfully stating that the U.S. government sympathized with the Mexican people in their quest for democracy and that he hoped Mexicans, in return, would respect U.S. properties in Mexico.[40] Regardless of his pleas, soldiers and locals used U.S.-owned mines to store munitions, looted their equipment, and sabotaged any working machinery. In addition, soldiers forced mule and donkey owners in Zacatecas to sell them their animals. Under military orders, Gen. Claro Hurtado ordered that locals present their animals in five days for sale on 14 July 1914, as the military needed new animals to haul munitions and supplies.[41] From a strategic point of view, the city offered respite for armies crisscrossing the country. In its north-central location, the state capital lay en route to the northern cities of Monterrey, Ciudad Juárez, and Durango. Soldiers took the opportunity to purchase, refresh, or replace their pack animals. The Villista rebels relied on the railroads for transport, and since the city served as a railway hub, it became clogged with refugees and armies in transit.

On 23 June 1914, Zacatecas witnessed one of the bloodiest battles of the conflict when Gen. Pánfilo Natera, Gen. Francisco "Pancho" Villa, and others attempted to capture the city from Gen. Luis Medina Barrón, an ally of Pres. Victoriano Huerta. Federal troops surrounded the city from atop the six major hills: La Bufa, El Sierpe, El Padre, El Capulín, El Grillo, and El Refugio. Revolutionary troops gained control of each hill despite considerable losses in the process. Federal troops lost six thousand men and took five thousand prisoners. The Constitutionalists, according to Villa, lost roughly a thousand men and suffered two thousand wounded.[42] With such a high number of casualties, including both soldiers and civilians, bodies littered the streets and the city lay in ruins.

The geography and terrain of the city influenced the military strategy and added to the mythology of the battle. Before the battle began, federal officer Ignacio Muñoz marveled at the city below from atop one of the hills. He noted that Zacatecas appeared to be a city in miniature and relatively quiet in the hours before battle.[43] On the Villa side of the conflict, soldiers besieged the hills of El Grillo and La Bufa, where the federal troops had placed their artillery.[44] Later, to commemorate the bloodshed, *corridos* recalled the battle, its heroics, and its casualties. Francisco Torres Rosales, a carpenter in the city, wrote "La Toma de Zacatecas," or "The Siege of Zacatecas," the day after the battle.[45] Friends had encouraged him to write a song describing the scene around them. Torres Rosales notably included the topography of the city in his song, as if the hills themselves had participated in the battle:

Les tocó atacar La Bufa
a Villa, Urbina y Natera,
porque allí tenía que verse
lo bueno de su bandera.
Las calles de Zacatecas
de muertos entapizadas,
lo mismo estaban los cerros
por el fuego de granada.

They had to attack La Bufa
Villa, Urbina, and Natera,
because there they had to see
the goodness of their flag.
The streets of Zacatecas
were carpeted by the dead,
the same as on the hills
by the blasts of grenades.

By incorporating the terrain into the song, the *corrido* not only eulogized the dead but also recognized the role of the famous landscape in the fight.

While the cultural history of the Battle of Zacatecas indicated an attempt to immortalize the event, locals struggled to contain a potential public health crisis in the aftermath of the battle. Dr. Luis Mora Castillo wrote to the local political boss on 2 July 1914 to request the removal of the hundreds of corpses.[46] Workers in the recovery effort continued to bring the dead to the hospital and sanitarium, most likely for identification or for an official recording of casualties. As the bodies mounted, Mora Castillo requested their removal. Meanwhile, locals struggled to find food. Even a year after the Battle of Zacatecas, the political leaders of the state posted a circular on 1 June 1915 that called for more maize to be introduced into markets. Locals struggled to find grain, as many had hoarded supplies with the hope of drawing a profit from its sale during desperate times.[47] Political leaders required hoarders to sell the grain at their residence or accept a fine of fifty pesos. Likewise, political leaders and generals in Zacatecas attempted to keep illegal activity to a minimum. Pancho Villa gave the Zacatecas post to a trusted general and native son, Pánfilo Natera, who explicitly warned citizens that destroyers of property and vandals would be executed if caught.[48] Villa and his demand subtly hinted at the protection of foreign property, suggesting that the revolutionary regime recognized it would eventually need outside capital to continue its efforts.

A Rebellious Nature

In addition to its striking mountain ranges and an arid altiplano, the landscape surrounding the city emerged as not only a contributing factor in how soldiers fought the Battle of Zacatecas but also a character in the cultural history of the revolution. The term "landscape" suggests a privileged point of view, but it also allows for artistic interpretations of it. As a character in Mariano Azuela's classic novel of the revolution, *The Underdogs*, the landscape becomes more than a plot device, as it shaped the feeling and mood of the novel, particularly after heavy military clashes. In effect, nature emerged as a crucial part of the novel's narrative.

Originally printed as a serial in the *El Paso del Norte* newspaper in 1915, the novel described the exploits of a small band of revolutionary soldiers as they wandered through the canyons of Coahuila, the deserts of Chihuahua, and finally into the Battle of Zacatecas. As the narrative progressed, the revolutionaries lost sight of why they fought as they grew more weary with every passing day. Paralleling their exhaustion, the terrain emerged as a second character, serving as a reminder of the struggle for land. Azuela included eloquent descriptions of the landscape and emphasized the hills, shrubs, and canyons of the north-central region of Mexico. Moreover, Demetrio Macías, the leader of this small band of rebels, employed the landscape in his strategy and tactics. The first skirmish narrated illustrates a battle in which soldiers used a small canyon near the Macías home as a death trap for the *federales*.[49] Also, the land voiced its own disenchantment with the conflict, paralleling that of the people. While the men rested at a *ranchería* early in the novel, the narrator details the flowing river and young crops growing in the *milpas* in the mild summer weather.[50] This fertile ground soon gave way to a desert-like environment by the end of the novel, which signaled a brooding refusal to bloom or to flow. Nature—fatigued, parched, and withered—refused to continue on its revolutionary march. With the arrival of drought, Macías and his men struggled to find water when there was "no pool or stream or well anywhere along the road."[51] Whereas food descriptions in the beginning of the novel indicated a cornucopia, they decreased significantly toward the end, hinting at an exhaustion of the food supply and the land as a consequence of the revolution.

Water and the Revolution

With extreme rates of landlessness among the poor and indigenous in 1910, Francisco Madero faced increasing pressure to ameliorate the situation by distributing land and reinstating communal land-holdings when he assumed the presidency in 1911. A splintering of factions began almost immediately. Emiliano Zapata wrote in the Plan de Ayala (1911) that "the lands, hills, and water usurped by *hacendados*, *científicos*, or *caciques* in the shadow of venal justice will henceforth enter into the possession of the villages or of citizens that have those titles."[52] In essence, water became part of the revolutionary demands of a faction, which later influenced its inclusion in the Constitution of 1917. The Constitution outlined protections for this resource, continuing the regulations regarding water use coded into legislation during the late nineteenth century.

Legislation on water spurred local and national tensions over how to designate or use available water sources, as laws changed frequently and added to existing laws. The first national legislation protecting water came during the regime of Porfirio Díaz. Enacted 5 June 1888, that law stated that navigable rivers fell under federal jurisdiction. Díaz expanded the scope of protection to include all rivers per the Law of Waters under Federal Jurisdiction (1910), which designated water as an inalienable right. The drafters of the Constitution of 1917 wrote Article 27, which stated that water sources belonged to the nation and formed part of national patrimony. The legislation on water emphasized both federal jurisdiction and the question of ownership, which pitted two interests against each other. The federal government therefore served as the grantor of access to private companies or individuals. Meanwhile, Article 27 allowed the public interest to supersede private property rights in order to facilitate the redistribution of resources already belonging to the nation, as historian Mikael Wolfe writes.[53] These codes inevitably clashed on the Zacatecas landscape. Mining and agriculture—the two pillars of the Zacatecas economy—collided once again as both sectors attempted to implement revolutionary reforms. In nineteenth-century Zacatecas, mining and agriculture were often at odds over water. In the twentieth century, those tensions grew and added to the conflict in the early days of the revolution and beyond.

The revolutionary federal government attempted to implement portions of the Constitution of 1917 broadly, which created tensions between itself and the Zacatecas state government. The state government defaulted to federal interests when it came to questions of water provenance. In 1919, municipal council members representing Mazapil, Zacatecas and nearby Salaverna petitioned to use water from abandoned mines in the region for consumption, not agriculture.[54] Mazapil, a remote city near the border with Coahuila, often faced water insecurity because of arid conditions as well as persistent interference from local mining interests. Municipal council members saw this petition as a potential conciliatory overture toward the mining sector. They suggested tapping the water of Mina San Eligio and Mina Nazareno, since both offered convenient access to underground water and were relatively close to the municipality. Therein emerged the problem: foreign mining companies laid claim to those mines. The infamous U.S. extraction corporation Mazapil Copper Company owned the former, while the Compañía Minera Nazareno y Alicante owned the latter. Mining engineer Amado Aguirre denied the water use request of the *junta municipal* on 23 December 1919 because the source of the water was on property belonging to the mining companies.[55]

By studying maps and letters held in Mexico City and the state capital, government officials attempted to identify the provenance of the water in question. The investigatory process revealed the complicated nature of water legislation in states with arid, mountainous topography and industrial interests. In searching for the provenance, the officials had to identify the source of waterways, whose property it traversed, and what interests claimed it, among other questions. Did the water flow from below the surface of the earth? From a mine? From a reservoir? If so, on whose property? In whose mine? Political rhetoric often identified water as the property of the nation, but the requests to use water set off a labyrinthine process of investigation into ownership. Meanwhile, in some cases, federal officials relied on local engineers to map the flow of water. In June 1921, Roberto Arriaga submitted a request to use water from a mine owned by La Fé Mining Company near Guadalupe, Zacatecas.[56] A series of letters details engineers' attempts to clarify the exact location of this mine. One local engineer, Octaviano Bustamente, mapped the flow and direction of the water. He noted that the water had been *tirada*, that is, dumped by accident or with intention, which was contrary to the conservation efforts of water legislation. Moreover, Genaro Bayona, another local engineer, noted evidence of previous use by the nearby Hacienda Trancoso, which had installed metal tubing to draw water to Presa de Pedernalillo, a reservoir.[57] Government officials therefore denied Arriaga's request because the water had become national property.

Engineering Solutions

Engineers in municipalities assisted the federal government in exploring these claims, yet they faced obstacles in the form of private mining companies. In the northern part of the state, three small towns—Mazapil, Concepción del Oro, and Salaverna—struggled to find water sources as mining interests encroached on a shared aquifer. Municipal officials in Concepción del Oro, about one hundred miles north of the state capital, sought to determine ownership of waters from Mina de Aranzazu, property of the Mazapil Copper Company, in 1923.[58] Set in an arid region, the *pueblo* continued its struggle to find water for its residents even four years after Amado Aguirre had denied the initial request. The Secretaría de Agricultura y Fomento ruled that the town had jurisdiction over the mine, even if the water did not flow into a larger body of water. Municipal officials found, to their despair, lower levels of water than expected. Local mayor Mauricio Cardona recounted how Mazapil Copper Company administrators had accused locals of wanting to take advantage of the water extracted and making themselves a nuisance, thus disrupting operations.[59] To silence the debate, the government simply responded that the Aranzazu mine did exist in the municipality. Just a year later a federal engineer suggested the extraction company had purposely trapped the underground water in order to keep it from flowing into a stream, which prevented locals from accessing the water. While this case did not contain a resolution, Mazapil residents continued to have a tense relationship with the extraction companies that gave their town life yet left them thirsty.

Engineers proved to be the constant in each dispute, often reducing complicated water claims to mathematical understanding in order to inform a ruling. In one case, Don Benjamín Gómez Gordoa, proud owner of the Hacienda de Trujillo, an estate on the left bank of the Río Aguanaval, about forty miles north of the state capital, boasted of his right to and ownership of the river's waters. He claimed his family had owned the water for more than one hundred years, according to engineer L. Penador.[60] Penador noted that Río Aguanaval had a "violent character," with a strong flow and water "difficult to capture." Thus, in March 1926, he called for a specific number of liters of water per second to be designated for the use of local farmers who needed it between November and May, for planting.[61]

By defaulting to objective mathematics, federal officials subjectively sidestepped local squabbles regarding water, which they were particularly wont to do if landholding interests, such as haciendas and mining companies, had a stake in the decision. Farmers and ranchers emerged as unwitting victims in the mathematical magic that made one party owner of a water source designated as a national resource. Engineers quantified the resource when water itself did not have a measurable value. Water is invaluable to human life but priced according to its availability. This perception made the federal government a determining judge in a morality play with engineers as counsel for all parties. Furthermore, engineers collected facts and reduced them to "neutral" mathematical formulas, which then informed biased decisions on social issues and land reform. In x number of liters per second, revolutionary leaders implemented math in an otherwise unfair landscape. Poor farmers or ejidatarios had little interest in water calculations when the season's crops hung in the balance and their cattle died of thirst. Because of its long legacy of mining, arid Zacatecas had an environment scarred by industry, with few forests and fewer aboveground sources of water. When sources on the surface dwindled, underground water offered the last resort. Consequently, water rulings and decisions made in Mexico City did not consider the larger social implications. Thus, the precision of mathematical formulas failed to capture the enormity of the water crisis and the imprecision of law.

Landowners and mine owners frequently countered petitions compiled by ejidatarios citing mining activity and its encroachment on their waterways, which exemplified the federal-local divide in interpretations of the water law. In Fresnillo, two ejido leaders lodged a complaint against the Fresnillo Mining Company and their exploitation of the Proaño hill in December 1932.[62] Rafael Uitrón and Petronilo Martínez alleged that the community had noticed changes in the canal's water level as it flowed through their land. Upstream, the company held the rights to the land bordering the communal tracts and frequently rented an adjacent parcel. Because of the mining firm's expansive landholdings and the canal that traversed them, engineers for the extractive company changed the amount of water delivered to the communal land downstream. While the lawsuit alleged purposeful manipulation of the flow, company engineer Thomas O'Bahn defended the company's consumption since it was for industrial purposes and because they had a lawful contract with Antonio Gordoa.[63] At first glance, this case appeared to dissolve into alternating accusations. However, in February 1933, lawyer Carlos Sánchez Mejorada sent a letter to José Parres, the secretary of agriculture and development, describing how the company threatened to suspend mining activity and fire workers if they did not have access to water sources.[64] This ominous note suggested not only the use of intimidation against workers but also the nefarious use of power behind the scenes. What did the company intend should they be denied the right to use water? Did they have any pull in the federal government? In order to slow the escalating conflict, Fresnillo Mining Company CEO Hugh Rose reiterated interest in the water for industrial purposes and sought a consensus in order to continue using the resource.[65] In his effort to move the case along, secretary José Parres told the ejidatarios that his office had no power to remedy the situation.[66] Meanwhile, lawyers stipulated that the ejidatarios needed to clarify their case and indicate how their community suffered harm from the canal changes. Federal lawyer José Balderas García stated that existing laws nullified Fresnillo Mining Company's claim but that to appeal to judges in Mexico City the locals needed to be far more specific as to how their ejido had been directly hurt by the company.[67] It worked. Despite the back and forth, Pablo Ferrat, in a regional water office, supported the mining company on 4 July 1933 because of bureaucratic rules, as he put it, which required additional maps to pursue the claim.[68]

The Extraction of Water

In searching for ways to water field crops, farmers and municipal officials found a new resource to exploit and in the process discovered a solution to water supply despite the drought. Previously, water in mines had served as an obstacle to further ore extraction; it often needed to be pumped into aboveground streams. In dire circumstances of drought and impending conflict, municipal officials increasingly found reasons to be convinced of its usefulness. Municipal officials proclaimed the water to be salvation for their parched cities. This water quenched the thirst of the people and the land. Moreover, the resource appeared to be bottomless. Where water once came from the sky in the form of rain, in some communities in Zacatecas, their water came mostly from underground. The mines often served as archaeological markers of former industrial activities. These scars on the landscape gave the appearance of an infertile region and did not hint at the wealth of water below. Nonetheless, farmers who laid claim to or petitioned for these waters demonstrated knowledge of agriculture and underground systems of water. The water from mines blurred the lines between Zacatecas above and the caverns below. Farmers employed water from the darkest corners of the earth to help grow crops aboveground.

After 1910, the federal government frequently had the last word regarding local fights over water. Although initially reticent to intervene between campesinos and mining investors, it often relied on an "on-the-ground" assessment by engineers, particularly in cases involving questions of provenance. However, escalating tensions found mining companies more willing to consistently fight rulings to achieve some degree of waterway use. With the legal head-butting, federal officials attempted to delay petitions with bureaucratic hurdles in order to avoid having to make a ruling. Coupled with mining companies' unrelenting persistence, many cases regarding water rights stretched over decades because of the labyrinthine legislation regarding the resource at the national, state, and local levels. The following two cases illustrate how the federal government stalled local efforts to access water in mines in arid regions in the state after the ratification of the Constitution of 1917 in February of that year.

In the first case, Ángel Nieto proposed an agreement between himself and La Fé Mining Company in May 1917 to share the water in a mine belonging to the latter. Specifically, he sought to use the water for agriculture and small-scale mining activities. He cited a 1909 mining law that allowed for the use of water in mines, especially if all parties agreed on the terms.[69] Federal officials wrote from Mexico City to remind Nieto of Article 27, which stated that all waters belonged to the nation, but they did not encourage or dissuade him from pursuing his case further. Moreover, federal officials requested he determine the provenance of this water and how many liters he required for his use. In addition, they indicated that the company would have to concede use of this water. Nieto pursued the case, but the company never relented. On the contrary, La Fé Mining greedily continued to use the water in its own mine, as well as from others. Eleven years later, La Fé Mining Company petitioned to use water from Mina La Purísima by accessing 170 liters per minute through the site's *socavón*, or drainage pit.[70] The federal government did not intervene in either party's petitions but merely withdrew from the discussion without offering a formal decision.

Although federal officials hesitated to intervene, they did implement "bureaucratic clumsiness" to frustrate requests for water access, especially those made by foreign parties. In 1924, the Mazapil Copper Company opened a mine called Mineral de Aranzazu in northern Zacatecas, near Concepción del Oro. The company agreed to honor an existing contract to pump water from the mine into a pond via tubing for the nearby residents of a settlement called El Cobre.[71] While successful at the beginning, El Cobre residents soon found the water noxious and too dangerous to drink. The water being pumped from the mine mixed with the "waste waters they use in washing the metals, which decomposes, and then flows to the Río Concepción de Oro."[72] Adding to these problems, Mazapil Copper Company officials had constructed a beneficiation facility to better the quality of the extracted metals, which further contaminated the waters, rendering them undrinkable. Local residents Agustín Beltrán and others wrote to the Secretaría de Industria, Comercio, y Trabajo in March 1923 explaining the insalubrious conditions with detailed descriptions of the *lama*, or the slime that came from these activities.[73] A local representative, Gen. Isidro Cardona, wrote to the

Secretaría de Agricultura y Fomento a month later to request the federal government's intervention and reminded the government of its obligation as outlined in the Constitution of 1917. Because of the isolation of the town, federal officials needed someone to inspect the situation firsthand, as the local *abasto de aguas* (water board) in Concepción del Oro had never filed notice of the contaminated waters. The government thus called on water board members from San Luis Potosí and Coahuila to resolve the situation. Months later, the representatives began arriving and often reported conflicting evidence. Several of them appeared to be vacillating in their reports, but a few completed thorough assessments of the situation. They visited the area frequently, conducted interviews, and filed several reports to update previous information. They reinforced the government position and assessed the water quality as they traced the water to its source while also displaying an understanding of local politics on the matter. Many of these representatives from surrounding water boards had some education or experience as engineers, which proved crucial to supervising water use when private companies took an interest. Faced with an onslaught of prying engineers and angry locals, the company relented after significant pressure and agreed to remedy the issue.

Ecologies of Extraction

Mining and farming communities repeatedly clashed over access to water across decades, as described in several legal cases. These cases are notable namely because of the deeply personal sentiments conveyed by townspeople regarding their land, as well as the lingering toxic legacy of mining in the region. These conflicts occurred during the so-called Mexican Miracle, an era of exponential growth in the population and heavy migration to urban centers such as Mexico City and Guadalajara. While petitioners continued to allude to the Constitution of 1917, officials penned new legislation and changes to the use of water sources that gave the federal government jurisdiction and rights. The persons involved in these cases also make salient their collective environmental memory and the precariousness of water resources. Environmental memory illustrated the awareness of resource quality and access changing over time.[74] Documentation of said changes did not exist, but the campesinos witnessed the changes firsthand. While science and technology attempted to measure or quantify these memories, humans interacted through their senses and collective experiences with the same resource at very different times. In addition, the villagers discussed unequal access to resources, outlining their definition of water precarity.

Environmental memory and water inequality in this context represent the lingering toxic legacies of mining in the region. With environmental memory, residents recalled the conditions of different resources, imbued those memories with sentiment, and reminisced on the beauty of those previous environments. Toxic legacies, meanwhile, represented the prevalence of harmful remnants from an industrialized past or present that invaded local ecologies—from rivers and soil to blood and nerves over the course of years, or centuries in the case of the city of Zacatecas. While toxic remnants manifested very real effects on human physiology, environmental memory represented the mind's own understanding of the environment and how it had changed. The campesinos recalled the characteristics of resource availability before the mining boom: the abundance of water, the fruits on trees, and more. Those who remembered how water ran in a stream, unencumbered and clean, similarly fed these memories. The unequal access to water also signaled toxic legacies because of the avaricious consumption of the resource by mining companies. In essence, campesinos informed memories of a past environment even as the toxic remains of the past remained very much alive around them.

This first case involved Mina La Nevada, located near the Río Mexicapam just outside Fresnillo. In September 1948, engineer Antonio Rodríguez suggested that the Secretaría de Recursos Hidráulicos, or Secretariat of Hydraulic Resources, examine water from the mine in order to classify the resource.[75] More than two years passed before senior engineer Hector Molina García noted the discovery of a vertical shaft, or *tiro*. Miners as well as local workers from Huerta del Padre Castillo (Orchard del Padre Castillo, an agricultural property) had used the shaft to access the water with *norias*, or horse-powered water winches.[76] More years passed. In 1951, Molina García reported water from various industries was emptying directly into the river, which already had been designated as national property. The engineer traced some of the effluvia to a site owned by the Fresnillo Mining Company, which used a 60-horsepower engine to draw water from an underground reservoir. By the time engineer Francisco Escobedo wrote with great alarm that the Río Mexicapam had largely disappeared over the course of three years, the debate had ended. He launched an investigation to see who owned the spring-fed water source, as Huerta workers also complained of the diminished resource. Workers and nearby farmers, including Emilia Reina, wrote letters of complaint to Pres. Adolfo Ruiz Cortines. Reina, a widow and owner of farmland, described the fruit trees that once lined the riverbank and the flowers growing alongside them.[77] While the workers and farmers received compensation for the loss of water access, they also lost a way of life as the region shifted from agriculture to a heavy focus on mining.

The incident at Mina La Nevada revealed bureaucratic entanglements, environmental memory, and technology changes. In a bureaucratic stumble, engineers Rodríguez and Escobedo had confused the mine with another of a similar name in the vicinity—Mina La Navidad. Administrators debated as to which mine the initial complaint referred and approximately how far it was from the river. Despite the confusion over the name, the engineers illustrated the meticulous methods used in determining ownership and provenance of the resource, with staff going so far as to ask several locals for letters affirming the name of the mine, which they later corrected to Mina La Nevada. In environmental memory, locals such as Emilia Reina cited fruit trees and flowers as lingering memories of how the river had shaped the landscape in their community, giving the river a sensory depth of description as she recalled the fruit they ate and the flowers they picked. These memories contrasted with the new reality. She tied the depletion of the river to the disappearance of these landscape characteristics. Subtly, the widow suggested an elimination of beauty by describing the joy she and others had experienced in eating the fruit and seeing the flowers, adding weight to her argument and the community's loss. Despite the attempt by engineers to eliminate this sentimentality, these environmental memories underscored the severity of the landscape's transformation from fruitful joy to wasteland. Finally, the workers and bureaucrats saw a dramatic shift in technology over the course of the six-year period from 1948 to 1954. Initially, the engineers wrote of water- and horse-driven hoists, but the narrative quickly shifted to new technology. With the arrival of the 60-horsepower pump, Río Mexicapam quickly dwindled as the Fresnillo Mining Company rapidly drew off much of the water. The engineers, to their credit, did make several maps to help identify the river, its origins, and its ownership, as they attempted to control on paper an increasingly elusive resource. Overall, workers, farmers, and miners butted heads in a bid to access the river over the course of several years, illustrating the interests of the individual parties as well as memories and the effects of industrial technology.

Another case revealed the long-term effects of competition over water resources between communities and mining companies. As in the Río Mexicapam case, residents living near the Mineral de Aranzazu site battled mining interests over several years. However, residents raised a more serious concern. In 1923, engineer Isidro Cardona relayed a petition from locals to use water from the mine and requested that the mining company set aside water for the locals.[78] He sought to build a tubing system to capture water from the local mine and to limit evaporation in order to provide for the four thousand residents of the community. Previously, the water from the mine served as the locals' only source, but Cardona noted that "the nature of these waters has changed, making them useless for what they should be used."[79] He asked the company to purify the water before returning it to the stream so it would "not jeopardize the health of residents in the barrio."[80] Although he did not clarify the purification method, he explicitly labeled the *lama*, or processing slurry, as dangerous to public health. In the face of threats to their health from mining activities, Cardona and the townspeople requested a daily total of twenty thousand liters of purified water. They noted how the people had used the stream previously but that the company now channeled water into a particular location and used it for the amalgamation process before returning the wastewater to the stream. The water was then, as the engineer described it, "not potable and dangerous to human health."[81]

Engineers and residents employed a stubborn approach when negotiating with mining companies. Whereas engineers cited legislation to give their arguments leverage, they began to approach companies directly for concessions. The politics changed according to the importance of mining in a particular community. Farmers and workers grew frustrated with the bureaucratic stalling in water disputes, while politicians deferred to mining interests since they invested in smaller communities. In the above case, mining operators contaminated a shared water source that had long been used by local farms. Residents recognized the baleful effects of the wastewater emerging from the mines. Consequently, they rejected this water for domestic use and consumption, recognizing a link between the environment and their health. They did not underscore this knowledge with scientific data but relied instead on empirical observation and miasma theory. Farmers and workers likely observed the opaque quality of the stream while at the same time noting a change in the smell or taste, especially since contamination altered the viscosity and clarity of the water. Engineers and farmers alike displayed little concern for the pollution of the resource from an ecological perspective. Instead, they emphasized the loss in the context of their use and their livelihoods. While they lacked the scientific understanding to list the dangerous metals contaminating their land, they likely emphasized the significance of the land to their economic status, rather than the ecological dangers it possessed in its waters.

Farmers and residents in the vicinity of mines also found little recourse in water legislation when seeking compensation. Although Article 27 of the Constitution of 1917 emphasized surface water, subsequent legislation raised questions regarding contamination and pollution of waterways. In the Ley de Aguas de Propiedad Nacional of 1929, the definition of *aguas de propiedad nacional*, or waters of national property, extends to water extracted from mines, according to Article 1, section IX. Likewise, the 1934 reiteration of the law covered water from mines per Article 1, section VIII. When mining companies used water from mines or local streams—even if it was in the category of "waters of national property"—for amalgamation or beneficiation work, its composition changed. After the processing was complete, they released the water back into waterways, contaminating them and the surrounding soils with industrial effluvia. In 1934, the government threatened to "punish administratively" any dumping of wastes from metal beneficiating plants or of any substances that could harm the riverbeds, human health, and the health of animals, in accord with Article 108, section I.[82] This admonishment, while effusive, did very little to protect those living within the ecology of extraction.

In the aftermath of the Río Mexicapam controversy, Zacatecas farmers continued to wrangle with the legal codes and definitions regarding local use of water for mining and farming. In particular, a legal battle loomed in Jiménez del Teul in 1937 as a fight over the local water source continued after years of fighting between locals, a mining company, and the federal government. One hundred and fifty farmers and villagers argued that the Mineral de La Candelaria polluted the local river with the waste of the mill and the mine. In addition, the Beneficiadora de Metales de la Compañía "Don Carlos" contaminated the river with wastewater from the treatment process, according to José Parres, head of agriculture and development.[83] On the back of the summary by Parres, Roberto Arriaga described the situation as "resolved" but noted the government's inability to impose a fine on the beneficiating company because the waters did not fall under the national property classification. In a telling bit of marginalia, Arriaga suggested following the case closely, as it proved "worth saving and archiving as precedent."[84]

Weeks before, on 30 January 1937, a group of townspeople in

Jiménez del Teul wrote to the secretary of agriculture and development to say that their cattle could no longer drink from the local stream because the effluvium was "thick and fetid." They also described the water from the stream as too dirty for domestic use.[85] Again farmers and villagers presented an environmental memory of clean water without three inches of sediment in it, and they wrote of their observations regarding animals. Cattle did not want to drink the water, and if they did drink it, they "stopped existing."[86] Many cattle and sheep died as a result of consuming the water, which led their owners to request compensation. Their efforts to pursue their claim due to water contamination ran into a maze of bureaucratic ineptitude or malfeasance. For example, it was discovered that someone from the federal government had thrown out a vital water sample taken from the stream in question. Agustín Ortíz Medina wrote that J. H. Ashley, an employee from the Compañía "Don Carlos," had collected the sample himself and offered it as evidence that there had been no wrongdoing on the company's part. The Jiménez del Teul residents had previously attempted to get the attention of the secretariat. In July 1936, General Lic. Arturo Reyes Robledo helped the campesinos write an initial letter demanding compensation for dead animals. That petition had observed that "nothing has been done to remedy the situation."[87] Reyes Robledo cited necropsy samples from seventeen small ungulates and sixty-three head of cattle to demonstrate the severity of the situation. In addition, he included the observations of locals who had used the water on their plants, which had soon died. He concluded that a link existed between humans and their surroundings. He also requested compensation for the animals: five pesos for a sheep or goat and thirty pesos per head of cattle. While his suggestion to stop mining went unheeded, Ortíz Medina argued how the mining activity near the farms violated Articles 118 and 119 of the law regarding water as national property. The law, passed in 1934 under Pres. Abelardo L. Rodríguez, had set out to clarify the means by which water could be accessed by locals and did indeed permit campesinos to use the contested water. Article 119 of the law stated that farmers had a right to access the water for small plot irrigation, and Article 120 went one step further by allowing campesinos of "little means [along with] small-time farmers and industrialists" to access the water. Despite the stated permission, farmers had to contract with notaries and set up a *procuraduría de aguas* to assess the use while also getting administrative and judicial permissions.[88] The impassioned arguments of Ortíz Medina and Reyes Robledo fell on deaf ears; the federal government ignored the requests of the townspeople of Jiménez del Teul well after 1937.

In the case of Jiménez del Teul, the debate over who owned and controlled the water emerged only after complaints of contamination. Specifically, the mining operators released the waste of their operations into the nearest stream, believing the stream to be part of the unregulated commons and within their right to use (or pollute). Many villagers also insisted on the stream's status as part of the commons or national property, and they had assumed they shared ownership of the water source. Alarmingly, the question of ownership arose only after the parties who used the source regularly began to insist on industry responsibility for its upkeep. Small community residents and farmers neglected collective duty for the health of the resource until they wanted to pin responsibility for the pollution on someone else. Indeed, they argued that the mining company put pollutants "in" the water they took "out." However, there had never been a discussion on how to use the water, where to employ it, and what (not) to dispose of in it.

The Animal Barometers

In the examples of agriculture being disturbed by mining, animals served as the barometer for human health. When animals died after consuming water, their death indicated a dangerous toxin in the resource. Animals had long served as indicators of the health of the environment, and if animals became ill or died suddenly, farmers or ranchers sought an environmental culprit. The animals most closely linked to mining were horses, mules, and burros. They dragged carts of ore from the mines, pulled water winches, dragged rakes that mixed the *tortas* in the patio process, or hauled supplies from one site to another. Before the arrival of the steam engine, miners relied heavily on these animals. Before any miner found themselves sick because of exposure in the mining workscape, animals typically died first. Oddly enough, writers and narrators traveling in Mexico in the nineteenth century did not describe sick miners. Instead, they discussed a number of horrifying animal stories, since miners went home to convalesce while the animals had to work until they died.

The "patio ponies" in the silver mining states of Mexico gained a degree of fame in U.S. travel literature because of their horrifying conditions. Thomas Wallace Knox in his book *The Boy Travellers in Mexico* (1890), a travel-adventure series written for youths, wrote of animals used in the mining process in Zacatecas and Guanajuato. The narrators, based on Knox's own world travels, described Zacatecas as "anything but attractive" and "poorly supplied with water."[89] In touring the mining sites, the fictional characters called the animals "sorry looking brutes" because of the shaved tails and the bodies splashed with mud as they pulled a rake through the *tortas*, the toxic circles where mercury and other chemicals were mixed together. The boys went on to describe the *tortas* as mining amalgamation ingredients used to determine the quality and richness of the silver being mined.[90] The animals used by mining operations, argued "Fred," often had little value because of age and proved "useless" for anything else. He observed that "the chemicals destroyed their hooves, and they do not last a great while."[91]

In addition to serving as a barometer of toxicity in the area, animals illustrated the consequences of contact with the toxins, their bodies demonstrating the effects of the chemicals on organic bodies. As the Knox book mentions, the hooves of horses and mules used in the amalgamation process deteriorated. John Stoddard, another world traveler, observed "green" mules in the patio pits in Guanajuato at roughly the same time.[92] The chemicals likely destroyed the keratin cells in hooves, eating away the fibers that gave them strength. Furthermore, the animals absorbed chemicals during the process of dragging a rake to mix mercury, salts, and alloys. A slow toxicity then spread through the animal's body, rendering it green. Toxic metals most often entered the organic body, whether it be human or animal, through ingestion or pulmonary intake.[93] Absorption through the skin depended on the duration of a body's exposure to the toxins as well as the purity of the toxins. Some substances, such as methylmercury, accumulated in the body with lipid-soluble properties and damaged the central nervous system.[94] Other compounds in the patio process, such as mercuric chloride, irritated skin in addition to being absorbed by the body.[95] The telltale signs of toxicity in horses offered insight into the dangers of the materials used in the silver refining process.

Ignacio Mena and other farmers in Jiménez del Teul wrote to Pres. Lázaro Cárdenas in April 1937 to underscore how contamination was affecting their animals. They indicated that their own health faced threats as well and cited as examples of not only the deaths of their animals but the resulting loss of their livelihoods.[96] The animals that drank from the stream, sickened, and died served as a dire warning of the locals' own peril if they consumed the water. Federal investigators attempting to prove the contamination of the water and the provenance of that contamination faced a number of hurdles in determining the water's danger to humans. Water diluted a contaminating substance while at the same time dispersing it, which made tracing toxins to a source difficult. Likewise, concentration relied on the topography of the region and riverbed as well as the composition of the soil (mud versus silt, sand versus rocks, etc.). So the dangers remained: unsuspecting animals continued to consume and suffer the effects of the toxins, inducing more fears among the human population of the deleterious effects of contaminated water.

Conclusion: Limited Legislation

As Mexico transitioned from the Porfiriato to the revolution, perceptions and approaches to public health changed. Epidemics promoted the idea of hygiene and the individual's duty to preserve the health of the community. Municipal guidelines attempted to prevent the spread of disease. Nonetheless, typhus and diphtheria found their way into the region via insect vectors and microbes. In contrast, water and public health became increasingly fraught in smaller agricultural and mining towns in the state of Zacatecas. Water remained the center of legislative questions on how to best balance conservation, agricultural use, and industrial consumption. Legislators and their efforts to protect water failed to be implemented evenly throughout the country, with bureaucratic burdens weighing down campesinos' efforts to seek redress for damages to their animals, farms, and livelihoods. While the federal government and local engineers largely bungled some of the cases presented here, the petitions unveiled a shift toward preserving private interests, despite revolutionary promises.

5

The Body as Nation

Silicosis-Tuberculosis, Unions, and Revolutionary Death

Tocan las seis y al tiro me presento
con paso lento y agitademente [*sic*]
yo me conduzco a las salas de la muerte
donde me dicen que es un puro afanar
Me voy, querida, para la mina vieja
sólo Dios sabe si ya no volveré.

At the stroke of six
the miner goes down to work
in the chambers of death.
It's a hard struggle and one must be very careful.
I go, my love, to work in the old mine.
Only God knows if I will ever return.
—"Corrido del Minero"

THE MELANCHOLY LYRICS OF THIS MEXICAN FOLK SONG, "Corrido del Minero," reflect the sense of dread in the daily, perilous workday for miners. Mine shafts became "chambers of death," and a miner despaired in not knowing if his time had run out. While this song suggests an acute awareness of the danger buried underground, many miners exited the mine with a menace already lodged in their lungs. Ailments such as silicosis and black lung for those working in coal pits trailed miners long after they returned to their homes, and these health issues pushed many to seek compensation from mining companies.

For Mexican miners, unions offered an opportunity to participate in the goals of the Mexican Revolution (1910–46), as outlined
in the Constitution of 1917. Emboldened by new ideals, mining
unions raised concerns of occupational health, specifically silicosis-
tuberculosis, to the new revolutionary government. Growing investment in mining offered reason to hope, but the government hesitated
to hire union workers to rebuild infrastructure as government and
labor relations soured. Exacerbating the already strained relationship,
union workers wanted the government to recognize both silicosis and
tuberculosis as diseases of occupation for miners. While the mining
companies relented on silicosis, workers insisted on the inclusion
of tuberculosis, or what they considered tuberculosis. Their efforts
illustrate the growing divide between those who championed the
miners' claim and those who viewed it as a threat to industry.

The debate over silicosis-tuberculosis signaled a turning point
for miners in the transition from the Porfiriato to revolutionary
Mexico. Miners began to embrace the tenets of the revolutionary
Constitution of 1917, as they had been among the most exploited
groups under Porfirio Díaz. The revolt and ensuing massacre in
the mine in Cananea, Sonora, in 1906 not only added fuel to revolutionary sentiment but also pitted miners as a group against the
Porfirian government. The persistent tensions between miners and
the government serve as an example of failures in implementing
the tenets of the Constitution's Article 123 in response to pressure
from transnational interests. The efforts of miners to have silicosis-
tuberculosis defined as an occupational disease coincided with a
global debate about it in the medical-legal community. Doctors
disagreed on methods of diagnosis and whether this disease should
be considered debilitating. Legal experts attempted to identify with
whom the fault lay. As a result, Mexican political leaders doubted
mining caused the disease, citing the medical debate while also supporting judicial inquiries on whether the industry was to blame.

This chapter focuses on the medical narrative and debate regarding the cause of silicosis-tuberculosis, which underscored tensions
relating to labor, class, and politics in revolutionary Mexico. Be-

cause no one knew the exact cause of the disease, politicians used the uncertainty to cast doubt on diagnoses, challenging medical experts for the sake of political gain. Thus, I argue that the bodies of miners became part of the ecology of extraction, as well as of revolutionary politics, while physicians and lawyers tried to mediate between different parties. As revolutionary politicians championed workers and unions, other politicians weighed the economic impact of silicosis on the industry itself. I therefore explore how mining unions and industry physicians formulated the argument regarding silicosis-tuberculosis as a disease of occupation. In a global context, the debate surrounding the disease in Mexico reflects only part of a global scramble to identify the causes of the illness in the 1930s and 1940s as miners around the world began showing symptoms. The chapter begins with a discussion of silicosis-tuberculosis and the confusing diagnoses that hindered compensation for sufferers. It continues with an examination of mining unions in the state of Zacatecas, as well as their frequent efforts to invoke and implement revolutionary tenets after the conflict. Furthermore, I examine how workers petitioned politicians in Mexico City to identify other lung ailments as diseases of profession and often alluded to their own travails with the disease, and I conclude with an analysis of silicosis in the ideological context of the revolution.

Silicosis-tuberculosis forms part of the ecology of extraction through its own physiology and through the concept of workscape. When working in the mines, workers suffer exposure to the dust of the pulverized rock they are excavating. When they leave the mine, the dust remains in their lungs. In effect, the ecology of extraction recognizes human physiology as subject to the process of mining, integrating human tissues with the physical act of digging and excavating. Moreover, this interaction spawns a debate on the disease's cause, exposing the extent of the human-nature interaction in the workscape. Workscape, as defined by Thomas Andrews, underscores the dynamic relationship between humans and their surroundings during labor, which challenges the perception that miners only remove the earth when in fact they carry the earth with them in their lungs. The subsequent diseases, silicosis and its derivative, silicosis-tuberculosis, demonstrate that mining not only extracts from the earth but also takes away the health of workers and surrounding communities.

Diagnosing Occupational Illnesses

Silicosis became the scourge of the working class beginning in the early twentieth century.[1] An ancient disease, it gained a foothold in mining communities around the world in the late nineteenth century with the adoption of modern mining technology, such as pneumatic hammers and drills. Workers in high-risk occupations included not only miners but also stonecutters, masons, and foundry workers. Silicosis-tuberculosis prolonged an inevitable death, with weakness, weight loss, and an ever-present cough characterizing the illness. Silicosis and tuberculosis share physical symptoms but remain separate diseases. The similarity of the symptoms sparked confusion among miners, legislators, and doctors themselves. Many miners thought themselves ill with one disease but actually ailed from the other.

Silicosis derives from the process of inhalation in dusty environs, with several factors affecting the severity of the disease and how quickly it progresses. The disease owes its name to "free silica," or the crystalline form of silicon dioxide, which makes up almost 90 percent of the earth's crust.[2] Inhaling fine particles of silicon dioxide creates fibrous lesions in the lungs that limit the absorption of oxygen, as well as the expansion of the lungs in breathing. Doctors diagnose the disease according to three factors of causality: level of exposure, latency period, and patient work history—all information that informs the pathological and physiological symptoms of the disease.[3] The three levels of silicosis are the chronic, the accelerated, and the acute. Patients with chronic (or classic) silicosis do not exhibit symptoms of the disease immediately but have a persistent cough that progresses for fifteen or more years after the initial exposure. The cough signals progressive massive fibrosis (PMF) in the lungs, which affects the pulmonary activities of carbon monoxide diffusion and reduces oxygen in the bloodstream even while at rest.[4] With more intense exposures of between five and ten years, accelerated silicosis diminishes lung function and limits mobility, while generating a more persistent cough. While chronic and accelerated silicosis have a latency period of years, the acute form of the disease develops in a matter of months to two years after silica exposure. Heavy coughing, lethargy, and rapid weight loss mark this form of the disease, and the patient suffers additional complications.[5] Low levels of oxygen in the blood, muscle spasms, and shallow breaths precede lung failure. With the ongoing obstruction of the airways, the sufferer has frequent bacterial infections and an increasing possibility of *Mycobacterium tuberculosis* entering the lungs.[6] Tuberculosis poses a serious risk to patients with acute and accelerated silicosis, as the weakened immune system and the deteriorated lung tissue become increasingly susceptible to the bacillus. This secondary disease was especially prevalent before the availability of antibiotics. Social factors, such as crowded living quarters and malnutrition, exacerbate the likelihood of contracting tuberculosis. When the silicosis patient becomes infected with the bacteria, the disease emerges as silicosis-tuberculosis.

Silicosis, as an occupational health issue, links labor history with environmental history. Workers hollowed out mountains with chisels, dynamite, and drills. They inhaled clouds of dust from the pulverized mountains into their lungs, which resulted in nodes of damaged tissue clusters, or fibroids. The degree and duration of exposure determined the severity of the disease, linking medical and environmental histories as well as humans and mountains. Environmental historians such as Richard White have argued that preindustrial laborers embraced nature, resources, and seasonal cycles and created a symbiotic relationship.[7] Industrialization broke this link and diminished the engagement with nature gained through old-fashioned physical labor. Liza Piper, in contrast, has asserted that industrialization never eroded the tie between labor and nature but instead moved the link deeper underground as workers excavated the earth with advanced technology.[8] Both arguments suggest that humans and nature remain bound during the labor process. However, as workers left mines or excavation sites, they took their labor home with them on their clothes, in their hair, in their lungs. As Brett Walker has suggested, even "bodies can be industrialized."[9] Indeed, just as mines filled with dust particles, so did the lungs of miners, illustrating an exchange on not only the physical level but also the microbial and microscopic plane. Thomas Andrews has argued in *Killing for Coal* that this workscape evinced the constant and dynamic exchange between worker and the surrounding elements of land, water, air, and microbes. In the biological and physiological relationship, the intrinsic tie between humans and nature grew through labor as well as the simple actions of breathing and walking.[10]

Industrial disease arose from the mutual exploitation of humans and nature by way of technology. Changing production methods, particularly with advances in extractive industries, often led to ailments in workers.[11] Drills, jackhammers, and crushers kicked up far more dust than previous techniques, which made respiratory diseases worse. Aware of the link between technology and health, mine owners contributed to miners' maladies through the implementation of new extraction methods, a relationship that mining investors hesitated to admit.

Labor Relations in Mexico

Physicians in Mexico as well as in the global medical community questioned the cause of silicosis in miners. Both unions and mining companies embroiled doctors in the debate over whether dusty mines contributed to the disease, skewing symptoms and diagnoses for their own benefit. Industry and union physicians presented only two sides of the debate as workers verbalized their symptoms in an attempt to gain compensation amid another global debate—the issue of indemnization for accidents and injuries on the job.[12] Indeed, "the environmental causes of diseases could prove hidden and deceptive," especially when tangled with the agendas of private interests, as Christopher Sellers writes.[13] Furthermore, the similarities in the symptoms of silicosis and tuberculosis spawned an advantageous confusion for industry doctors.

Industrial workers and farmers resented the size and power of foreign properties and investments in the early years of the revolution, and they frequently targeted U.S., British, and French businesses with looting and sabotage.[14] Local government leaders confronted abusive foreign owners by speaking up for the exploited employees of those foreign-owned firms. Municipal heads argued that the new government did not tolerate the mistreatment of workers.[15] Foreign investors watched as the number of unions rose after the ratification of the Constitution of 1917. Its Article 123 underscored the workers' right to form unions, a dramatic change from the Porfiriato, which discouraged union activity. While some workers' organizations in Coahuila, Durango, and Chihuahua registered with the Pan-American Federation, official mining unions appeared to be largely absent from central mining states due to the ongoing violence of the revolution and to the itinerant nature of mining work. As Claude T. Rice of the *Engineering and Mining Journal (EMJ)* explained, Zacatecas had largely been abandoned by the mining industry in 1908, suggesting a loss of capital and workers.[16] With few mines operational, many miners sought work elsewhere. Conversely, Guanajuato experienced a silver boom and consequent foreign investment in the first two decades of the twentieth century, which drew miners from other mining regions.[17] As the military phase of the revolution wore on, villages emptied of men as they joined the ranks willingly or by force.

By 1920, Jesús Agustín Castro, governor of Durango, and Donato Moreno, governor of Zacatecas, had sought to reassure foreign investors wary of the volatile political, economic, and labor situation. They emphasized the security of their states to a reporter from the *Engineering and Mining Journal.*[18] Castro noted that any delay in investment only resulted in missed opportunity. He pushed for an active propaganda campaign to encourage investors to return and underscored the new government's commitment to protect mining operations.[19] Both Castro and Moreno emphasized a reorganization of railroads as well. Rebuilding rail infrastructure facilitated access to mining camps and limited the rising freight rates hampering the mining industry. Moreno assured the reporter of the government's willingness to intervene when labor unions paralyzed operations.[20] He cited recent examples of tensions between labor and capital; in response, the government had sent mediators to resolve such situations. He added a prophetic note: with the new peace, he hoped to see mining operations at their maximum activity within a year.[21] Moreno's and Castro's reassurances demonstrated how politicians intended to lure foreign investment while trying to renew an aging industry and present the image of stability.

Revolutionary leaders portrayed workers as central to the livelihood of the nation, the ideology, and the future of Mexico. Presidents, generals, and bureaucrats held them up as the beneficiaries of the revolution, pointing to the protections for them enshrined in the Constitution of 1917. Article 123 guaranteed workers an eight-hour workday, medical care, and shift limits, while stipulating that foreign industrial companies had to obtain government consent to mine, drill, or excavate. The Constitution specifically ensured that employees were to receive compensation for injuries received on site, and it granted them eligibility for disability claims.

In 1921, economic conditions improved considerably in the state of Zacatecas, as was widely reported in the United States. According to the *Engineering and Mining Journal*, employment increased and held steady at a high level.[22] While work in southeastern Zacatecas was stopped, miners had begun to pump water out of flooded mines in other regions.[23] In 1924, the *EMJ* reported a considerable output of copper, silver, and silver-lead ore from the state.[24] Two years later, in the same publication, Arthur Barrette Parsons championed the output as a "revival of Zacatecas," reassuring potential investors of continued production.[25]

In order to encourage and support mining ventures across Zacatecas and across the country, the government sought a workforce to contribute to the shared goals of economic progress, particularly in valuable sectors such as mining. Tensions between miners and mining companies grew under added pressure from government authorities to limit union labor. Mining relied on the railroads and infrastructure to bring workers and supplies in and send raw materials out, so when transportation problems arose, mine operators felt a sense of urgency. In November 1922, the office of Pres. Álvaro Obregón received a telegram indicating irregularity of work on the Zacatecas/Coahuila railroad.[26] There was heavy turnover in the workforce. Workers who remained complained of low pay. Four years later, that railroad project continued to have the same problems. J. M. Aguirre, the leader of the Confederación de Sociedades "Ferrocarriles de la República," sent a letter to Pres. Plutarco Elías Calles in August 1926 "supplicating" him to reconsider the use of "common workers."[27] Luis Napoleón Morones, former head of the Confederación Regional Obrera Mexicana (CROM) and the nation's secretary of economy at the time, also received a copy of Aguirre's letter to Calles, as well as a letter of support for Aguirre's argument sent by the Sociedades Ferrocarriles de Conductores, Jefes de Patio y Garroteros, Orden de Maquinistas y Fogoneros de Locomotoras, a syndicate that also requested that its workers to be reinstated to their old positions. The record did not indicate the government's response. Aguirre never specified the incidents leading to the break but emphasized how the federal government had issued a more favorable contract with other railway companies in Veracruz. In response, union workers might have continued work stoppages, which imply a start-stop pace on the railway. As presidents sought a quick economic recovery in the railroad sector, they grew increasingly frustrated with obstinate workers clamoring for fairer contracts.

Into the 1930s, the relationship between miners and the government remained tenuous, especially when the influence of foreign interests trumped the power of local mines. Miners and workers continued to pressure the government to support union workers in their negotiations with foreign-owned mining companies. Adolfo Calderón of Río Grande, Zacatecas, sent a letter to Pres. Abelardo Rodríguez in September 1934, accusing German mine owner Ernesto Boheringer of manipulating miners in Mina La Alianza.[28] Boheringer refused to let miners access the ore they mined, emphasizing their role as merely excavators. Calderón requested that the president remind the foreign parties to respect the rights of workers, which would settle the matter quickly. The situation escalated when Boheringer's son, Alejandro Otto Boheringer, claimed ownership of Mina Xolot and used his Mexican citizenship to claim the mine. Manuel Abrego of Río Grande, Zacatecas, filed a complaint in an angry letter to the president on October 1934, barely a month after the elder Boheringer refused to pay workers for their labor. Abrego, and later Ramos, denounced the younger Boheringer's claims, citing that he had only German citizenship and, at nineteen years old, was too young to own land.[29] President Rodríguez's office did not respond.

Closer to the state capital, workers clashed with foreign mining companies that continued to drill and excavate. Many foreign and domestic companies had closed during the military phase of the revolution because workers had challenged company policies. In the aftermath, workers for the Fresnillo Mining Company, a U.S. firm in Zacatecas, began a series of strikes and talks with their employer in 1934. With tensions high, José María Próspero Alderete of the Sindicato Único de Obreros, Mineros, y Similares of the San Luis Mining Company in Socavón, Durango, requested government mediation, as his workers wanted to participate in mining Zacatecas too.[30] While some complained about foreign interests blocking local ventures, mining *sindicatos* and *sociedades* pressured the national government to uphold its revolutionary promises by recognizing workers' rights in negotiations. In Zacatecas, the regional isolation, politically charged workers, and sluggish pace of promised reforms emboldened miners. Antonio Treviño and Francisco Solís of the Sociedad Cooperativa Industrial "Concepción del Oro" in the northern part of the state wrote to President Rodríguez in September 1932. They stated how mining activities had stirred to life once again after a series of work stoppages due to lack of capital, rather than union activity.[31] From the state capital, Bonifácio Reyes sent a telegram to Rodríguez in October 1932 seeking government investment in mines.[32] He requested 100,000 pesos in order to invest in technology and to contribute to workers' funds in the Sociedad Cooperativa Minera de Zacatecas. He believed the new technology of drills, refining equipment, and excavation tools only encouraged the productivity workers, who with such advanced means could possibly excavate up to fifty tons of ore a day.[33]

Other miners pursued a more aggressive approach, outlining new methods to distribute mineral wealth. J. Jesús Ortíz and Ernestina Salazar Méndez formed the Primer Congreso Obrero y Campesino de Concepción de Oro in January 1934. They suggested that abandoned mines with indeterminate ownership be worked by the poorer miners, who then paid a percentage of the profits to the state.[34] While Rodríguez and his government did not respond, illegal mining, or excavating without permit, had been practiced since the colonial era and most likely continued during and after the revolution, when the permit agencies had little time to take notice of such activities.[35] Rather than wait for government decisions regarding land distribution and mine ownership, Ortíz and Salazar's proactive suggestion hinted at a growing frustration with smaller-scale mining.

In the late 1930s, workers, with their new political awareness, embraced the campaign to receive compensation for their occupational diseases, while the government compiled a list of ailments that menaced the health of workers in various settings. The debate challenged the government to uphold revolutionary ideology and its goals for workers. Although there was support for compensation of workers sickened by their labors, the government had to weigh the possibility of sacrificing economic investment for the sake of workers' health.

Silicosis and Labor in Mexico

Discussions of occupational disease hinged on questions over which party assumed responsibility for the workers' health. Silicosis-tuberculosis raised concerns that the government would have to assume responsibility for the medical care of injured or ill workers and that it might have to compensate thousands of people for the work-related illness they had suffered. Politicians found themselves inundated with information from a new wave of public health authorities who cited the role of silica in the deteriorating health of workers in mining communities, towns with quarries, and populations downwind from smokestacks. The use of technology also increased in this period, which played an increasing role in North American mining sites.[36] Drills expedited the mining of ore underground and generated even more dust than older excavation methods. While some mines adopted the practice of misting the mine walls with water to reduce dust clouds, silicosis continued to worry mine owners and workers alike.

In addition to government and company questions about compensation for sickened workers, the debate on silicosis-tuberculosis centered largely on the pathology of the disease itself because of advancing medical knowledge as well as variations in how the illness affected sufferers. Underscoring these conundrums, silicosis-tuberculosis featured similarities to other diseases. Since the rise of germ theory, medical science had shifted focus from miasmas to how bacilli and other microbes contributed to this chronic, irreversible disease.[37] Silicosis, originally called "miners' phthisis" in the United States, often led doctors to confuse or conflate the disease with tuberculosis, commonly called consumption.[38] Adding to the confusion, silicosis was frequently referred to as "miners' consumption" before it was properly identified. Yet, unlike tuberculosis, silicosis patients did not suffer from fevers, nor did their radiographies share any similarities. Instead, patients had a persistent cough that grew worse with time. Coupled with dramatic weight loss and limited expansion of the lungs in often-malnourished individuals, the symptoms culminated in a painful end. Physicians frequently misdiagnosed their patients, as some patients experienced the rapid onset of chronic symptoms, while others did not display respiratory symptoms until years later. Doctors tended to patients with chronic and acute silicosis, but their diagnoses varied because of patients' inconsistent history in terms of work conditions, work hours, frequency of exposure, and the amount of dust they faced on any given workday. Moreover, medical institutions failed to recognize and to circulate consistent information among doctors on how to distinguish between the two pathologies, especially among those who served a mining population. Perhaps indicating the lack of medical infrastructure and diagnostic progress, medical debates did not highlight this crucial difference. Workers themselves misunderstood their illnesses and often conflated the three pulmonary diseases. The misdiagnoses of silicosis, tuberculosis, and their combined spawn, silicosis-tuberculosis, only added fuel to the tensions between labor and the federal government over occupational health.

Diagnosing a Global Disease

In an effort to dispel the confusion surrounding silicosis proper, the global medical community sought to understand and control the disease. In the wake of continuing industrialization and technology advances, as well as in the context of the Great Depression, silicosis became a sudden health crisis in the United States, leading many miners to seek government compensation.[39] Anthony Lanza, a public health specialist, conducted a landmark study of chronic industrial disease in 1914 with the support of the U.S. Public Health Service and the Bureau of Mines. Lanza determined the link between the initial exposure to mining dust and the onset of the symptoms. His research, paired with Alice Hamilton's advocacy on the part of workers, argued in favor of new clinical models that sought to pinpoint how work conditions, particularly dust, contributed to the cause of lung diseases. Lawsuits engulfed mining companies, insurance firms, and public health specialists for the next decade.

In 1930, medical doctors, public health specialists, and mining executives met in Johannesburg, South Africa, for a conference on silicosis hosted by the International Labor Organization (ILO) and the Transvaal Chamber of Mines. In addition to representatives from governments and corporations, the gathering amassed an impressive amount of data, including the world's largest collection of x-rays for workers from one occupation. The meeting was well attended, its publications widely circulated, and its findings mentioned frequently in Mexican government documents. The proceedings focused primarily on hard rock mining, how it contributed to silicosis, and the disease's tie to tuberculosis. While the chamber wished for the meeting to determine the causes of silicosis and possible remedies, the meeting had an economic undercurrent. Because of the ubiquitous presence of chronic pneumonia among South African miners, the government imposed a ban on mining recruitment in 1913. The ban devastated the industry in the region. Chamber officials attempted to broaden their understanding of the disease at the conference in an effort to resolve the confusion surrounding the workers' health and safety and to reassure mining interests of the industry's eventual return.[40] Moreover, the conference targeted three areas: prevention; silicosis and its pathology along with diagnosis; and prognosis, compensation, and maintenance.[41] Physicians and industrial health specialists debated when silicosis began, with some suggesting it began while workers labored in the mines and others insisting the disease manifested itself in the lungs only years later. Attendees did agree on the need for further research into the association of dust with the disease, as well as the need to collect more data from initial medical examinations to facilitate monitoring and prevention.[42] Yet, conference speakers still dealt with unreliable methods of diagnosis. For example, although radiography remained the best method of diagnosing the disease, not every doctor or mining community had access to the new technology, particularly in Mexico.[43]

Recommendations for workplace supervision fell short at the Johannesburg conference. Physician Andrew Watt argued that miners contended with two kinds of dust, appropriately labeled in economic terms. The "income" dust arose from a day's work underground, while "capital" dust existed in the mine's air, regardless of the practice of misting walls.[44] The reduction of workers' biomechanisms to economic terminology highlighted their disposability in the capitalist push to extract as much as possible, as fast as possible. If one asset was lost, another quickly stepped in to take up the hammer in their stead, indicating the bone-crushing exploitation of industry. Historian Jock McCulloch has suggested that the Transvaal Chamber of Mines suppressed Watt's report in the last days of the conference because his opinion that dust was inherent in mine work presented the increased possibility of liability.[45] Without an accurate measure of dust in a mine, doctors and union representatives lacked data to leverage mining companies for compensation.

So, why the industry preoccupation with disease? Employers indicated their determination to create distance between their culpability, the industry's faults, and the long-term prognosis. They educated themselves and foresaw the direction of the discussion. When they found cracks in workers' arguments, they drilled until the legal cases broke apart. While the conference in South Africa attempted to define the disease, it also demonstrated the inseparability of the human body from nature. Miners' bodies reflected the amount of dust in the air and the seeming inescapability of inhaling it. As with the economic rhetoric applied to underground spaces, miners employed the lingo of the body to refer to their workspace. Furthermore, miners in their workscape entered a place in which human labor and natural processes intertwined in a dynamic exchange.[46] In this space, boundaries blurred in the relationships between land, air, water, bodies, and organisms. This constant transfer extended well past the mine and into the homes of miners. Miners carried dust home on their clothes and in their lungs, and wind carried the dust from the mining site over large areas, scattering it across communities. The exchange of course created a physiological response with every inhalation: silicosis. Residents who never entered a mine but lived in a mining community also experienced symptoms of silicosis. The nebulous understanding of the disease, its symptoms, and how dust contributed to it only further blurred the line between "human" and "nature" in this ecology of extraction.

Silicosis and Occupational Health in Mexico

Silicosis and occupational health in Mexico introduced debate regarding the disease, the rights of workers, and the definition of disability in workers. Because the disease shared so many similarities with tuberculosis and other lung ailments, the confusion spawned questions about which disease infected workers, when they contracted the ailment, and how the malady manifested itself in the human body. Silicosis and other chronic pulmonary diseases like it kill slowly. Its progressive character subjects the patient to a protracted period of pain and misery. Workers who pursued claims of indemnization against their employer for contracting the disease underwent a series of clinical studies to complete the analysis of their ailment. Despite these initial tests, the attempt to resolve a worker's claim was subject to the whims of courts, meetings, corporate boards, and government bureaucracies. Coupled with the obfuscation of symptoms, workers had to first survive, physically and financially, in order to pursue compensation. Under the supervision of Departamento Autónomo del Trabajo, workers negotiated their claims through their syndicates or lawyers. The department worked in tandem with the Junta de Conciliación y Arbitraje, a federal arbitrage group that attempted to find a solution for the workers and companies involved. The department provided the foundation for what later became the Secretaría de Trabajo y Previsión Social (Secretariat of Labor and Social Security) in 1941.

With workers pursuing indemnization, the government grappled with the concept of disability, or *incapacidad*, and how it informed the occupational health cases in its judicial system.[47] Both the government and the business community asked at what point workers are incapacitated and thus unable to perform their duties. The case of Antonio Lechuga and Jesús Rodríguez forced the Departamento Autónomo del Trabajo to define disability with silicosis to determine the amount of compensation owed to workers suffering from occupational diseases. A 1940 internal memorandum from the department on Lechuga and Rodriguez's case against the yarn and weaving factory La Trinidad in Veracruz revealed the debate over disability, with three principal opinions emerging. Dr. Erasmo González Ancira opined that, with regard to silicosis or anthracosis, disability is largely anatomical and not functional. While the disease diminished the vitality of an individual, the patient could continue working as long as the disease did not progress or an infection set in.[48] Dr. Luis Cervantes, however, stated that silicosis patients suffered from an ailment that rendered them unable to perform their work.[49] From these two contrasting opinions, the officials at the department deferred to Dr. Ubaldo Roldán. Dr. Roldán suggested that Lechuga and Rodríguez suffered from a "partial and permanent organo-functional invalidity estimated to be at 15%."[50] In his analysis of the two workers, he concluded that they were still able to perform the necessary movements in their work as long as the disease did not progress. Roldán also noted that workers mutilated on the job could find a profession that enabled them to work despite their physical impairments. In particular, this last definition appealed to the department because it employed percentages to determine *incapacidad*. A higher percentage signaled a higher degree of disability to the department. This method of assessment was not uncommon and will be discussed further later.

Silicosis emerged as an occupational disease in Mexico before the name of the disease even existed. Dr. Amadeo Betancourt wrote in a government memorandum that Dr. Luis Lara first identified the physical maladies of workers in 1898. Lara noted how workers emerged from mines coughing, with pains in their chest and back.[51] While silicosis is not mentioned, Lara's description in the memo suggests a pulmonary disease associated with extraction. After Anthony Lanza's study in 1914 for the U.S. Public Health Service and Bureau of Mines identified dust as the cause of silicosis, governments and mining companies became increasingly attuned to the compensation claims of workers from across the globe. In the early 1920s, miners began to file a number of silicosis claims for compensation in Mexico. A young lawyer, Miguel Alemán, who later was president of Mexico (1946–52), represented many sick miners and textile workers seeking compensation before he turned to politics.[52] Textile workers soon joined miners in pursuing silicosis compensation.

With the global discussion of compensation and silicosis in full swing, miners in Mexico filed an increasing number of claims in the 1930s. Jalisco miners Margarito and Candelario Gómez frequently wrote to Pres. Lázaro Cárdenas to plead that he pay attention to their case files regarding their claims against the Ámparo Mining

Company. They sent desperate telegrams to the president in which they described their dire circumstances.[53] Margarito noted in a 31 July 1939 telegram that they had sought compensation for silicosis back in 1934.[54] Sick and unable to work, they struggled to make ends meet. In addition, the mine refused to give them any employment, either in retribution for their claim or to protect themselves from further litigation.

In order to square compensation claims from workers with their actual physical condition, doctors performed clinical studies on claimants to determine how far silicosis had advanced. In 20 December 1939, Departamento Autónomo del Trabajo head Antonio Villalobos met with William Gooch, the head of the Cananea Consolidated Copper Company, based in the northern state of Sonora. More than 600 workers had filed silicosis compensation claims in the Cananea area, arguing that they had been stricken with silicosis during their time in the mines. Villalobos coordinated the federal government's response through arbitrage, and he, like Gooch, wanted an effective resolution of the remaining claims. Both parties agreed with the miners' syndicate that the workers' health should be evaluated in order to negotiate compensation.[55] Consequently, the department sent Dr. Antonio Delgado to Cananea, Sonora, to examine workers in May 1940. Delgado quickly noted that only a handful of the 140 miners from the case had received a thorough clinical exam. Each miner required an hour-long examination, bacteriological study of the sputum, blood work, radiological study, and a detailed medico-legal opinion.[56] Despite the long hours that Delgado put in at the Hospital del Ronquillo, he noted that local authorities had failed to notify several of the claimants because many lived outside Cananea and were not aware of Delgado's presence.[57] In the end, only 66 workers saw a doctor. Of that total, 37 workers had the full clinical study and written medico-legal opinion.[58] From this total, 7 workers received the diagnosis of "silicosis simple," which possibly refers to chronic silicosis. Dr. Delgado and his colleague, Dr. Ubaldo Roldán, listed these workers as incapacitated in ranges of 10 to 20 percent. One worker was diagnosed with silicosis and partial infection with tuberculosis. Three unfortunate claimants received the diagnosis of silicosis-tuberculosis, with one deemed 80 percent incapacitated.

Mining companies quantified disability in order to determine compensation despite the pathological aspects of chronic disease. Doctors, particularly Dr. Roldán, assessed the condition of a sick worker at the time of their examination in order to estimate compensation. The assigned percentage of disability at specific time weighed disease at that particular moment. It failed to consider the progressive nature of silicosis that eventually necessitated medical care and that incapacitated workers to the point they could not work. In effect, Dr. Roldán echoed the work of Luigi Carozzi (1875–1963), the former head of the Industrial Hygiene Section at the International Labor Organization. As historians Paul-André Rosental and Bernard Thomann have noted, Carozzi's system of classification placed significant emphasis on a doctor's own medical opinions and highlighted workers' earning capacity.[59] Thus, doctors made medical judgments at a point when the disease was at a particular stage, thus sidestepping the chronic nature of the disease. Earning capacity outweighed *incapacidad* in this assessment. Furthermore, physicians misdiagnosed or emphasized the medical gray area in which silicosis existed. Pulmonary symptoms among diseases overlapped, a weak point in workers' arguments that mining companies exploited. This medical obfuscation further affected workers' claims.

In Mexico, tuberculosis also appeared in impoverished areas and in many mining communities, which leveraged mining companies' arguments. Company lawyers argued that workers confused the diseases, despite their very different pathologies. In effect, mining companies used the poverty of workers to cast doubt on diagnoses because of the similarity of tuberculosis and silicosis. Pres. Manuel Ávila Camacho (1940–46) wrote in 1943 that miners contracted tuberculosis because of the "deficiencies" in their living conditions; similarly, Dr. Amadeo Betancourt had described the country in the grips of a crisis of hygiene. He argued that mining bosses would dismiss silicosis because of the "anger they hold" toward hygiene guidelines.[60] Despite the conflation of the pulmonary ailments, tuberculosis-stricken workers found success briefly in having the illness recognized as an occupational disease.

The history of occupational health in Mexico is one that largely emphasizes blame. When miners suffered injuries in Zacatecas mines, company supervisors quickly blamed the injured in legal briefs, citing negligence, clumsiness, recklessness, or ignorance. In this case, silicosis, tuberculosis, and silicosis-tuberculosis patients alike blamed companies for their chronic illnesses. Mine owners and supervisors, workers argued, had failed to provide proper ventilation in the shaft or to mist the interior walls of the mine consistently in an effort to minimize dust.

Miners and politicians continued to confuse the separate pathophysiologies of silicosis and tuberculosis as well as how quickly silicosis turned into silicosis-tuberculosis. J. Buenaventura Lara, a senator from the mining state of Guanajuato, pushed for tuberculosis to be recognized as an occupational disease among miners, and the Cámara de Diputados did so in December 1942; an amendment to the existing law added mining to the list of occupations that already recognized tuberculosis as an occupational disease. *Mineros* thus joined doctors, nurses, butchers, and *mozos de anfiteatro*, or medical school amphitheater workers, on the list of those who could become infected in the course of their work. The other professions in the list all treated the sick, handled cadavers, came into contact with human bodily fluids, or touched raw beef, which raised the possibility of contracting human or bovine tuberculosis. Miners, in contrast, acquired tuberculosis through a separate infection or through a weakened immune system already ravaged by silicosis. The Departamento Médico Consultiva reviewed the law and suggested a change in order to avoid confusion. Doctors argued in favor of adding the clause "when following silicosis or after ten years in [a] mine or in dusty surroundings produced by machines."[61] The Consultiva's report, which outlined occupational health measures, suggested twenty-two thousand cases of tuberculosis in arbitrage with silicosis lawsuits, which created confusion as well as a backlog. Consequently, many miners did not receive final decisions regarding indemnization for two to three years after their initial claim.[62] This point raised troublesome questions, however. If the pulmonary system served as the point of entry for this disease, did this mean that miners working underground for longer periods should receive greater compensation than nonminers afflicted with the disease? Did townspeople inhale the dust? If so, should they be compensated? Did it matter if the dust came from a silver, gold, or lead mine? In September 1943, miner Pablo Bretado Sánchez of Fresnillo, Zacatecas, wrote a letter to Ávila Camacho in support of the addition of tuberculosis to the list of occupational diseases. He wrote that tuberculosis had claimed "innumerable victims of workers and the companies evade responsibility even though workers labor for twelve to fifteen years or more."[63] In contrast, TB expert Leopold Brahdy blasted the concept of compensation laws that covered tuberculosis in the *American Review of Tuberculosis*; in his estimation, the disease could not result from working in industry. Brahdy reiterated that no country in the world covered tuberculosis as an occupational disease in its compensation laws.[64] However, lung ailments in general remained the scourge of miners. And the number of affected miners proved incalculable, especially in states where agriculture competed with mining for workers. Moreover, how would the disease affect children, like those pictured in a wide group shot from circa 1910?

Medical experts for mining companies gave opinions that only added to the twisting narrative regarding the pathologies of silicosis, tuberculosis, and silicosis-tuberculosis. In July 1943, Drs. Ernesto Rangel y Frías and Miguel Vera, employed by the Compañía Metalúrgica Peñoles, insisted in a medical brief that tuberculosis in miners required a previous diagnosis of silicosis. Employing Senator Lara's initial argument, they offered a rebuttal to the senator's principal points. Specifically, they rejected Lara's comment that silicosis need not precede tuberculosis. Moreover, the twenty-two thousand existing cases, which Lara cited, had not been published or peer-reviewed in a medical journal.[65] As for the South African model of compensation Lara presented, Drs. Rangel and Vera called

13. Zacatecas miners pose for a photograph. Note the mine entrances to the far left on the hillside. Courtesy of DeGolyer Library, Southern Methodist University, Giesecke Collection.

tuberculosis an indemnifiable occupational disease, but not among miners. South Africa, the Mexican doctors argued, declared the disease an indication of the environmental and hygiene concerns in the region, that is, dust, cramped public quarters, and the endemic state of the disease.[66] In short, South Africa preemptively declared the illness a general danger in order to remedy other concerns in mining communities. In contrast, Rangel and Vera argued that the Mexican Ley de Trabajo already included silicosis as an occupational disease. Indeed, the law acknowledged that repetitive exposure to dust endangered workers' health. Moreover, doctors underscored the lack of medico-legal briefs in discussing the differences, similarities, and physiological causalities between silicosis and tuberculosis.[67] Nevertheless, according to medical texts from the era, many factors caused silicosis and tuberculosis, including dust, gas, lack of ventilation systems, and the decomposition of wooden beams in mines. Rangel and Vera argued to the contrary, positing that only silica in the earth caused silicosis and the resultant tuberculosis infection.[68] Despite reluctance to declare tuberculosis to be among

the occupational diseases covered by the Ley Federal del Trabajo, many local mining companies caved to union pressure to add the illness to their lists, as Article 127 stipulated in the collective work contract (Contrato Colectivo de Trabajo). The inclusion of tuberculosis allowed for direct negotiation between unions and mining companies, as in the case of the Ámparo Mining Company in 1935, which recognized both diseases and agreed to pay compensation to those who had received such diagnoses.[69]

Rangel and Vera refuted Senator Lara's initial arguments, alleviating the concerns of foreign mining companies, which feared calls for indemnization, and skewing general disagreements in the medical community in favor of the mining industry. In July 1943, Francisco Rohde y Herrera entered the fray. Considered an expert in pulmonary illnesses, Dr. Rohde y Herrera quickly became a favorite with the mining industry. He reiterated that Rangel and Vera's argument pointed to tuberculosis at epidemic levels, nationally and globally, which made the disease not exclusive to mine workers.[70] He likewise questioned Lara's figure of twenty thousand cases of tuberculosis and silicosis-tuberculosis, contending that the senator offered no samples for peer review nor did he provide information on the medical outcomes of the patients sampled.[71] Moreover, he argued how new workers should receive an initial medical examination prior to entry into the mine, in order to determine responsibility for disease and illness. If workers received a medical examination as part of their employment orientation, doctors would later be able to identify what hazardous working conditions contributed to silicosis or silicosis-tuberculosis. In turn, the description of the occupational hazards would help identify which employers owed workers compensation for occupation-related illness.

In a damning statement, Rohde y Herrera questioned the personal hygiene of workers and dismissed the medical-legal debate surrounding the addition of tuberculosis to the Ley de Trabajo. Tuberculosis, he suggested, stemmed from the poor hygiene and unsanitary home life of workers.[72] In Rohde y Herrera's estimation, workers who lived in unsanitary conditions were to blame for their illnesses, not the company. He proposed that sanitation inspectors and company officials visit the workers' homes to rule out endemic tuberculosis in the community. Downplaying the responsibility of the company, he further introduced doubt into the role of tuberculosis as an occupational disease by arguing that, by his estimation, roughly 30 percent of the twenty thousand cases presented by Lara suggested only "minor irritations."[73] He calculated that only 15 percent had incipient silicosis and only 4.5 percent had advanced silicosis, given their symptoms and the margin of error.[74] Rohde y Herrera did not provide evidence to justify these statistics and instead insisted that the frequency of the disease among miners indicated a widespread conspiracy. He cited the skewed nature of the debate at the 1937 Congreso Nacional de Higiene y Medicina del Trabajo medical conference. He noted the contentiousness among the crowd of union workers that had attended and how seminar chairs frequently hushed the crowd to prevent interruptions during questions.

Efforts to legally identify tuberculosis as an occupational disease failed via self-sabotage. Rather than emphasizing tuberculosis as an infection of silicosis-affected lungs, politicians and unions had neither the medical expertise nor the medical data to highlight the diagnostic differences between the two diseases. Workers suffered from similar symptoms: persistent cough, weight loss, and malaise,

among others. However, their legal arguments neglected to emphasize the lack of certainty in diagnosis. Why this disease and not
the other? Does one not lead to the other? The case also stumbled
with Lara's exaggerated data count, a damning lie costing workers
possible compensation. While the lack of radiography machines
made diagnosis difficult, the absent technology did demonstrate
how little medical infrastructure existed around mining cities, which
made some companies' promises to offer x-rays to new employees
doubtful at best.

In writing on the legislation regarding tuberculosis in the workers'
protection law for miners, Pres. Manuel Ávila Camacho in 1943
indicated that he shared global concerns about the victims of tuberculosis. He stated that pulmonary tuberculosis in miners, not
preceded by silicosis, did not constitute an occupational disease,
but he recommended a thorough study into the pathology of the
disease to assess its threat to the community. The president also
recognized how Mexico's occupational health measures remained
some of the most progressive in the world.[75] The president cited
medical professionals in his decision and emphasized the epidemiology studies that examined tuberculosis as a contagion. In short,
he echoed many of the conclusions made by Rohde y Herrera that
tuberculosis was not an occupational disease.[76]

While the confusion surrounding compensation laws and tuberculosis ended in 1943, miners of coal had begun the process of
exploring compensation for their pulmonary ailments. Presidential
secretary and future Jalisco governor (José) Jesús González Gallo
responded to workers' queries on tuberculosis in an evasive manner
and cited a number of studies that dismissed tuberculosis as an
occupational disease from the outset. He suggested the severity of
tuberculosis in workers depended largely on the materials miners
excavated, arguing that different metals produced distinct effects
on miners' lungs. He noted that metal-producing mines created
an enormous amount of dust and silica, whereas coal mines did
not.[77] In later parts of his report, he stretched the truth through
argumentation, indicating his legal expertise but not mentioning

any medical studies. He argued how inhaled coal dust created an antiseptic environment for the tuberculosis bacteria, citing Dr. A. Oller, a doctor from Mitholz, Switzerland.[78] Oller had interpreted statistics that illustrated a relatively minor mortality rate for coal miners with tuberculosis compared to those who mined for metals.[79] Indeed, González Gallo emphasized that only a few miners had not suffered silicosis prior to contracting tuberculosis, arguing that the two illnesses were "reciprocal diseases."[80] González Gallo then argued that government officials should distinguish between coal miners and miners in metal-producing enterprises. Moreover, he pushed for the law to recognize the disease as an occupational illness only in workers who had toiled ten years or more in mines.[81]

The discussion over how to categorize various pulmonary ailments in Mexico revealed complex arguments among miners, bureaucrats, and doctors along with the president of Mexico. No one fully understood the role of disease in mining communities. Diseases, symptoms, and pathologies appeared as indeterminate and as difficult to grasp as the air miners sought with each raspy breath. Miners viewed themselves as sufferers of serious illnesses, while Mexico City politicians considered them expendable, inactive contributors to the economy. Doctors, meanwhile, saw patients as unwitting participants in the debate over the diagnosis of silicosis-tuberculosis or as sources of confusion in the endless search for a diagnosis for their pulmonary ailments. Workers saw themselves as heirs to revolutionary ideas about their role in the new Mexican republic. The Constitution of 1917 provided them with wages, hours, and workplace guidelines, yet confusion about the diagnostic interpretations of silicosis-tuberculosis raised once again the question of who was responsible for public health. The government? The worker? The employer? What if miners worked for foreign employers? The growing bureaucracy and red tape signaled a challenge in understanding not only disease in the workplace but also the role of the revolution in workers' lives. Politicians had begun to change.[82] The days of the sweeping reforms of Lázaro Cárdenas, who nationalized land and expropriated foreign interests, slowed to a trot and ground to a halt with the new generation of Mexican presidents. Indeed, the inclusion of tuberculosis, or what miners thought to be tuberculosis, as an occupational disease seemed doomed from the start. With the amendment to recognize TB as an occupational disease of miners in congressional debate, Gustavo P. Serrano, head of the Cámara Minera de México, wrote a confidential telegram to President Ávila Camacho on 29 December 1942. Although only a few sentences long, the message rang loud and clear: the law requiring compensation for workers who had developed silicosis-tuberculosis would devastate the mining industry.[83] Two weeks before he dismissed the amendment, the president received another communiqué from Serrano. In a letter, Serrano reiterated Dr. Rohde y Herrera's conclusion that tuberculosis could not be considered an occupational disease.[84]

In sum, it bears repeating that mining companies encouraged doubt about workers' claims by underscoring the differences in pulmonary diseases. While some miners truly suffered from silicosis and its cousin silicosis-tuberculosis, many workers recognized only coughing as a tell-tale symptom for pulmonary diseases. Doctors also added to the debate by creating such a nuanced argument based on pathology and epidemiology that it dismissed worker claims on the basis of diagnosis (or misdiagnosis). As to the question of misdiagnosis: how many workers received the tuberculosis diagnosis when they suffered from silicosis? Just as lung capacity was reduced to a percentage, so too were workers' claims for compensation.

Why Silicosis Matters

Occupational health, or rather the illusion of safety in the mines of Mexico, illustrated a convergence of engineering and medicine, in part due to a number of changes in what miners expected to encounter in their work, as well as in what citizens expected of their country. First, the value of trades and occupations shifted during the late nineteenth century and early twentieth century due to the introduction of technology. While there existed a hierarchy that championed jobs that did not involve digging, workers gained social status when they used steam-powered technology to demonstrate skill. The introduction of this technology evinced a portrait of control over the environment, which created an illusion of safety. As engineers completed the professionalization process, workers entrusted them to make decisions on the infrastructure of the mine, such as beams, while also continuing to read the veins. Moreover, engineers guided their drills and jackhammers in other directions, creating greater distance between workers and the process of extraction. Thus, when accidents happened, when cave-ins occurred, workers recognized the mirage of safety and false trust in the engineer. In other words, death and mishaps at work demonstrated the failure to prevent and to control, an unnerving possibility for miners hundreds of feet underground.

Second, while technology increased production and extraction, it also provided the image of a modern country, further associating technology with modernity. Extraction technology drove workers into new corners of mountains or farther into the depths of existing mines with steam-powered drills and hammers, while at the same time steam-powered pumps emptied aquifers in the search for silver. However, engineers did not account for the human factor in the introduction of new gadgets and apparatuses. Without proper training or knowledge on how the machines worked, workers grew confident or careless with the technology, which led to failures in the reliability of technology.

Third, occupational safety limited the influence of foreign companies in revolutionary Mexico at least on paper, leveling economic power dynamics to a degree. Whereas the Porfiriato saw exploitation on the part of mining companies, miners and union heads used revolutionary ideology to establish workers' rights as defined in the Constitution of 1917. For example, from 1860 to 1910, miners in Batopilas, Chihuahua, worked for the Batopilas Consolidated Mining Company, a U.S. firm. As John Mason Hart has written, the U.S. interests had introduced "high technology" while disrupting the "cultural traditions and economic system."[85] In the end, the miners in Porfirian-era Mexico presumably contracted pulmonary diseases in addition to their meager wages, leaving them poor and in ill health with little recourse due to the uneven power dynamics plaguing the venture during that period.[86]

Finally, insurance men and risk assessors emerged as the new empiricists in global occupational safety. They came armed with medical-legal jargon and scientists ready and able to reduce complex ecological questions to numbers.[87] Engineers in the early twentieth century faced new demands as insurance companies called for safety precautions to be incorporated into new construction as well as existing businesses, to prevent bodily injury or occupational disease. In the United States, new medical and legal workplace regulations, worker safety guidelines, and compensation for injured or sickened workers arose from a series of tragedies in the first half of the century. In 1911, a fire at the Triangle Shirtwaist Factory in New York City killed 146 women due to the lack of fire exists and shoddily built stairs. The American Society of Safety Engineers was established later that year. From 1917 to 1926, young women in a watch factory painted watch dials with a glowing paint made from radium. In order to make the paintbrush fine-tipped, they rolled it between their lips and in the process absorbed and ingested the radioactive element. Their legal case forced companies to acknowledge the toxicity of materials handled in day-to-day work activities.[88]

Occupational safety took a prominent place in Mexican legislation, prompting medico-legal discourse on every disease and ailment attributed to labor in a particular sector. According to the Constitution of 1917, as outlined in Article 123, section XIV, employers were to be held liable for workers' on-the-job accidents and occupational diseases "contracted because of or in the performance of their work or occupation."[89] In addition, the Ley Federal de Trabajo of August 1931 laid out the specific ailments associated with trades and crafts. It also argued that employers must pay an indemnity to a family in case of a worker's on-the-job death or to injured workers rendered disabled, either temporarily or permanently.[90] Still, pamphleteers and union leaders questioned whose rights the government protected with this legislation: those of the workers or the companies.[91]

While initial legislation reflected Mexico's progressivism toward occupational health, medical-legal rhetoric muddied cases and the lack of accountability marred the success of the law's application. When workers demanded compensation for workplace injury, mining companies took two approaches: one with doctors and one that focused on discrediting workers. With medical doctors, insurance companies hired physicians to cast doubt on the patient's diagnosis. The doctors questioned whether workers' behavior possibly contributed to their ailments or if they lived in poor conditions. Through obfuscation with medical jargon, they exculpated companies by offering diseases with similar symptoms, eliminating the direct link between the trade and the illness. In the second approach, mining companies sought to blame the workers themselves for injuries. They cited carelessness and reckless behavior in a dangerous work environment in order to make workers responsible for their own injuries, shifting blame once again. Meanwhile, the importance of rhetoric grew all the more when insurance companies became involved, adding another layer of medical-legal discourse. Engineers entered the fray when insurance firms hired them to serve as witnesses in their favor. With physics and chemistry, engineers attempted to re-create accidents or falls in order to direct or misdirect blame. Overall, where engineers and physicians initially attempted to protect workers, they later became absorbed in building legal arguments against workers.

Conclusion: A Prognosis for the Revolution

While the revolution presented labor issues and social justice as central to its ideological goals, workers in the 1920s and 1930s witnessed how reforms fell short, as the government's need for economic stability trumped the demands of railroad workers and miners. The mining industry in Zacatecas had struggled early on to keep pace with new refining techniques as well as the Guanajuato silver boom that began at the turn of the century. The revolution erupted and unnerved potential investors. In the Battle of Zacatecas in 1914, the hills teemed with armies instead of miners, further slowing silver production. Despite fears that the state's industry would not recover, several positive reports printed in U.S. publications reiterated the political and financial security of an investment in Zacatecas mining. While Claude Rice, Arthur Barrette Parsons, and other *Engineering and Mining Journal* writers reassured foreign investors, union workers felt the backlash as state-funded projects, such as the railroads, did not employ them. Adding insult to injury, mining unions tested Article 123 and its blueprint for compensation in the event of occupational injury or disease. The silicosis-tuberculosis compensation laws mediated the relationship between disease and labor, but they also contributed to debates over the diagnosis and potential remedies for such an illness. As the *grito* of the revolution lifted high into the air, it dissipated in the wracking coughs and scarred lungs of workers.

Conclusion
Toxic Legacies

Wealth flowed like water.

—Eduardo Galeano, *Open Veins of Latin America*

IN JULY 2002, A CANADIAN ENVIRONMENTAL ENGINEER named Ron Pearson and his team mapped seven sites in Zacatecas, nearby Guadalupe, and the reservoir La Zacatecana. Reflecting activities common in the lives of Zacatecanos, the sites included a school, a playground, farm fields, and the shoreline of a lake. The team took seven samples, some from the soil and some from vegetation. They then analyzed the collections to measure pH, mercury, methylmercury, arsenic, cadmium, and lead, among others. Using Ontario site data as a model to determine the environmental and health risks, they found four of the sites in violation of ecological and human health criteria.[1] The highest level of mercury found in soil from Ontario was 10 μg (micrograms); in Zacatecas, Pearson and his team found 13 μg of mercury at site 2 (a school), 12 μg at site 3 (a road), and 28 μg at site 4 (a farm field).[2]

The lingering effects of silver mining in these samples illustrate how more than four hundred years of industry had affected the surrounding region. The results demonstrate that mining is not an industry limited to its extraction sites but one that consumes an entire region. Mining transcends space. The ecology of extraction extends well beyond the borders of the mine and involves macroscopic as well as microscopic ecosystems. It involves water systems above and below the ground. Horses, cattle, and goats are affected by it.

Humans come in contact with it or are subjected to it by those in power. However, mining also transcends time. Toxic metals leaked into the soil or waterways and remained there to expose future ecologies to toxins. The state of Zacatecas faces the consequences of the legacy of mining.

This research has examined the interaction between mining, water, and public health at various levels in the decades before and after the Mexican Revolution. The process of extraction exposed Zacatecanos and the surrounding environments to heavy metals, water insecurity, and public health crises. The human body's permeability allows it to absorb toxins from contaminated water. Meanwhile, the widespread use of mercury in refining led to toxic runoff from patio amalgamation sites, thus contaminating local water sources. This exchange underscored how extraction affected the human body. Even as Porfirian Mexico City implemented fountain systems and drainage canals, Zacatecas locals found their water sources in constant danger from mining. Scrambling to keep up with the model set by the national capital, locals also found the climate and topography of the region difficult to manage in times of drought. With water disappearing on the surface, they soon turned to water in underground aquifers to quench their thirst and to water their farms. The Porfirian-era legislation that had allowed them to use this water and the laws that imbued a nationalist purpose to water management vanished in the wake of the revolution. Farmers and *ejidatarios* paid most dearly for their belief that revolutionary-era statutes would protect them. As a result, this is a story of continuities from the colonial era to the Porfiriato to revolutionary Mexico. While the center of the country generally benefited from the wealth extracted, it also dictated how farmers used water and how mining companies affected locals' ability to use the water. In order to grasp this disparity, historians must study the many regions of the country and not solely the national capital.

After 1946, Zacatecanos continued to rely on agriculture and cattle ranching to supplement their economy while mining remained small in scale. Investment in mining stalled as Zacatecas locals relocated

14. A view of the historic center of Zacatecas. Library of Congress, Prints and Photographs Division, Detroit Publishing Company Collection, LC-D 43-1577.

to larger cities during the midcentury economic boom known as the Mexican Miracle. In the late twentieth century, the state attracted the interest of foreign mining conglomerates that invested heavily in extraction. With new technology and financial resources, these mines supplanted the drift mines (horizontal entry into mountains), slope mines (sloped entry into a mountain), and vertical shafts with open-pit mining. Despite the mining industry being the backbone of the economy of Zacatecas, locals cheered when the city's historic center, pictured here, was recognized as a UNESCO World Heritage Site in 1993, ensuring that its architecture and cultural sites would be preserved.

The New Extraction

Because the historiography on Zacatecas emphasizes the colonial period, historians, scholars of Mexico, and indeed the public cannot fathom that mining continues in the city to this day. It is a common misconception that mining stopped when the Spanish left. While this research fills that gap in the historiography, the state of Zacatecas remains a state of extraction even today. In addition to large-scale pit mining, new companies now extract water from aquifers and mercury from contaminated soil.

With climate change and a rapidly growing population, the city of Zacatecas continues to have problems with water access. As a growing city, it serves as the primary economic draw in the region in addition to cities like Aguascalientes, Aguascalientes, and larger cities like Guadalajara, Jalisco. New arrivals into the city of Zacatecas build on the outskirts and stretch city infrastructure projects even farther into the hills. In July 2013, politicians and residents monitored the drought that parched the region and dropped aquifer levels significantly. Mayors and state governors of Chihuahua, Zacatecas, Coahuila, and Durango appealed for natural disaster funds as dust storms swept the area.[3] Because of the growing dependence on aquifers in the region, the Comisión Nacional del Agua, or CONAGUA, listed the aquifers in Zacatecas as overexploited.[4]

That same year, residents began competing with a new extraction company: a brewery. The Cervecería Modelo factory soon expanded to an area beyond the state capital. In order to meet the demand for water in the production of beer, engineers drilled eight large wells into the aquifer and built large pumps to draw water into the brewery facilities. Head brewmaster Arturo Cadena told producers of the National Geographic television program *Megafactories* that the factory draws almost eight million U.S. gallons of water a day from below the surface when operating at full capacity to produce popular brands of beer such as Corona, Pacífico, and Modelo.[5] The extraction of water raises questions about the industrialization of the resource with new technology that does not just consume but rather drains water sources. With aquifers as the primary source for water, the region faces a looming choice between city growth and business investment.

A new extraction also takes advantage of the long-standing re-gional history of silver mining by harvesting the heavy metals left over from the patio amalgamation system. While these heavy metals menace human health, some harvesters profit by gathering these toxins—not as remediation or cleanup but rather as a business. Like the Pearson study cited at the beginning of this chapter, scientists Tetsuya Ogura and others also found high levels of mercury (Hg) in Zacatecas soil. With the heavy metal at such high concentra-tions throughout the state, they tracked growing investments among mercury harvesters in the region.[6] These harvesters quite literally bake the mercury out of soil in a large adobe oven, rendering the mercury liquid and collectable. With more than 450 years' worth of mercury waste in the soil, the harvesters have an abundance from which to draw.

In addition, Zacatecanos have continued to contend with heavy metals in water sources. Scientist Felib Iskander and his colleagues examined the possibility of cleanup efforts at La Zacatecana, a reser-voir on the outskirts of the city.[7] Because of its location, the reservoir collected heavy metals from surrounding patio amalgamation systems through dumping or runoff. Consequently, at the bottom of the lake scientists found mercury, silver, and other metals in the sediment. The city then launched an environmental restoration effort to make the reservoir a recreational spot for locals. Initially considered too expensive, the project soon attracted locals who found the heavy metals in La Zacatecana and its watershed a worthwhile enterprise. Many ejidatarios in the region attempted to dredge the remaining mercury, gold, and silver from the watershed with some ill effects, as María del Carmen Zetina Rodríguez describes.[8]

Farther north, sharing this same expansive aquifer network, the Mina GoldCorp company, operator of the Peñasquito Polymetallic mine outside Mazapil, Zacatecas, also contaminated the aquifers in late 2016.[9] The open-pit mines from this mining complex, visible on Google Earth, are sites of excavation for lead, copper, and tin. During this excavation process, their holding ponds leeched selenium into the aquifer, a finding the company initially attempted to dismiss, according to a report by Reuters.[10] Farmers in the region expressed their anger because this same water fed their irrigation canals and stock tanks. Although multivitamins include a trace of selenium (roughly 400 µg), persons who absorb selenium through their skin or get it from food, air, or water in high quantities can suffer respiratory problems, gastrointestinal symptoms, hair loss and brittle nails, and neurological problems, according to the National Institutes of Health.[11] Moreover, locals in the Mazapil and Concepción del Oro region cited limited water availability as a prime reason for slow economic development and diversification beyond mining.

Despite the challenges, the city continues to grow and new economic opportunities are cropping up in the region. Along with the brewery, the local university, Universidad Autónoma de Zacatecas, as well as its lauded School of Mines, also provides many jobs. Numerous residents of Zacatecas commute to Aguascalientes (roughly an hour away) to work at the Nissan factory. In addition, the city remains a favorite with domestic tourists, who flock to the city to take a mine tour or walk its colonial streets. Pres. Enrique Peña Nieto invited King Felipe VI and the Royal Consort Letizia of Spain to Zacatecas to visit the city in February 2015. The royals toured La Bufa, the Museum of Guadalupe, and area churches. The city also hosts an annual international festival in the arts, an annual *charreada* (Mexican rodeo), and the Morisma de Bracho, a reenactment of the Reconquest of Moorish Spain, with more than a thousand participants. Overall, the city continues its path forward in spite of the environmental challenges in the region.

While this research may present a declensionist narrative, the story of Zacatecas and Mexico does offer some hope. Mexicans increasingly embrace sustainability efforts and welcome investments in renewable energy, such as the new wind turbine parks in the state of Tamaulipas. The country also produces more engineers than Germany in any given year.[12] Politicians and other government officials have promised to keep this important talent from leaving the country and thus limit brain drain. While all of these advances may seem like empty promises, the election of Andrés Manuel López

Obrador as president in 2018 has raised the potential of growth in environmental regulation enforcement and the alternative energy sector, per his campaign platform. Moreover, declensionist narratives outline mistakes and failures of the past so that the country can avoid them in the future.

Zacatecas, with its *rostro de cantera con corazón de plata* (face of stone with a heart of silver), emerged as a crown jewel in the colonial period and maintained its identity as a stalwart city in north-central Mexico to the present. While historians focus primarily on its colonial history, the city offers insight into its relationship with mining through a political and social ecology framework. The interaction between mining, water, and public health demonstrates the all-consuming nature of the industry along with how history informs locals' perceptions of extraction. Zacatecanos embraced mining as part of their industrial heritage. Even so, they proved resilient in challenging extractive interests even when their government officials failed them.

Notes

Introduction

1. Emilia Reina to Secretaría de Recursos Hidráulicos, 24 July 1954, AHA, Fondo Aguas Nacionales, Caja 1067, Exp. 14050.

2. Santiago, "Extracting Histories."

3. See Santiago, *Ecology of Oil*; and Vitz, *City on a Lake*.

4. Douglas, *Risk and Blame*, 51.

5. Aboites Aguilar, *El agua de la nación*, 13–15.

6. See Vitz, *City on a Lake*; Aboites Aguilar, *El agua de la nación*; Wolfe, *Watering the Revolution*; Mendoza García, "Resistencia a la 'federalización'"; and Birrichaga Gardida, "Modernización del sistema hidráulico rural en el Estado de México."

7. See Santiago, *Ecology of Oil*; Piper, *Industrial Transformation of Subarctic Canada*; Van Horssen, *Town Called Asbestos*; and Leech, *City That Ate Itself*.

8. See Velasco Murillo, *Urban Indians*; and Bakewell, *Silver Mining and Society in Colonial Mexico*, 122–24.

9. See, for example, Schell, "Silver Symbiosis."

10. See Lane, *Potosí*, for a social and environmental history of the colonial mining city; and Robins, *Mercury, Mining, and Empire*, for a discussion of colonial mining conditions in Potosí.

11. See Agostoni, *Monuments of Progress*; Boyer, *Land between Waters*; and Tortolero Villaseñor, *El agua y su historia*.

12. See Hempel, *Strange Case of the Broad Street Pump*. The term "little creatures" refers to bacteria seen in the Broad Street pump water samples when magnified under a microscope. Hempel notes the popularity of the term for the microscopic beings.

13. Nash, "Writing Histories of Disease and Environment," 800–801.

14. Beatty, *Technology and the Search for Progress*, 146.

15. See Sellers, *Hazards of the Job*; and Rosner and Markowitz, *Deadly Dust*.

16. White, "Are You an Environmentalist?," 172–73.

17. Andrews, *Killing for Coal*, 125.

18. Langston, *Toxic Bodies*, xiii. In addition to Langston, the term comes from Mitman, Murphy, and Sellers, "Landscapes of Exposure."

19. Santiago, *Ecology of Oil*, 4.

20. See Liceaga, *Las inoculaciones preventivas*.

21. See Garner, "Long-Term Silver Mining Trends in Spanish America"; and Brading, "Colonial Silver Mining."

22. Amador, *Bosquejo histórico*, 2:411–12.

1. Underground Bodies

1. Ferrusquía-Villafranca, "Geology of Mexico," 50–51.

2. Ferrusquía-Villafranca, "Geology of Mexico," 14.

3. Nieto-Samaniego, Alaniz-Álvarez, and Camprubí, "Mesa Central of Mexico," 56, 64.

4. Ferrari, Valencia-Moreno, and Bryan, "Magmatism and Tectonics," 3.

5. Ferrari, Valencia-Moreno, and Bryan, "Magmatism and Tectonics," 3.

6. Hansen et al., "Silver and Palladium Help Unveil the Nature of a Second R-Process."

7. Bakewell, *Silver Mining and Society*, 150.

8. In addition, Amador notes that Spanish accounts of the region labeled many indigenous groups *chichimecas*, despite there being a group by that name. Amador, *Bosquejo histórico*, 1:31.

9. See García García and Solar Valverde, *Proyecto Arqueológico Cerro del Teúl, Zacatecas*.

10. Brown, *Mining History of Latin America*, 6.

11. Brown, *Mining History of Latin America*, 7.

12. Brown, *Mining History of Latin America*, 7.

13. See Krech, *Ecological Indian*; and Ellingson, *Myth of the Noble Savage*.

14. Bakewell, *Silver Mining and Society*, 4–5.

15. Amador, *Bosquejo histórico*, 1:89.

16. Amador, *Bosquejo histórico*, 1:83.

17. Amador, *Bosquejo histórico*, 1:83.

18. Bakewell, *Silver Mining and Society*, 5–6.

19. Bakewell, *Silver Mining and Society*, 5.

20. Chipman, *Moctezuma's Children*, 105–6.

21. Stein and Stein, *Silver, Trade, and War*, 21; Bakewell, *Silver Mining and Society*, 138.

22. Stein and Stein, *Silver, Trade, and War*, 30.

23. Velasco Murillo, *Urban Indians*, 39.

24. Velasco Murillo, *Urban Indians*, 42.

25. Stein and Stein, *Silver, Trade, and War*, 28. *Mita* is used to denote a forced labor draft in Peru. In New Spain, it was known as the *repartimiento*.

26. Velasco Murillo, *Urban Indians*, 56.

27. Velasco Murillo, *Urban Indians*, 56–57.

28. Brading, *Miners and Merchants in Bourbon Mexico*, 97.

29. Brading, *Miners and Merchants in Bourbon Mexico*, 97.

30. Bakewell, *Silver Mining and Society*, 150–56.

31. Brown, "Workers' Health," 468, 471.

32. Brown, "Workers' Health," 481, 488.

33. Robins, *Mercury, Mining, and Empire*, 141. For a general discussion of mercury and mining in Latin America, see Kris Lane, "Dangerous Attractions."

34. See Cronon, "Place for Stories," for a discussion of environmental history as a struggle between progressive or declensionist narratives.

35. Guerrero, "History of Silver Refining," 8.

36. For the chemistry behind silver production, see Guerrero, *Silver by Fire*.

37. Howe, *Mining Guild of New Spain*, 310; Motten, *Mexican Silver and the Enlightenment*, 47.

38. Motten, *Mexican Silver and the Enlightenment*, 46–47; Fisher, *Silver Mines*, 55–56.

39. Motten, *Mexican Silver and the Enlightenment*, 46–47.

40. Fisher, *Silver Mines*, 55.

41. Born, *Born's New Process*, 81–87.

42. Amador, *Bosquejo histórico*, 2:269. Amador writes that by 1822 forests had largely disappeared in the region. See Studnicki-Gizbert and Schecter, "Environmental Dynamics of a Colonial Fuel-Rush." For an excellent discussion of wood resources in a mining district, see Avalos-Lozano and Aguilar Robledo, "Reconstructing the Environmental History of Colonial Mining."

43. Motten, *Mexican Silver and the Enlightenment*, 47.

44. Motten, *Mexican Silver and the Enlightenment*, 49.

45. Halleck, *Collection of Mining Laws*, 405–6. Halleck offers translations of the primary sources in English. He translates mercury as "quicksilver" in reference to *azogue*.

46. Halleck, *Collection of Mining Laws*, 411–12.

47. Quoted in Halleck, *Collection of Mining Laws*, 426.

48. Halleck, *Collection of Mining Laws*, 427–30.

49. Halleck, *Collection of Mining Laws*, 508.

50. Halleck, *Collection of Mining Laws*, 514.

51. Halleck, *Collection of Mining Laws*, 555, 560.

52. Martínez Baca, *Reseña histórica*, 380 (my translation).

53. Halleck, *Collection of Mining Laws*, 514.

54. Martínez Baca, *Reseña histórica*, 380.

55. Martínez Baca, *Reseña histórica*, 380.

56. Halleck, *Collection of Mining Laws*, 403–4.

57. Melitón to Diputación Minera, 21 June 1825, AHEZ, Fondo Ayuntamiento, Serie Diputación, Subserie Minería, Caja 2 (1808–91), Exp. 40.

58. Ramírez to Diputación Minera, 21 June 1825, AHEZ, Fondo Ayuntamiento, Serie Diputación, Subserie Minería, Caja 2 (1808–91), Exp. 40.

59. Melitón to Diputación Minera, 15 September 1825, AHEZ, Fondo Ayuntamiento, Serie Diputación, Subserie Minería, Caja 2 (1808–91), Exp. 40.

60. Halleck, *Collection of Mining Laws*, 403–4, 418.

61. Amador, *Bosquejo histórico*, 2:413.

62. Fowler, *Santa Anna of Mexico*, 157–60.

63. Bernstein, *Mexican Mining Industry*, 19–20.

64. *Ley minería y ley de impuesto*, 7.

65. "Ministry of Development, Colonization, and Industry," as seen in the side-by-side English and Spanish translations in *Mining Laws of the United States of Mexico/Ley Minería de los Estados Unidos Mexicanos*.

66. Bernstein, *Mexican Mining Industry*, 49–50.

67. Halleck, *Collection of Mining Laws*, 239–40.

68. "Libro de Denuncios," 30 January 1882, AHEZ, Fondo Ayuntamiento, Serie Minería, Subserie Denuncios, Caja 7, Exp. 124.

69. Macmillan and Plomley, "American Surveyor," 7.

70. Macmillan and Plomley, "American Surveyor," 7.

71. Macmillan and Plomley, "American Surveyor," 7.

72. Carlos Birkbeck to Ayuntamiento, 6 January 1866, AHEZ, Fondo Ayuntamiento, Serie Minería, Subserie Denuncios, Caja 7, Exp. 115.

73. Macmillan and Plomley, "American Surveyor," 8. Death and relationship confirmed via Family Search, https://www.familysearch.org/ark:/61903/1:1:QL7N-HC2P.

74. Macmillan and Plomley, "American Surveyor," 4.

75. Macmillan and Plomley, "American Surveyor," 7.

76. "Libro de Denuncios," 5 January 1879, AHEZ, Fondo Ayuntamiento, Serie Minería, Subserie Denuncios, Caja 7, Exp. 120.

77. Statement by Antonio Kimball, 26 April 1877, AHEZ, Fondo Ayuntamiento, Serie Varios, Caja 3, Exp. 77.

78. Hart, *Revolutionary Mexico*, 143; Pletcher, "Fall of Silver in Mexico," 33–54; Bernstein, *Mexican Mining Industry*, 29, 51–52, 128.

79. See Art. 5 in *Ley minería y ley de impuesto*, 47.

80. Kimball to Jefatura Política, 17 October 1877, AHEZ, Jefatura Política, Serie Correspondencia General, Subserie Minería, Caja 1, Exp. n/a.

81. Fernando Calderón, lawsuit, 1 March 1889, AMdeZac, Serie Jefatura Política, Subserie Denuncios de Terrenos, Caja 1, Exp. 13.

82. El Porvenir may be translated as "The Future."

83. Fernando Calderón, lawsuit, 19 March 1889, AMdeZac, Serie Jefatura Política, Subserie Denuncios de Terrenos, Caja 1, Exp. 13.

84. Pascual López Velarde to Jefe Político Ponce, 3 May 1889, AMdeZac, Serie Jefatura Política, Subserie Denuncios de Terrenos, Caja 1, Exp. 13.

85. López Velarde to Ponce, 3 May 1889.

86. A. G. Castellanos to Diputación Minera, 18 March 1891, AHEZ, Fondo Ayuntamiento, Serie Diputación Minera, Caja 2, Exp. 79.

87. Pedro Espejo to Diputación Minera, 21 May 1891, AHEZ, Fondo Ayuntamiento, Serie Diputación Minera, Caja 2, Exp. 79.

88. Buiza to Asamblea Municipal, 19 September 1891, AHEZ, Fondo Ayuntamiento, Serie Diputación Minera, Caja 2, Exp. 80. According to the Mining Code of 1884, owners gained possession of the water sources that passed above or under the purchased property. Article 1 acknowledges the minerals that may be gathered, as well as the water, which was used in refining, for drinking, or to power the operation, as part of the claim. In addition, it stipulated that water sources discovered in the process (*aguas termales o medicinales*) would belong to the owner. The law did not provide legal recourse should the claimant's right to the water abrogate the ability of locals or municipalities to use the water.

89. For a discussion of cholera in Mexico City, see Stevens, *Mexico in the Time of Cholera*. For a discussion of the disease in the Yucatán, see McCrea, *Diseased Relations*.

90. Agostoni, *Monuments of Progress*, 75.

91. Rosenberg, *Cholera Years*, 5, 17.

92. Rosenberg, *Cholera Years*, 206–7.

93. List of victims in Sauceda, August 1849 to July 1850, AHEZ, Fondo Ayuntamiento, Serie Hospitales y Sanidad, Caja 4, Exp. 147.

94. Pedro Hernández to Asamblea Municipal, 17 November 1853, AHEZ, Fondo Ayuntamiento, Serie Hospitales y Sanidad, Caja 4, Exp. 137.

95. Agostoni, *Monuments of Progress*, 72–75. See also Stevens, *Mexico in the Time of Cholera*.

96. Hernández and Villegas, 10 March 1854, AHEZ, Fondo Ayuntamiento, Serie Abasto de Agua, Caja 1, Exp. 52.

97. Corristan to Asamblea Municipal, 10 April 1861, AHEZ, Fondo Ayuntamiento, Serie Abasto de Agua, Caja 1, Exp. 60.

98. Córdova to Asamblea Municipal, 14 September 1885, AHEZ, Fondo Ayuntamiento, Serie Hospitales y Sanidades, Caja 4, Exp. 171.

99. Timoteo Macías and others to Asamblea Municipal, 8 May 1877, AHEZ, Fondo Ayuntamiento, Serie Hospitales y Sanidad, Caja 4, Exp. 168. For a history of alcohol in Mexico, see Toner, *Alcohol and Nationhood*; and Toxqui and Pierce, *Alcohol in Latin America*.

100. Asamblea Municipal to Macías and others, 10 May 1877, AHEZ, Fondo Ayuntamiento, Serie Hospitales y Sanidad, Caja 4, Exp. 168.

2. The Home

1. "Estadística de San José de la Isla," 26 September 1903, AMdeZac, Fondo Jefatura Política de Zacatecas, Serie Estadísticas, Caja 3 (1903), Exp. 40. My translation for the engineer's response would be "There aren't any."

2. See Mill, *Auguste Comte and Positivism*; Agostoni, *Monuments of Progress*, 25.

3. Tortolero Villaseñor, *El agua y su historia*, 52.

4. Candiani, *Dreaming of Dry Land*, xxvi. See Hardin, "Tragedy of the Commons," for a discussion of resource use and conservation on public lands.

5. Benidickson, *Culture of Flushing*, 3.

6. Selee, "Municipalities and Policymaking," 103–5.

7. González Ortega to Sebastián Lerdo de Tejada, in González Ortega, *Presidency of Mexico*, 9–11.

8. Flores Olague et al., 113–15; Vidal, *Bosquejo histórico*, 3:391–99.

9. "Gobernantes de Zacatecas," UNAM Archivo Jurídico, accessed May 2017, https://archivos.juridicas.unam.mx/.

10. Mather, "On the principles involved," 218.

11. See Garner, "Long-Term Silver Mining Trends," for a comparative discussion about Potosí and Zacatecas in the colonial period. For a discussion of modern Zacatecas silver, see Pletcher, "Fall of Silver in Mexico"; or Schell, "Silver Symbiosis."

12. Mather, "On the principles involved," 220.

13. Mather, "On the principles involved," 216.

14. "Diario de Garitas," 1–30 June 1886, AHEZ, Fondo Ayuntamiento, Serie Comercio, Subserie Diario de Garitas (June 1886), Caja 6 (1880–86), Exp. n/a.

15. Mather, "On the principles involved," 219.

16. Carrillo to Jefatura Política, 3 October 1884, AHEZ, Colección Jefatura Política de Zacatecas, Serie Correspondencia General, Caja 1 (1823–99), Subserie Minería, Exp. n/a.

17. Ramírez, *Datos para la historia*, 373; Azuela Bernal, "La geología en la formación de los ingenieros," 101.

18. Carrillo to Jefatura Política, 3 October 1884.

19. Carrillo to Jefatura Política, 3 October 1884.

20. Gutiérrez to Jefatura Política, 13 June 1890, AHEZ, Fondo Jefatura Política, Serie Correspondencia General, Subserie Abasto de Agua, Caja 1, Exp. n/a.

21. Cordary to Jefatura Política, 21 November 1899, AHEZ, Colección Jefatura Política de Zacatecas, Serie Correspondencia General, Subserie Minería, Caja 1 (1823–99), Exp. n/a.

22. Agostoni, *Monuments of Progress*, 115–17.

23. Agostoni, *Monuments of Progress*, 110–12.

24. Tomás Lorck to Jefatura Política, 14 July 1884, AHEZ, Colección Jefatura Política de Zacatecas, Serie Correspondencia General, Subserie, Obras Públicas, Caja 2 (1876–93), Exp. n/a.

25. Lorck to Jefatura Política, 14 July 1884.

26. Ma. del Refugio Lamadrid de Mourell, letter, 29 November 1884, AHEZ, Colección Jefatura Política, Serie Correspondencia General, Subserie Obras Públicas, Caja 2 (1876–93), Exp. n/a.

27. Memorandum to Enrique Carrillo, 29 November 1884, AHEZ, Colección Jefatura Política, Serie Correspondencia General, Subserie Obras Públicas, Caja 2 (1876–93), Exp. n/a.

28. Rosa Aparicio, report to Jefatura Política, 30 April 1891, AHEZ, Colección Jefatura Política, Serie Correspondencia General, Subserie Abasto de Agua, Caja 1, Exp. n/a.

29. Arteaga to Jefatura Política, 20 October 1891, AHEZ, Fondo Jefatura Política de Zacatecas, Serie Correspondencia General, Subserie Obras Públicas, Caja 2 (1876–93), Exp. n/a.

30. Arteaga to Jefatura Política, 20 October 1891.

31. Petition from various neighbors, 4 March 1893, AHEZ, Fondo Jefatura Política de Zacatecas, Serie Correspondencia General, Subserie Obras Públicas, Caja 2 (1876–93), Exp. n/a.

32. Gen. Trinidad García de la Cadena (1823–86) served as governor on four separate occasions between 1869 and 1880, while also investing in mines and agriculture. Readers should not confuse this politician with Trinidad García (1831–1906), author of *Los mineros mexicanos* (1895), mine owner, and *jefe político* in Fresnillo, Zacatecas. Adding further confusion, Governor García de la Cadena often hired author García as a political advisor. Biographical notes do not mention any family ties between them, with the former being

from the southern city of Tabasco, Zacatecas, and the latter being from the western city of Sombrerete, Zacatecas.

33. "Algunos indicadores demográficos y sociales" (figure), in Flores Olague et al., *Zacatecas*, 191. By haciendas, I refer to the large, autonomous estates, which depended on participation in diverse economic sectors to survive. Many sold cattle, sheep, horses, agricultural products, and more while also participating in mining if viable veins were found on site. Ranches, in contrast, often dealt exclusively with cattle, horses, sheep, and their products, such as milk, hides, and beef.

34. Comparative summary, *Censo General de 1910*, inegi.org.mx.

35. "Población según la ocupación principal," *Censo General de 1895*, inegi.org.mx.

36. See Ferry, *Not Ours Alone*.

37. Ferry, *Not Ours Alone*, 117–20. For discussions of women and mining, see Gier and Mercier, *Mining Women*; Johnson, *Roaring Camp*; and Finn, *Tracing the Veins*.

38. "Área, población total, urbana y rural," *Censo General de 1910*, inegi.org.mx.

39. Amador, *Elementos de geografía del estado de Zacatecas*, 18–19.

40. Kuntz Ficker, "La República Restaurada y el Porfiriato," 142.

41. Roque Llamas and others to Asamblea Municipal, 4 March 1893, AHEZ, Fondo Jefatura Política, Serie Correspondencia General, Subserie Obras Públicas, Caja 2 (1876–93), Exp. n/a; Rosenberg, *Cholera Years*, 40–42.

42. Bermiso to Asamblea Municipal, 16 July 1886, AHEZ, Fondo Ayuntamiento, Serie Abasto de Agua, Caja 1, Exp. 73.

43. Bermiso to Asamblea Municipal, 16 July 1886.

44. Martínez to Carrillo, 23 August 1886, AHEZ, Fondo Ayuntamiento, Serie Abasto de Agua, Caja 1, Exp. 74.

45. Maps and plans by Rico, 26 May 1888, AHEZ, Fondo Jefatura Política de Zacatecas, Serie Correspondencia General, Subserie Abasto de Agua, Caja 1, Exp. n/a.

46. Luis Córdova to Asamblea Municipal, 5 January 1889, AHEZ, Fondo Ayuntamiento, Serie Abasto de Agua, Exp. 76.

47. Córdova to Asamblea Municipal, 5 January 1889.

48. Asamblea to Córdova and Berliner, 8 January 1889, AHEZ, Fondo Ayuntamiento, Serie Abasto de Agua, Exp. 76.

49. "Railroad Notes," *Arizona Weekly Citizen*, 23 September 1895.

50. "A Big Insurance Verdict," *San Francisco Call*, 31 August 1898.

51. Luis Córdova to Asamblea Municipal, 14 May 1889, AHEZ, Fondo Ayuntamiento, Serie Abasto de Agua, Exp. 77.

52. Various documents reflecting contract negotiations between Liebes and Liebes and the Asamblea Municipal, May 1889, AHEZ, Fondo Ayuntamiento, Serie Abasto de Agua, Exp. 77.

53. Various documents and correspondence between Carrillo and the Liebes brothers, 1889, AHEZ, Fondo Ayuntamiento, Serie Abasto de Agua, Caja 1, Exps. 78, 80–82.

54. Velasco memorandum to Carrillo, October 1889, AHEZ, Fondo Ayuntamiento, Serie Abasto de Agua, Caja 1, Exp. 84.

55. G. Liebes to Asamblea Municipal, 29 December 1889, AHEZ, Fondo Ayuntamiento, Serie Obras Públicas, Caja 3 (1849–99), Exp. n/a. While the Liebes brothers proved difficult to track down, there was a Liebes family in San Francisco that held mining interests in Zacatecas. It is unclear if this is the same family. Luis Liebes appears in the *Actas de Cabildo* for Mexico City in 1890. His contract with the national capital stipulates that he would implement a drainage plan.

56. Rougroy and Fischweiler to Asamblea Municipal, 17 November 1890, AHEZ, Fondo Ayuntamiento, Serie Abasto de Agua, Caja 1, Exp. 87.

57. Jesús María Castañeda to Jefatura Política, 28 April 1891, AHEZ, Fondo Jefatura Política, Serie Correspondencia General, Subserie Obras Públicas, Caja 2 (1876–93), Exp. n/a.

58. Rosa Aparicio, water report, 2 March 1891, AHEZ, Fondo Jefatura Política de Zacatecas, Serie Correspondencia General, Subserie Abasto de Agua, Caja 1, Exp. n/a.

59. Rosa Aparicio, water report, 30 August 1891, AHEZ, Fondo Ayuntamiento, Serie Abasto de Agua, Caja 1, Exp. 91.

60. Circular, August 1891, AMdeZac, Fondo Jefatura Política, Serie Impresos, Caja 1 (1853–98), Exp. 36.

61. Floressi to Jefatura Política, 4 August 1893, AHEZ, Fondo Jefatura Política de Zacatecas, Serie Correspondencia General, Subserie Abasto de Agua, Caja 1, Exp. n/a.

62. Floressi to Jefatura Política, 4 August 1893.

63. Tortolero Villaseñor, *El agua y su historia*, 74–76.

64. Tortolero Villaseñor, *El agua y su historia*, 57–58.

65. Jefe Político Salazar to Asamblea Municipal, 8 December 1893, AHEZ, Fondo Jefatura Política de Zacatecas, Serie Correspondencia General, Subserie Abasto de Agua, Caja 1, Exp. n/a.

66. Salazar, pump schematics to Villaseñor, 13 April 1894, AHEZ, Fondo Jefatura Política de Zacatecas, Serie Correspondencia General, Subserie Abasto de Agua, Caja 1, Exp. n/a.

67. Salazar, pricing layout to Villaseñor, 18 April 1894, AHEZ, Fondo Jefatura Política de Zacatecas, Serie Correspondencia General, Subserie Abasto de Agua, Caja 1, Exp. n/a.

68. Circular, April 1894, AMdeZac, Fondo Jefatura Política, Serie Impresos, Caja 1 (1853–98), Exp. 44.

69. Stoddard, *John L. Stoddard's Lectures*, 249.

70. Stoddard, *John L. Stoddard's Lectures*, 249–50.

71. Water test results, June 1893, AHEZ, Fondo Jefatura Política, Serie Correspondencia General, Subserie Abasto de Agua, Caja 1, Exp. n/a.

72. Water test results, February 1894, AHEZ, Fondo Jefatura Política, Serie Correspondencia General, Subserie Abasto de Agua, Caja 1, Exp. n/a.

73. Pascual López Velarde to Jefatura Política, 29 May 1894; Elorduy to Jefe de Policía, 9 June 1894, both in AHEZ, Fondo Jefatura Política, Serie Correspondencia General, Subserie Abasto de Agua, Caja 1, Exp. n/a.

74. Villaseñor to Rafael García, 14 February 1896, AHEZ, Fondo Jefatura Política, Serie Correspondencia General, Subserie Abasto de Agua, Caja 1, Exp. n/a.

75. This act of taking one community's water to quench another's thirst still occurs. Water policy scholars, such as Raúl Pacheco-Vega at CIDE in Mexico, argue that bottled water companies perpetuate inequality among those seeking access to potable water.

76. Agostoni, *Monuments of Progress*, 116–18; Vitz, *City on a Lake*, 19–21.

77. Tortolero Villaseñor, *El agua y su historia*, 111.

78. Tortolero Villaseñor, "Transforming the Central Mexican Waterscape," 125–26.

79. Document on the planting of trees, 10 February 1906, AMdeZac, Fondo Jefatura Política de Zacatecas, Serie Estadísticas, Caja 8 (1908), Exp. 5.

80. Document on the planting of trees, 9 August 1908, AMdeZac, Fondo Jefatura Política de Zacatecas, Serie Estadísticas, Caja 13 (1908), Exp. 6.

81. Schell, "Silver Symbiosis," 89; Carlson, *Causes of Bank Suspensions*, 7.

82. Sandoval to Jefatura Política, 19 October 1893, AHEZ, Fondo Jefatura Política de Zacatecas, Serie Correspondencia General, Subserie Industria y Comercio, Caja 4 (1893–1894), Exp. n/a.

83. Sandoval to Jefatura Política, 3 November 1893, AHEZ, Fondo Jefatura Política de Zacatecas, Serie Correspondencia General, Subserie Industria y Comercio, Caja 4 (1893–1894), Exp. n/a; Sandoval to Jefatura Política, 13 November 1891, AHEZ, Fondo Jefatura Política de Zacatecas, Serie Correspondencia General, Subserie, Industria y Comercio, Caja 3 (1890–1892), Exp. n/a.

84. Notices of closure, November 1895, AHEZ, Fondo Jefatura Política de Zacatecas, Serie Correspondencia General, Subserie Industria y Comercio, Caja 4 (1893–94), Exp. n/a; AHEZ, Fondo Ayuntamiento, Serie Comercio (1895–97), Exp. 10.

85. Palacios to Asamblea Municipal, November 1895, AHEZ, Fondo Ayuntamiento, Serie Minería, Subserie Varios, Caja 3, Exps. 96, 97.

86. Apestegui petition, 16 February 1897, AHEZ, Fondo Ayuntamiento, Serie Comercio, Caja 9 (1895–97), Exp. 26.

87. Quoted in García, *Los mineros mexicanos*, 242–43.

88. García, *Los mineros mexicanos*, 243.

89. Esparza Sánchez, *Historia de la ganadería en Zacatecas*, 17.

90. Esparza Sánchez, *Historia de la ganadería en Zacatecas*, 66.

3. The City

1. García, *Los mineros mexicanos*, 67–69.

2. Turner, *Ritual Process*, 94–98.

3. Bulfinch, *Bulfinch's Mythology*, 176–79.

4. García, *Los mineros mexicanos*, 67–68.

5. Turner, *Ritual Process*, 89–90.

6. Ferry, *Not Ours Alone*, 23.

7. Mumford, *Technics and Civilization*, 4.

8. Williams, *Notes on the Underground*, 22–23; Merchant, *Death of Nature*, 1.

9. García, *Los mineros mexicanos*, 25.

10. Andrews, *Killing for Coal*, 125–27.

11. Witness Gabriel Gaitan to Teófilo García, 26 February 1883, AHEZ, Fondo Poder Judicial, Serie Criminal, Caja 2, Exp. n/a.

12. Juan Briseño, criminal case logbook, 24 March 1883, AHEZ, Fondo Poder Judicial, Serie Criminal, Caja 2, Exp. n/a.

13. Briseño criminal case logbook, 24 March 1883.

14. Briseño criminal case logbook, 24 March 1883.

15. Luis Mora Castillo, testimony, 16 May 1882, AHEZ, Fondo Poder Judicial, Serie Criminal, Caja 36, Exp. 924.

16. Esteban Buzola, testimony, 16 May 1882, AHEZ, Fondo Poder Judicial, Serie Criminal, Caja 36, Exp. 924.

17. Suárez and Herta, testimony, 19 May 1882, AHEZ, Fondo Poder Judicial, Serie Criminal, Caja 36, Exp. 924.

18. Murvato confession, 29 May 1882, AHEZ, Fondo Poder Judicial, Serie Criminal, Caja 36, Exp. 924.

19. García, *Los mineros mexicanos*, 45.

20. Witness Canales, testimony before Juzgado, 28 April 1891, AHEZ, Fondo Poder Judicial, Serie Criminal, Caja 6, Exp. 150.

21. Zarate and Córdova, report, 18 January 1891, AHEZ, Fondo Poder Judicial, Serie Criminal, Caja 6, Exp. 150.

22. Judge F. Henriquez, memorandum, 13 February 1891, AHEZ, Poder Judicial, Serie Criminal, Caja 21, Exp. 537.

23. Judge F. Henriquez, memorandum, 27 February 1891, AHEZ, Poder Judicial, Serie Criminal, Caja 21, Exp. 537.

24. Crecensio Ríos, testimony before Judge Jesús Zamora, 31 October 1891, AHEZ, Poder Judicial, Serie Criminal, Caja 22, Exp. 575.

25. Ríos testimony before Judge Zamora, 31 October 1891.

26. See, for example, Mumford, *Technics and Civilization*, 10. See also Worster, *Dust Bowl*; and Isenberg, *Mining California*.

27. Mumford, *Technics and Civilization*, 10.

28. See "Ingersoll Rock Drill," *Manufacturer and Builder Magazine*.

29. Isenberg, *Mining California*, 32–33.

30. Rice, "Zacatecas, a Famous Silver Camp of Mexico," 401.

31. García, *Los mineros mexicanos*, 241.

32. Andrews, *Killing for Coal*, 33–34.

33. Tinajero and Freeman, *Technology and Culture*, 2.

34. Beatty, *Technology and the Search for Progress*, 3.

35. Austin, *Metallurgy of the Common Metals*, 153–55.

36. Beatty, *Technology and the Search for Progress*, 150–51; Julian and Smart, *Cyaniding Gold and Silver Ores*, 160–61.

37. Beatty, *Technology and the Search for Progress*, 146; Rice, "Zacatecas, a Famous Silver Camp of Mexico," 401.

38. My thanks to Dra. Patricia Lira Gómez of the Universidad Autónoma de Zacatecas Escuela de Minas for explaining this to me in an interview in 2011.

39. See Ramazzini, *Treatise of the diseases of tradesmen*.

40. Avalos-Lozano and Aguilar Robledo, "Reconstructing the Environmental History of Colonial Mining," 62–64.

41. "Public Health Statement: Mercury," March 1999, Agency for Toxic Substances and Disease Registry, Centers for Disease Control and Prevention, https://www.atsdr .cdc.gov/phs/phs.asp?id=112&tid=24.

42. See Roumagnac, *Los criminales de México*; and Buffington, *Criminal and Citizen in Modern Mexico*.

43. See Speckman Guerra, *Crimen y castigo*; and Ríos Molina, *Los pacientes del Manicomio La Castañeda*.

44. Adelaida B. Bernal, statement, 29 November 1890, AHEZ, Serie Poder Judicial, Subserie Criminal, Caja 1, Exp. 7.

45. Bernal statement, 29 November 1890.

46. Various testimonies, 29 November 1890, AHEZ, Serie Poder Judicial, Subserie Criminal, Caja 1, Exp. 7.

47. Wasik and Murphy, *Rabid*, 128–29.

48. Leung et al., "Rabies," 33–35.

49. Wasik and Murphy, *Rabid*, 10.

50. "Anexo 12: Reglamento del Gabinete Anti-Rábico," in *Memorias de Eduardo G. Pankhurst*.

51. "Anexo 12," in *Memorias de Eduardo G. Pankhurst*.

52. "Anexo 12," in *Memorias de Eduardo G. Pankhurst*.

53. *Memorias de Eduardo G. Pankhurst*, 299.

54. "Anexo 12," in *Memorias de Eduardo G. Pankhurst*.

55. *Memorias de Eduardo G. Pankhurst*, 299.

56. *Memorias de Eduardo G. Pankhurst*, 299.

57. *Memorias de Eduardo G. Pankhurst*, 299.

58. *Memorias de Eduardo G. Pankhurst*, 299.

59. Jesús López, report to D. Enrique, 13 April 1913, AMdeZac, Serie Jefatura Política de Zacatecas, Subserie Sanidad, Caja 2 (1907–15), Exp. 37.

60. D. Enrique, note, 13 April 1913, AMdeZac, Serie Jefatura Política de Zacatecas, Subserie Sanidad, Caja 2 (1907–15), Exp. 37.

61. López report to Enrique, 13 April 1913.

62. Ponce, reports on slaughterhouse conditions, October–November 1898, AHEZ, Fondo Jefatura Política de Zacatecas, Serie Correspondencia General, Subserie Industria y Comercio, Caja 6 (1897–98), Exp. n/a.

63. Ponce, report on slaughterhouse conditions, July 1898, AHEZ, Fondo Jefatura Política de Zacatecas, Serie Correspondencia General, Subserie Industria y Comercio, Caja 6 (1897–98), Exp. n/a; Ponce, report on slaughterhouse conditions, August 1898, AHEZ, Fondo Jefatura Política de Zacatecas, Serie Correspondencia General, Subserie Industria y Comercio, Caja 7 (1899), Exp. n/a.

64. *Memorias de Eduardo G. Pankhurst*, 378.

65. Pilcher, *Sausage Rebellion*, 17–18; 91–94.

66. *Memorias de Eduardo G. Pankhurst*, 379.

67. Nichols, *Santos, duraznos y vino*, 15.

68. *La Escuela de Medicina*, 162.

69. *Memorias de Eduardo G. Pankhurst*, 49.

70. Correspondence from anonymous authors to Asamblea Municipal, 23 January 1892, AHEZ, Fondo Ayuntamiento, Serie Diversiones Públicas, Caja 3, Exp. 197.

71. For a discussion of houses of tolerance and prostitution as well as public health in Mexico City, see Bliss, *Compromised Positions*.

72. Correspondence from anonymous authors to Asamblea Municipal, 23 January 1892.

73. Beltrán Perelló, *Violación*, 10–11.

74. Beltrán Perelló, *Violación*, 12–13.

75. Beltrán Perelló, *Violación*, 12–13.

76. Bliss, *Compromised Positions*, 28–29.

77. Kimball to Davis, 5 May 1884, Consular Reports for Zacatecas, Mexico (1860–88), Record Group 84, Records of the Foreign Service Posts of the Department of State, 1788–ca. 1991, National Archives, Washington DC, microfilm.

78. Kimball to Davis, 5 May 1884.

79. Kimball to Davis, 5 May 1884.

80. For a discussion of railroads and mining, see Hart, *Empire and Revolution*, 122–23.

81. Kimball to Davis, 5 May 1884.

4. The Body as Land

1. Mendoza, memorandum to Dir. General de Aguas, 20 March 1944, AHA, Fondo Aguas Nacionales, Caja 237, Exp. 2391.

2. San Marcos can be found northeast of Durango, Durango, while Miguel Auza, Zacatecas, sits at the state line with Durango. The Santiago mentioned here is believed to be an *ejido* in western Zacatecas and not a municipality. .

3. Ontiveros to President Alemán, 25 May 1949, AHA, Fondo Aguas Nacionales, Caja 237, Exp. 2391.

4. Zapata et al., "Plan de Ayala," 342.

5. Tortolero Villaseñor, "Water and Revolution," 126–28.

6. Tortolero Villaseñor, "Water and Revolution," 126–28; Tortolero Villaseñor, "Entre las revoluciones," 160-161; Wolfe, "Climate of Conflict," 469.

7. Diez, "El cultivo e industria," 55.

8. Tutino, *Mexican Heartland*, 11–13.

9. Raleigh, "Absence of Water Conflicts," 550–51. See also Ashcraft and Mayer, *Politics of Fresh Water*.

10. McGrew, *Encyclopedia of Medical History*, 350.

11. McGrew, *Encyclopedia of Medical History*, 350.

12. McGrew, *Encyclopedia of Medical History*, 351.

13. McGrew, *Encyclopedia of Medical History*, 351.

14. Francisco Árbol y Bonilla to Junta de Sanidad de Zacatecas, 13 February 1852, AHSS, Fondo Salud Pública III, Sección Epidemiología, Caja 1, Exp. 45.

15. Árbol y Bonilla to Junta de Sanidad de Zacatecas, 13 February 1852.

16. Junta de Sanidad de Zacatecas, report on the typhus epidemic, 13 April 1892, AHSS, Fondo Salud Pública III, Sección Epidemiología, Caja 1, Exp. 45. The compiling of both

reports in the same file indicates a thematic organization on the archivist's part (i.e., Zacatecas typhus).

17. McMichael, *Health of Nations*, 3–5.

18. McMichael, *Health of Nations*, 5.

19. McMichael, *Health of Nations*, 141–45.

20. Charles Scudder, "Health Officials Warn of Increased Flea-Borne Typhus Risk in Dallas, Houston," *Dallas Morning News*, 2 December 2017.

21. Burns, Acuña-Soto, and Stahle, "Drought and Epidemic Typhus," 442–47.

22. Atenógenes Llamas, circular, 21 October 1892, AMdeZac, Serie Jefatura Política, Subserie Impresos, Caja 1 (1853–98), Exp. 39.

23. *Agua en la Filarmónica Presa*, circular, April 1893, AMdeZac, Serie Jefatura Política, Subserie Impresos, Caja 1 (1853–1898), Exp. 36; *Se pretende introducir a las fuentes de San Juan de Dios y Tacuba*, circular, April 1894, AMdeZac, Serie Jefatura Política, Subserie Impresos, Caja 1 (1853–98), Exp. 44.

24. José M. Echeverría and Pedro Espejo, *Al público auxilios a los atacados*, circular, 30 November 1892, AMdeZac, Serie Jefatura Política, Subserie Impresos, Caja 1 (1853–98), Exp. 30.

25. Echeverría and Espejo, *Al público auxilios a los atacados*.

26. Ocampo to Jefatura Política, 27 May 1905, AMdeZac, Fondo Jefatura Política, Serie Sanidad, Caja 1 (1895–1906), Exp. 70.

27. Ocampo to Jefatura Política, 27 May 1905.

28. McGrew, *Encyclopedia of Medical History*, 93.

29. McGrew, *Encyclopedia of Medical History*, 93.

30. McGrew, *Encyclopedia of Medical History*, 93.

31. McGrew, *Encyclopedia of Medical History*, 93; Nichol, *Diseases of the Nares*, 320–21.

32. McGrew, *Encyclopedia of Medical History*, 93; Nichol, *Diseases of the Nares*, 320–21.

33. Dr. Rosalío Torres, written opinion, 22 August 1898, AHEZ, Fondo Ayuntamiento, Serie Hospital y Sanidad, Caja 4, Exp. 206.

34. Knight, *Mexican Revolution*, 1:40.

35. Rodríguez, "El tifo." See also Alexander, "Fever of War."

36. "Gobernantes de Zacatecas," UNAM Archivo Jurídico, accessed May 2017, https://archivos.juridicas.unam.mx/.

37. Knight, *Mexican Revolution*, 1:28.

38. "Gobernantes de Zacatecas."

39. See Speckman Guerra, *Crimen y castigo*; and Ríos Molina, *Los pacientes del Manicomio La Castañeda*.

40. Secretary of State Philander C. Knox, statement printed as a circular, 13 February 1912, AMdeZac, Fondo Jefatura Política de Zacatecas, Serie Impresos, Caja 4 (1912–15), Exp. 4.

41. Claro Hurtado, circular issued 9 July 1914, AMdeZac, Fondo Jefatura Política, Serie Impresos, Caja 4 (1912–15), Exp. 48.

42. Katz, *Pancho Villa*, 350.

43. Muñoz, *Verdad y mito*, 2:185.

44. Katz, *Pancho Villa*, 350.

45. Esparza Sánchez, *El corrido zacatecano*, 140–41 (my translation).

46. Mora Castillo to Jefatura Política, 2 July 1914, AMdeZac, Fondo Jefatura Política de Zacatecas, Serie Hospitales, Caja 6 (1912–15), Exp. 40.

47. F. Cabral, circular, 1 June 1915, AMdeZac, Fondo Jefatura Política de Zacatecas, Serie Impresos, Caja 4 (1912–15), Exp. 84.

48. Natera circular, 20 June 1915, AMdeZac, Fondo Jefatura Política de Zacatecas, Serie Impresos, Caja 4 (1912–15), Exp. 85.

49. Azuela, *Underdogs*, 22–24.

50. Azuela, *Underdogs*, 58.

51. Azuela, *Underdogs*, 133.

52. Zapata et al., "Plan de Ayala," 345–46.

53. Wolfe, *Watering the Revolution*, 17–18.

54. Municipal Council of Mazapil, petition, 10 November 1919, AHA, Fondo Aprovechamientos Superficiales, Caja 1053, Exp. 14840.

55. Aguirre to municipal council of Salaverna, 23 December 1919, AHA, Fondo Aprovechamientos Superficiales, Caja 1053, Exp. 14840. No information could be found to ascertain if this was Gen. Amado Aguirre of the División del Occidente, who went on to serve in the Obregón government in 1920.

56. Arriaga to Secretaría de Agricultura y Fomento, 16 June 1921, AHA, Fondo Aprovechamientos Superficiales, Caja 1223, Exp. 16983.

57. Bayona to Agente General, División de Aguas, 28 September 1921, AHA, Fondo Aprovechamientos Superficiales, Caja 1223, Exp. 16983.

58. Mauricio Cardona to Secretaría de Agricultura y Fomento, 16 June 1923, AHA, Fondo Aprovechamientos Superficiales, Caja 1821, Exp. 27208.

59. Cardona to Secretaría de Agricultura y Fomento, 16 June 1923.

60. Penador to Secretaría de Agricultura y Fomento, 4 March 1926, AHA, Fondo Aguas Nacionales, Caja 237, Exp. 2391.

61. Penador to Secretaría, 4 March 1926.

62. Petition from ejidatarios to Secretaría de Agricultura y Fomento, 15 December 1932, AHA, Fondo Aguas Nacionales, Caja 1881, Exp. 26459.

63. O'Bahn to Secretaría de Agricultura y Fomento, 18 January 1933, AHA, Fondo Aguas Nacionales, Caja 1881, Exp. 26459.

64. Sánchez Mejorada to José Parres, 11 February 1933, AHA, Fondo Aguas Nacionales, Caja 1881, Exp. 26459.

65. Rose to Ortíz Segura and Sánchez Mejorada, 10 February 1933, AHA, Fondo Aguas Nacionales, Caja 1881, Exp. 26459.

66. Parres to [H]uitrón and Martínez, 26 April 1933, AHA, Fondo Aguas Nacionales, Caja 1881, Exp. 26459.

67. Balderas García to Ferrat, 27 June 1933, AHA, Fondo Aguas Nacionales, Caja 1881, Exp. 26459.

68. Ferrat to [H]uitrón and Martínez, 4 July 1933, AHA, Fondo Aguas Nacionales, Caja 1881, Exp. 26459.

69. Nieto to Secretaría del Estado y del Despacho de Fomento, 14 May 1917, AHA, Fondo Aguas Nacionales, Caja 883, Exp. 11042.

70. La Fé Mining Company to Secretaría de Agricultura y Fomento, 8 November 1928, AHA, Fondo Aguas Superficiales, Caja 4863, Exp. 67610.

71. Isidro Cardona to Secretaría de Agricultura y Fomento, 14 April 1928, AHA, Fondo Aguas Superficiales, Caja 4869, Exp. 67753.

72. Cardona to Secretaría de Agricultura y Fomento, 14 April 1928.

73. Agustín Beltrán and others to Secretaría de Industria, Comercio, y Trabajo, 9 March 1933, AHA, Fondo Aguas Superficiales, Caja 4869, Exp. 67753.

74. The term has been used in ecocriticism and literature with regard to nature writing. Here, I emphasize archival sources, especially those materials locals sent to federal institutions, to illustrate power dynamics and local advocacy. See Buell, "Uses and Abuses of Environmental Memory," for a literary understanding of the term. Knoeller uses "ecological memory" in *Reimagining Environmental History*.

75. Rodríguez to Octaviano Garay, 17 September 1948, AHA, Fondo Aguas Nacionales, Caja 1494, Exp. 20452.

76. Molina García to Director General de Aprovechamientos, 10 October 1948, AHA, Fondo Aguas Nacionales, Caja 1494, Exp. 20452.

77. Reina to Secretaría de Recursos Hidráulicos, 24 July 1954, AHA, Fondo Aguas Nacionales, Caja 1067, Exp. 14050.

78. Cardona to Secretaría de Agricultura y Fomento, 23 April 1923, AHA, Fondo Aguas Superficiales, Caja 4869, Exp. 67753.

79. Cardona to Secretaría de Agricultura y Fomento, 23 April 1923.

80. Cardona to Secretaría de Agricultura y Fomento, 23 April 1923.

81. Cardona to Secretaría de Agricultura y Fomento, 23 April 1923. Cardona argued that the water emerged as "impotables y perjudícales a la salud" (my translation).

82. Ley de Aguas de Propiedad Nacional, 1934, in *Evolución de la Legislación de aguas en México*, https://siaps.colmex.mx/documentos/legislacion/Evolucion%20de%20la%20legislacion%20de%20aguas%20en%20Mexico.pdf.

83. José Parres, summary, 2 February 1937, AHA, Fondo Aguas Superficiales, Caja 1899, Exp. 28597.

84. Roberto Arriaga, note, 10 February 1937, AHA, Fondo Aguas Superficiales, Caja 1899, Exp. 28597.

85. Agustín Ortíz Medina, summary for subsecretary of agriculture and development, 30 January 1937, AHA, Fondo Aguas Superficiales, Caja 1899, Exp. 28597.

86. Ortíz Medina summary for subsecretary of agriculture and development, 30 January 1937.

87. Reyes Robledo to José Parres, 15 July 1936, AHA, Fondo Aguas Superficiales, Caja 1899, Exp. 28597.

88. Articles 118, 119, 120, in Ley de Aguas de Propiedad Nacional, 1934.

89. Knox, *Boy Travellers in Mexico*, 85.

90. Knox, *Boy Travellers in Mexico*, 91.

91. Knox, *Boy Travellers in Mexico*, 92.

92. Stoddard, *John L. Stoddard's Lectures*, 256.

93. Foulkes, "Metal Disposition," 5.

94. Foulkes, "Metal Disposition," 14.

95. Lidén, Maibach, and Wahlberg, "Skin," 456.

96. Mena and other petitioners to Lázaro Cárdenas, 19 April 1937, AGN, Serie Presidencial, Fondo Lázaro Cárdenas, Caja 339, Exp. 40.2/394.

5. The Body as Nation

1. For silicosis in the United States, see Rosner and Markowitz, *Deadly Dust*; Sellers, *Hazards of the Job*; and Derickson, *Workers' Health, Workers' Democracy*.

2. Parker and Wagner, "Silicosis," 10.43–10.45.

3. Parker and Wagner, "Silicosis," 10.43–10.45.

4. Parker and Wagner, "Silicosis," 10.43–10.45.

5. Parker and Wagner, "Silicosis," 10.43–10.45.

6. Parker and Wagner, "Silicosis," 10.43–10.45.

7. White, *Organic Machine*, 4.

8. Piper, *Industrial Transformation*, 4.

9. Walker, *Toxic Archipelago*, 11.

10. Andrews, *Killing for Coal*, 125.

11. Rosner and Markowitz, *Deadly Dust*, 119.

12. Sellers, *Hazards of the Job*, 121.

13. Sellers, *Hazards of the Job*, 121.

14. Hart, *Empire and Revolution*, 275–78.

15. Hart, *Empire and Revolution*, 275.

16. Rice, "Zacatecas, a Famous Silver Camp," 403.

17. Previsor (pseud.), "Prospects at Zacatecas."

18. "Governors of Zacatecas and Durango," *EMJ*, 918–19.

19. "Governors of Zacatecas and Durango," *EMJ*, 918–19.

20. "Governors of Zacatecas and Durango," *EMJ*, 919.

21. "Governors of Zacatecas and Durango," *EMJ*, 919.

22. "Mexico," *EMJ*, 603.

23. "Mexico," *EMJ*, 603.

24. "Regional Summaries," *EMJ*, 122.

25. Parsons, "Revival of Zacatecas," 324.

26. J. M. Aguirre to Obregón, 22 November 1922, Archivo General de la Nación, Serie Obregón-Calles, Caja 159, 422-C-3.

27. Aguirre to Calles, 19 August 1926, AGN, Serie Obregón-Calles, Caja 129, 407-C-45. Aguirre wrote, "Le suplico a Usted" in his letter, as well as "trabajadores comunes." The English translations are my own.

28. Calderón to Rodríguez, 8 September 1934, AGN, Colección Minería Zacatecas, Serie 564.5/123.

29. Abrego to Rodríguez, 8 October 1934, AGN, Colección Minería Zacatecas, Serie 564.5/123.

30. Próspero Alderete, telegram to Rodríguez, 3 May 1934, AGN, Colección Minería Zacatecas, Serie 561.8/253.

31. Treviño and Solís to Rodríguez, 26 September 1932, AGN, Colección Minería Zacatecas, Serie 561.8/253.

32. Reyes to Rodríguez, 7 October 1932, AGN, Colección Minería Zacatecas, Serie 564.5/4.

33. Reyes to Rodríguez, 7 October 1932.

34. Ortíz and Salazar, telegram to Rodríguez, 5 January 1934, AGN, Colección Minería Zacatecas, 564.5/53.

35. Bernstein, *Mexican Mining Industry*, 12.

36. Derickson, *Workers' Health, Workers' Democracy*, 39–40. Derickson calculates the number of drills used in mining between 1880 and 1902 to have risen from 257 to 3,329.

37. Rosner and Markowitz, *Deadly Dust*, 14.

38. Rosner and Markowitz, *Deadly Dust*, 31.

39. Rosner and Markowitz, *Deadly Dust*, 5.

40. McCulloch, *South Africa's Gold Mines*, 75.

41. McCulloch, *South Africa's Gold Mines*, 75.

42. McCulloch, *South Africa's Gold Mines*, 76.

43. McCulloch, *South Africa's Gold Mines*, 77.

44. Watt, "Personal Experiences," 596.

45. McCulloch, *South Africa's Gold Mines*, 78–79.

46. Andrews, *Killing for Coal*, 125.

47. It is worth noting that two words in Spanish suggest lacking ability, physical or otherwise. On one hand, *incapacidad* is defined as the lack of ability to do, receive, or learn something, in addition to the lack of intelligence, or lack of preparation or means to realize an act, according to the Real Academia Española dictionary (https://dle.rae.es /incapacidad; my translation). Similarly, *incapacidad laboral* more clearly defines disability brought about by occupational diseases. It is defined as a "scenario in which illness or psychiatric or physical suffering impedes a person, in a definitive manner, from completing a professional activity and that normally it awards a person" (https://dle.rae.es /incapacidad; my translation). On the other hand, *discapacidad* is defined as the condition or manifestation of disability, and it is the most common word used to express disability in the current context (https://dle.rae.es/discapacidad). I will use the word *incapacidad* in this section, as "incapacidad laboral" is the term the documents use.

48. Memorandum on Antonio Lechuga y Jesús Rodríguez vs. La Trinidad, 20 February 1940, AGN, Departamento Autónomo del Trabajo (hereafter DAT), Caja 41, Exp. 8, p. 2.

49. Memorandum on Antonio Lechuga y Jesús Rodríguez vs. La Trinidad, 20 February 1940, p. 2.

50. Memorandum on Antonio Lechuga y Jesús Rodríguez vs. La Trinidad, 20 February 1940, p. 2b. Roldán uses the term *invalidez*, an antiquated term used to refer to a physical disability that makes someone an "invalid."

51. Memorandum from Dr. Amadeo Betancourt to Departamento Autónomo del Trabajo, AGN, DAT, Caja 406, Exp. 33. Betancourt did not provide a full name for Dr.

Lara. I hypothesize that he is referring to Dr. Luis Lara y Pardo, a public health specialist. Lara y Pardo wrote extensively on prostitution and public health in the 1930s. However, he also wrote a dictionary on geography, history, and biography with criminologist and pseudoscientist Carlos Roumagnac in 1910.

52. Alexander, *Sons of the Mexican Revolution*, 47.

53. Margarito Gómez, telegrams to Lázaro Cárdenas, 25 November 1937, 21 February 1938, 11 August 1938, 15 January 1939, 15 March 1939, 31 July 1939, 29 January 1940, 26 April 1940, 18 August 1940, AGN, Serie Lázaro Cárdenas del Río (hereafter, LCdR), 434.1/253. Funnily enough, Gómez shares the same name as a federal deputy that represented the state of Hidalgo from 1930 to 1932, according to Camp, *Mexican Political Biographies 1884–1934*. Both wrote to Cárdenas at this time, but the miner was based in Etzatlan, Jalisco.

54. Margarito Gómez to Cárdenas, 31 July 1939, AGN, Serie LCdR, 434.1/253.

55. Antonio Villalobos, William Gooch, and others, meeting notes, 20 December 1939, AGN, DAT, Caja 298, Exp. 2.

56. Dr. Antonio Delgado, reports to Departamento Autónomo del Trabajo, 6 May 1940, 13 May 1940, both in AGN, DAT, Caja 298, Exp. 2.

57. Antonio Delgado to Departamento [Autónomo del Trabajo], 27 June 1940, AGN, DAT, Caja 298, Exp. 2.

58. "Lista Nominal de Obreros Examinados en el Mineral de Cananea por el suscrito del 6 de mayo al 3 junio del presente," 27 June 1940, AGN, DAT, Caja 298, Exp. 2.

59. McCulloch and Rosental, with Melling, "Johannesburg and Beyond," 74–76; Rosental and Thomann, "Silicosis and 'Silicosis,'" 143–44.

60. Ávila Camacho, memorandum to Congress, 10 September 1943, AGN, Serie MAC, Caja 750, 545.2/6; Dr. Amadeo Betancourt, memorandum to Departamento Autónomo del Trabajo, AGN, DAT, Caja 406, Exp. 33.

61. "Reforma a la fracción X del Artículos de la Ley Federal del Trabajo," report issued January 1943, AGN, Serie MAC, Caja 750, 544.2/6.

62. Drs. Ernesto Rangel and Miguel Vera, "La tuberculosis pulmonar de los mineros no procedida de silicosis no es enfermedad profesional," report issued July 1943, AGN, Serie MAC, Caja 750, 545.2/6.

63. Pablo Bretado Sánchez, letter, 2 September 1943, AGN, Serie MAC, Caja 750, 545.2/6.

64. Brahdy, "Occupation, Tuberculosis and Compensation Laws," 509.

65. Rangel and Vera, "La tuberculosis pulmonar."

66. Rangel and Vera, "La tuberculosis pulmonar."

67. Rangel and Vera, "La tuberculosis pulmonar."

68. Rangel and Vera, "La tuberculosis pulmonar."

69. Rangel and Vera, "La tuberculosis pulmonar."

70. Rohde y Herrera, "La tuberculosis como enfermedad profesional de los mineros," report issued July 1943, AGN, Serie MAC, Caja 750, 545.4/6.

71. Rohde y Herrera, "La tuberculosis."

72. Rohde y Herrera, "La tuberculosis."

73. Rohde y Herrera, "La tuberculosis."

74. Rohde y Herrera, "La tuberculosis."

75. Ávila Camacho, memorandum to Congress, 1 September 1943, AGN, Serie MAC, Caja 750, 545.2/6.

76. Ávila Camacho, memorandum to Congress, 1 September 1943.

77. González Gallo, report to Atanasio Vizcaya, 25 March 1941, AGN, Serie MAC, Caja 750, 545.2/6.

78. González Gallo report to Vizcaya, 25 March 1941.

79. González Gallo report to Vizcaya, 25 March 1941.

80. González Gallo report to Vizcaya, 25 March 1941.

81. González Gallo report to Vizcaya, 25 March 1941.

82. See Alexander, *Sons of the Mexican Revolution.*

83. Serrano, telegram to Ávila Camacho, 29 December 1942, AGN, Serie MAC, Caja 750, 545.2/6.

84. Serrano to Ávila Camacho, 18 August 1943, AGN, Serie MAC, Caja 750, 545.2/6.

85. Hart, *Silver of the Sierra Madre,* 195.

86. Hart, *Silver of the Sierra Madre,* 195.

87. Markowitz and Rosner, "Why Is Silicosis So Important?," 14–29.

88. See Clark, *Radium Girls.*

89. "Constitution of 1917," Article 123, section XIV, https://www.constituteproject .org/constitution/Mexico_2015?lang=en.

90. "Ley Federal del Trabajo," *Diario Oficial.*

91. For a discussion on the law, see Suárez-Potts, *Making of Law.*

Conclusion

1. Pearson, "Preliminary Findings," 11–12, 15.

2. Pearson, "Preliminary Findings," 15.

3. Pedro Rocha y Sida, "Declaran desastre natural en Durango por la sequía," *El Sol de Durango,* 5 June 2013.

4. "Acuíferos sobreexplotados 2009," diagram 2.4 in chapter 2 of *Estadísticas del agua en México, edición 2011,* 34, CONAGUA, accessed June 2015, http://www.conagua.gob.mx /CONAGUA07/Contenido/Documentos/Sina/Capitulo_2.pdf.

5. "Corona Mega Factory," *Megafactories,* aired 10 March 2013 on National Geographic Channel.

6. Ogura et al., "Zacatecas (Mexico) Companies," 168–70.

7. Iskander, Vega-Carrillo, and Manzanares Acuna, "Determination of Mercury," 45–48; Zetina Rodríguez, "La controversia ambiental," 167–71.

8. See Zetina Rodríguez, "La historia de un tesoro"; and Zetina Rodríguez, "La controversia ambiental."

9. Allison Marte, Frank Jack Daniel, and Noe Torres, "GoldCorp Struggles with Filtering Out Selenium in Mine Ponds," *Reuters Mexico,* 24 August 2016, https://www.reuters .com/article/us-goldcorp-leak/exclusive-goldcorp-struggles-with-leak-at-mexican-mine -idUSKCN10Z1YN.

10. Marte, Daniel, and Torres, "GoldCorp Struggles."

11. See MacFarquhar et al., "Acute Selenium Toxicity Associated with a Dietary Supplement."

12. William Booth, "Mexico Is Now a Top Producer of Engineers, but Where Are Jobs?," *Washington Post*, 28 October 2012, https://www.washingtonpost.com/world/the_americas /mexico-is-now-a-top-producer-of-engineers-but-where-are-jobs/2012/10/28/902db93a -1e47-11e2-8817-41b9a7aaabc7_story.html?utm_term=.fbfa512a04a0.

Bibliography

Archives

AGN   Archivo General de la Nación, Mexico City
AHA   Archivo Histórico del Agua, Mexico City
AHEZ   Archivo Histórico del Estado de Zacatecas
AHSS   Archivo Histórico de la Secretaría de Salud, Mexico City
AMdeZac   Archivo Municipal de Zacatecas

Published Materials

Aboites Aguilar, Luis. *Demografía histórica y conflictos por el agua: Dos estudios sobre 40 kilómetros de historia del río San Pedro, Chihuahua*. México DF: Centro de Investigaciones y Estudios, 2000.

———. *El agua de la nación: Una historia política de México (1888–1946)*. México DF: CIESAS, 1998.

———. "En busca del centro: Una aproximación a la relación centro-provincias en México, 1921–1949." *Historia Mexicana* 59, no. 2 (2009): 711–54.

Agostoni, Claudia. *Monuments of Progress: Modernization and Public Health in Mexico City, 1876–1910*. Calgary AB: University of Calgary Press, 2003.

Alexander, Ryan M. "The Fever of War: Epidemic Typhus and Public Health in Revolutionary Mexico City." *Hispanic American Historical Review* (February 2020), forthcoming.

———. *Sons of the Mexican Revolution: Miguel Alemán and His Generation*. Albuquerque: University of New Mexico Press, 2016.

Amador, Elías. *Bosquejo histórico de Zacatecas*. Volume 1, *Desde los tiempos remotos hasta el año de 1810*. 1943. Zacatecas: Instituto Zacatecano de Cultura "Ramón López Velarde," 2009.

———. *Bosquejo histórico de Zacatecas*. Volume 2, *Desde el año de 1810 a 1857*. 1943. Zacatecas: Instituto Zacatecano de Cultura "Ramón López Velarde," 2009.

———. *Elementos de geografía del estado de Zacatecas: Obra expresamente arreglada para uso de las escuelas oficiales del mismo estado*. Zacatecas: Tipografía de la escuela de Artes y Oficios en Guadalupe, 1894.

Amaro Peñaflores, René. "Educación popular, ilustración y escuelas de artes y oficios en Zacatecas, 1780–1870." In *Entre la tradición y la novedad: La educación y la formación de hombres "nuevos" en Zacatecas en el siglo XIX*, edited by Sonia Pérez Toledo and René Amaro Peñaflores, 133–45. Zacatecas: Universidad Autónoma de Zacatecas y Universidad Autónoma Metropolitana, 2003.

———. *Los gremios acostumbrados: Los artesanos de Zacatecas 1780–1870*. Zacatecas: Universidad Pedagógica Nacional, 2002.

Andrews, Thomas G. *Killing for Coal: America's Deadliest Labor War*. Cambridge MA: Harvard University Press, 2010.

Ashcraft, Catherine M., and Tamar Mayer, eds. *The Politics of Fresh Water: Access, Conflict and Identity*. New York: Routledge, 2017.

Austin, Leonard Strong. *The Metallurgy of the Common Metals: Gold, Silver, Iron, Copper, Lead, and Zinc*. San Francisco: Mining and Scientific Press, 1909.

Avalos-Lozano, Antonio, and Miguel Aguilar Robledo. "Reconstructing the Environmental History of Colonial Mining: The Real de Catorce Mining District, Northeastern New Spain/Mexico, Eighteenth and Nineteenth Centuries." In *Mining North America: An Environmental History since 1522*, edited by John R. McNeill and George Vrtis, 47–70. Oakland: University of California Press, 2017.

Azuela, Mariano. *The Underdogs*. New York: Signet Classic, 1963.

Azuela Bernal, Luz Fernanda. "La geología en la formación de los ingenieros mexicanos del siglo XIX." In *Formación de ingenieros en el México del siglo XIX*, edited by María de la Paz Ramos Lara and Rigoberto Rodríguez Benítez. México DF: Universidad Nacional Autónoma de México, 2007.

Bakewell, Peter J. *Silver Mining and Society in Colonial Mexico: Zacatecas, 1546–1700*. Cambridge: Cambridge University Press, 1971.

Beatty, Edward. *Technology and the Search for Progress in Modern Mexico*. Oakland: University of California Press, 2015.

Beltrán Perelló, Karolina. *Violación: El fracaso del ideal de orden y progreso durante el Porfiriato en Zacatecas*. Zacatecas: Programa de Estímulos a la Creación y al Desarrollo Artístico, 2013.

Benidickson, Jamie. *The Culture of Flushing: A Social and Legal History of Sewage*. Vancouver: UBC Press, 2007.

Bensusan Areous, Graciela Irma. *El modelo mexicano de regulación laboral*. México DF: Plaza y Valdés, 2000.

Bernstein, Marvin D. *The Mexican Mining Industry, 1890–1950: A Study of the Interaction of Politics, Economics, and Technology*. Albany: State University of New York Press, 1964.

Birrichaga Gardida, Diana. "El dominio de las 'aguas ocultas y descubiertas': Hidráulica colonial en el centro de México, siglos XVI–XVII." In *Mestizajes tecnológicos y cambios culturales en México*, edited by Enrique Florescano and Virginia García Acosta, 91–128. México DF: CIESAS, 2004.

———. "Modernización del sistema hidráulico rural en el Estado de México (1935–1940)." In *La modernización del sistema de agua potable en México, 1810–1950*, edited by Diana Birrichaga Gardida, 193–217. México DF: El Colegio Mexiquense, 2007.

Bliss, Katherine E. *Compromised Positions: Prostitution, Public Health, and Gender Politics in Revolutionary Mexico City*. University Park: Pennsylvania State University Press, 2001.

Born, Ignaz von. *Born's New Process of Amalgamation of Gold and Silver Ores and Other Metallic Mixtures*. Translated by R. E. Raspe. London: printed for T. Cadell, 1791.

Boyer, Christopher R., ed. *A Land between Waters: Environmental Histories of Modern Mexico*. Tucson: University of Arizona Press, 2014.

Brading, D. A. *Miners and Merchants in Bourbon Mexico, 1763–1810*. Cambridge: Cambridge University Press, 1971.

Brading, D. A., and Harry E. Cross. "Colonial Silver Mining: Mexico and Peru." *Hispanic American Historical Review* 52, no. 4 (1972): 545–79.

Brahdy, Leopold. "Occupation, Tuberculosis and Compensation Laws." *American Review of Tuberculosis* 44, no. 5 (1941): 509–19.

Brown, Kendall W. "The Curious Insanity of Juan de Alasta." *Colonial Latin American Review* 13 (December 2004): 199–211.

———. *A History of Mining in Latin America: From the Colonial Era to the Present*. Albuquerque: University of New Mexico Press, 2012.

———. "Workers' Health and Mercury Mining in Huancavelica, Peru." *The Americas* 57, no. 4 (2001): 467–96.

Bryant, Keith L., Jr. "The Importation of Anglo Culture, 1850–1900." Chapter 2 in *Culture in the American Southwest: The Earth, the Sky, the People*. College Station: Texas A&M University Press, 2001.

Buell, Lawrence. "Uses and Abuses of Environmental Memory." In *Contesting Environmental Imaginaries: Nature and Counternature in a Time of Global Change*. Leiden: Brill, 2017.

Buffington, Robert. *Criminal and Citizen in Modern Mexico*. Lincoln: University of Nebraska Press, 2000.

Buffington, Robert, and Pablo Piccato. *True Stories of Crime in Modern Mexico*. Albuquerque: University of New Mexico Press, 2009.

Bulfinch, Thomas. *Bulfinch's Mythology*. 1855–63. New York: Barnes and Noble Classics, 2006.

Burns, Jordan, Rodolfo Acuña-Soto, and David W. Stahle. "Drought and Epidemic Typhus, Central Mexico, 1655–1918." *Emerging Infectious Diseases* 20, no. 3 (2014): 442–47.

Camp, Roderic A. *Mexican Political Biographies, 1884–1935*. Austin: University of Texas Press, 1991.

Candiani, Vera S. *Dreaming of Dry Land: Environmental Transformation in Colonial Mexico City*. Stanford: Stanford University Press, 2011.

Carlson, Mark. *Causes of Bank Suspensions in the Panic of 1893*. Washington DC: Federal Reserve Board, 2002.

Cherniack, Martin. *The Hawk's Nest Incident: America's Worst Industrial Disaster*. New Haven: Yale University Press, 1986.

Chipman, Donald E. *Moctezuma's Children: Aztec Royalty under Spanish Rule, 1520–1700*. Austin: University of Texas Press, 2005.

Clark, Claudia. *Radium Girls: Women and Industrial Health Reform, 1910–1935*. Chapel Hill: University of North Carolina Press, 1997.

"Corrido del Minero." Performed by Joe Glazer and included on the album *We Just Come to Work Here, We Don't Come to Die: Songs of Occupational Health and Safety*. Cataloged by Smithsonian Institution Folkways. Collector Records, 1975. Compact disc.

Cronon, William. "A Place for Stories: Nature, History, and Narrative." *Journal of American History* 78, no. 4 (1992): 1347–76.

Cross, Harry E. "Dieta y nutrición en el medio rural de Zacatecas y San Luis Potosí (siglos XVIII y XIX)." *Historia Mexicana* 31, no. 1 (1981): 101–16.

———. "Living Standards in Rural Nineteenth-Century Mexico: Zacatecas, 1820–1880." *Journal of Latin American Studies* 10, no. 1 (1978): 1–19.

Derickson, Alan. *Workers' Health, Workers' Democracy: The Western Miners' Struggle, 1891–1925*. Ithaca: Cornell University Press, 1989.

Diez, Domingo. "El cultivo e industria de la caña de azúcar: El problema agrario y los monumentos históricos y artísticos del estado de Morelos." In *Dos conferencias sobre el Estado de Morelos por el Señor Domingo Diez*, 1–104. México DF: Imprenta Victoria, 1919.

Douglas, Mary. *Risk and Blame: Essays in Cultural Theory*. London: Routledge, 1992. ProQuest eBook, 2015.

Ellingson, Ter. *The Myth of the Noble Savage*. Berkeley: University of California Press, 2001.

Esparza Sánchez, Cuauhtémoc. *El corrido zacatecano*. México DF: SEP, Instituto Nacional de Antropología e Historia, 1976.

———. *Historia de la ganadería en Zacatecas, 1531–1911*. Zacatecas: Universidad Autónoma de Zacatecas, 1988.

Ferrari, L., M. Valencia-Moreno, and S. Bryan. "Magmatism and Tectonics of the Sierra Madre Occidental and Its Relation with the Evolution of the Western Margin of North America." In *Geology of México: Celebrating the Centenary of the Geological Society of Mexico*, edited by Susana A. Alaniz-Álvarez and Ángel F. Nieto-Amaniego, 1–39. Boulder CO: Geological Society of America, 2007.

Ferrusquía-Villafranca, Ismael. "Geology of Mexico: A Synopsis." In *Biological Diversity of Mexico: Origins and Distribution*, edited by T. P. Ramamoorthy, Robert Bye, Antonio Lot, and John Fa, 3–107. New York: Oxford University Press, 1993.

Ferry, Elizabeth. *Not Ours Alone: Patrimony, Value, and Collectivity in Contemporary Mexico*. New York: Columbia University Press, 2005.

Finn, Janet. *Tracing the Veins: Of Copper, Culture, and Community from Butte to Chuquicamata*. Berkeley: University of California Press, 1998.

Fisher, John. *Silver Mines and Silver Miners in Colonial Peru, 1776–1824*. Liverpool: University of Liverpool, 1977.

Flores Olague, Jesús, Mercedes de Vega, Sandra Kuntz Ficker, and Laura del Alizal. *Zacatecas: Historia breve*. 2nd ed. México DF: El Colegio de México, 2011.

Foulkes, Ernest. "Metal Disposition: An Analysis of Underlying Mechanisms." In *Metal Toxicology*, edited by Robert A. Goyer et al., 3–29. San Diego CA: Academic Press and Harcourt Brace, 1995.

Fowler, Will. *Santa Anna of Mexico*. Lincoln: University of Nebraska Press, 2007.

Galeano Eduardo. *Open Veins of Latin America: Five Centuries of the Pillage of a Continent*. Translated by Cedric Belfrage. 1973. New York: Monthly Review Press, 1997.

Garay Hernández, María del Carmen, María del Rosario Paredes Lara, and José Hernández Martínez. "Acumulación de As-Cd-Pb en suelo y cultivos afectados por jales mineros en la cuenca de Calera-Zacatecas, México." In *Medio ambiente y insustentabilidad en Zacatecas*, edited by Patricia Rivera and Guillermo Foladori, 161–75. Tijuana: Colegio de la Frontera, 2012.

García, Trinidad. *Los mineros mexicanos*. 1895. México DF: Editorial Porrúa, 1968.

García García, Enrique, and Laura Solar Valverde. *Proyecto Arqueológico Cerro del Teúl, Zacatecas*. México DF: Instituto Nacional de Antropología e Historia, 2010.

Garner, R. L. "Long-Term Silver Mining Trends in Spanish America: A Comparative Analysis of Peru and Mexico." *American Historical Review* 93, no. 4 (1988): 898–935.

Garza, James A. *The Imagined Underworld: Sex, Crime, and Vice in Porfirian Mexico City*. Lincoln: University of Nebraska Press, 2007.

Gibson, Charles. *The Aztecs under Spanish Rule: A History of the Indians of the Valley of Mexico, 1519–1810*. 1964. Stanford: Stanford University Press, 2006.

Gier, Jaclyn J., and Laurie Mercier, eds. *Mining Women: Gender in the Development of a Global Industry, 1670 to the Present*. New York: Palgrave Macmillan, 2006.

"Gobernantes de Zacatecas." Biblioteca Jurídica Virtual, Universidad Nacional Autónoma de México. https://archivos.juridicas.unam.mx/www/bjv/libros/6/2863/11.pdf.

Gomez, Rocio. "Fountains of Modernity: Water, Mining, and Public Health in Zacatecas, 1882–1898." In "Historias Ambientales," special issue edited by Michael K. Bess and Raúl Pacheco-Vega. *ISTOR: A Journal of History* 69 (Summer 2017): 9–24.

Gonzalez Ortega, Jesús. *The Presidency of Mexico: Protest of General Jesús González Ortega, President of the Supreme Court of Justice, against the decrees of Señor Benito Juárez, Ex-President of the Mexican Republic*. New York: Russell's American Steam Printing House Presses, 1866.

"Governors of Zacatecas and Durango Define Attitude towards Mining Industry." *Engineering and Mining Journal* 110, no. 19 (6 November 1920): 918–19.

Guerrero, Saul. "The History of Silver Refining in New Spain, 16th c. to 18th c.: Back to the Basics." *History and Technology: An International Journal* 32, no. 1 (2016): 2–32.

———. *Silver by Fire, Silver by Mercury: A Chemical History of Silver Refining in New Spain and Mexico, 16th to 19th Centuries*. Leiden: Brill, 2017.

Hall, Linda. "La Frontera y las minas en la revolución mexicana (1910–1920)." *Historia Mexicana* 32, no. 3 (1983): 389–421.

Halleck, H. W. *A Collection of Mining Laws from Spain and Mexico*. Compiled and translated by H. W. Halleck. San Francisco CA: O'Meara and Painter, 1859.

Hansen, C. J., et al. "Silver and Palladium Help Unveil the Nature of a Second R-process." *Astronomy and Astrophysics* 545 (September 2012): A31.

Hardin, Garrett. "The Tragedy of the Commons." *Science* 162 (1968): 1243–48.

Hart, John Mason. *Empire and Revolution: The Americans in Mexico since the Civil War*. Berkeley and Los Angeles: University of California Press, 2002.

———. *Revolutionary Mexico: The Coming and Process of the Mexican Revolution*. Berkeley and Los Angeles: University of California Press, 1987.

———. *The Silver of the Sierra Madre: John Robinson, Boss Shepherd, and the People of the Canyons*. Tucson: University of Arizona Press, 2008.

Hempel, Sandra. *The Strange Case of the Broad Street Pump: John Snow and the Mystery of Cholera*. Berkeley: University of California Press, 2007.

Howe, Walter. *The Mining Guild of New Spain and Its Tribunal General, 1770–1821*. Cambridge MA: Harvard University Press, 1949.

Índice de las leyes de aguas nacionales y sus reformas. Provided by El Colegio de México. Accessed June 2015. http://siaps.colmex.mx.

"The Ingersoll Rock Drill." *Manufacturer and Business Magazine*, 4 April 1874, 78–79.

Isenberg, Andrew C. *Mining California: An Ecological History*. New York: Hill and Wang, 2005.

Iskander, Felib Y., Hector René Vega-Carrillo, and Eduardo Manzanares Acuna. "Determination of Mercury and Other Elements in La Zacatecana Dam Sediment in Mexico." *Science of the Total Environment* 148, no. 1 (May 1994): 45–48.

Johnson, Susan L. *Roaring Camp: The Social World of the California Gold Rush*. New York: Norton, 2000.

Julian, H. Forbes, and Edgar Smart. *Cyaniding Gold and Silver Ores: A Practical Treatise*. London: Charles Green and Company, 1921.

Katz, Friedrich. *The Life and Times of Pancho Villa*. Stanford: Stanford University Press, 1998.

Knight, Alan. *The Mexican Revolution*. 2 vols. Lincoln: University of Nebraska, 1990.

Knoeller, Christian. *Reimagining Environmental History: Ecological Memory in the Wake of Landscape Change*. Reno: University of Nevada Press, 2017.

Knox, Thomas Wallace. *The Boy Travellers in Mexico*. New York: Harper and Brothers, 1890.

Krech, Shepherd, III. *The Ecological Indian: Myth and History*. New York: Norton, 2000.

Kuntz Ficker, Sandra. "La República Restaurada y el Porfiriato." In *Zacatecas: Historia breve*, edited by Jesús Flores Olague et al., 115–45. 2nd ed. México DF: El Colegio de México, 2011.

La Escuela de Medicina: Periódico dedicado a las ciencias médicas. Volume 5. México DF: Imprenta librería, y litografía de E. Dublan, 1884.

Lane, Kris. "Dangerous Attractions: Mercury in Human History." In *Mercury Pollution: A Transdisciplinary Treatment*, edited by Sharon L. Zuber and Michael C. Newman, 13–31. Boca Raton FL: CRC Press, 2012.

———. *Potosí: The Silver City That Changed the World*. Oakland: University of California Press, 2019.

Langston, Nancy. *Toxic Bodies: Hormone Disrupters and the Legacy of DES*. New Haven: Yale University Press, 2011.

Leavitt, Judith W. *Typhoid Mary: Captive to the Public's Health*. Boston: Beacon Press, 1998.

LeDuc, Albert, Luis Lara y Pardo, and Carlos Roumagnac. *Diccionario de Geografía, Historia, y Biografías Mexicanas*. París: Librería de la Viuda de C. Bouret, 1910.

Leech, Brian. *The City That Ate Itself: Butte, Montana and Its Expanding Berkeley Pit*. Reno: University of Nevada Press, 2018.

Leung, Alexander K. C., James S. C. Leung, H. Dele Davies, and James D. Keller. "Rabies: Epidemiology, Pathogenesis, and Prophylaxis." In *Rabies: Symptoms, Treatment, and Prevention*, edited by John G. Williamson, 33–47. New York: Nova Science, 2010.

"Ley Federal del Trabajo." *Diario Oficial de la Federación* 67, no. 51 (28 August 1931).

Ley minería y ley de impuesto a la minería con sus respectivos reglamentos. México DF: Secretaría de Fomento, 1893.

Liceaga, Eduardo. *Las inoculaciones preventivas de la rabia.* México DF: Imprenta de Ignacio Escalante, 1888.

Lidén, Carola, Howard I. Maibach, and Jan E. Wahlberg. "Skin." In *Metal Toxicology*, edited by Robert A. Goyer, Curtis D. Klaasen, and Michael P. Waalkes, 447–64. San Diego CA: Academic Press and Harcourt Brace, 1995.

Loewenberg, Samuel. "The Plight of Mexico's Indigenous Women." *The Lancet* 375, no. 9727 (May 2010): 1680–82.

López, Fernando. *Conferencia sobre higiene pública y privada para evitar y combatir las enfermedades infecto-contagiosas por el Dr. Fernando López.* Zacatecas: Talleres de N. Espinosa, 1910.

MacFarquhar, Jennifer K., et al. "Acute Selenium Toxicity Associated with a Dietary Supplement." *Archives of Internal Medicine* 170, no. 3 (2010): 256–61.

Macmillan, David S., and Brian Plomley. "An American Surveyor in Mexico, 1827–1860." *New Mexico Historical Review* 34, no. 1 (1959): 1–9.

Malone, Michael. *The Battle for Butte: Mining and Politics on the Northern Frontier, 1864–1906.* Seattle: University of Washington Press, 2006.

Markowitz, Gerald, and David Rosner. "Why Is Silicosis So Important?" In *Silicosis: A World History*, edited by Paul-André Rosental, 14–29. Baltimore: Johns Hopkins University Press, 2017.

Martin, Percy. *Mexico of the Twentieth Century.* 2 vols. London: Edward Arnold, 1907.

Martínez Baca, Eduardo. *Reseña histórica de la legislación minera en México.* México DF: Oficina Tipográfica de la Secretaría de Fomento, 1901.

Mather, W. W. "On the principles involved in the Reduction of Iron and Silver Ores, with a supplementary notice of some of the principal Silver Mines of Mexico and South America." *American Journal of Science and Arts* 24, no. 2 (January 1833): 213–37.

McCrea, Heather. *Diseased Relations: Epidemics, Public Health, and State-Building in Yucatán, Mexico, 1847–1924.* Albuquerque: University of New Mexico Press, 2011.

McCulloch, Jock. *South Africa's Gold Mines and the Politics of Silicosis.* London: Boydell and Brewer, 2012.

McCulloch, Jock, and Paul-André Rosental, with Joseph Melling. "Johannesburg and Beyond: Silicosis as a Transnational and Imperial Disease, 1900–1940." In *Silicosis: A World History*, edited by Paul-André Rosental, 64–104. Baltimore: Johns Hopkins University Press, 2017.

McGrew, Roderick. *Encyclopedia of Medical History.* New York: McGraw-Hill, 1985.

McMichael, Anthony J. *Climate Change and the Health of Nations: Famines, Fevers, and the Fate of Populations.* Oxford: Oxford University Press, 2017.

McNeill, John R. and George Vrtis, eds. *Mining North America: An Environmental History since 1522.* Oakland: University of California Press, 2017.

Memorias de Eduardo G. Pankhurst. Colección Especial "Arturo Romo Gutiérrez." Zacatecas, Zacatecas, 1908.

Mendoza García, Edgar. "Resistencia a la 'federalización': Propiedad y control local de las aguas subterráneas en Tehuacán, Puebla (1917–1946)." In *La modernización del sistema de agua potable en México, 1810–1950*, edited by Diana Birrichaga Gardida, 171–92. México DF: El Colegio Mexiquense, 2007.

Merchant, Carolyn. *The Death of Nature: Women, Ecology and the Scientific Revolution.* San Francisco: Harper & Row, 1980.

"Mexico: Zacatecas, Conditions Good Owing to Activities of Mexican Corporation and Bote Mining Co." *Engineering and Mining Journal* 111 (2 April 1921): 603.

Mill, John Stuart. *Auguste Comte and Positivism.* 1865. Project Gutenberg eBook, 2005.

Mining Laws of the United States of Mexico/Ley Minería de los Estados Unidos Mexicanos. 4th ed. México DF: F. P. Hoeck & Co., 1901.

Mitman, Greg, Michelle Murphy, and Christopher Sellers, eds. "Landscapes of Exposure: Knowledge and Illness in Modern Environments." Special issue of *Osiris* 19 (2004).

Molina del Villar, América. "El tifo en la ciudad de México en tiempos de la Revolución Mexicana, 1913-1916." *Historia Mexicana* 64, no. 3 (2015): 1163–1247.

Motten, Clement G. *Mexican Silver and the Enlightenment.* New York: Octagon Books, 1972.

Mumford, Lewis. *Technics and Civilization.* 1934. Chicago: University of Chicago Press, 2010.

Muñoz, Ignacio G. *Verdad y mito de la Revolución Mexicana, relatada por un protagonista.* 3 vols. México DF: Ediciones Populares, 1961.

Nash, Linda L. *Inescapable Ecologies: A History of Environment, Disease, and Knowledge.* Berkeley: University of California Press, 2007.

———. "Writing Histories of Disease and Environment in the Age of the Anthropocene." *Environmental History* 20, no. 4 (2015): 796–804.

Nichol, Thomas. *Diseases of the Nares, Larynx, and Trachea in Childhood.* New York: A. L. Chatterton, 1884.

Nichols, Sandra L. *Santos, duraznos y vino: Migrantes mexicanos y la transformación de Los Haro, Zacatecas, y Napa, California.* México DF: Universidad Autónoma de Zacatecas, 2006.

Nieto-Samaniego, Ángel F., Susana A. Alaniz-Álvarez, and Antoni Camprubí. "Mesa Central of Mexico: Stratigraphy, Structure, and Cenozoic Tectonic Evolution." In *Geology of México: Celebrating the Centenary of the Geological Society of Mexico*, edited by Susana A. Alaniz-Álvarez and Ángel F. Nieto-Amaniego, 41–70. Boulder CO: Geological Society of America, 2007.

Ogura, Tetsuya, et al. "Zacatecas (Mexico) Companies Extract Hg from Surface Soil Contaminated by Ancient Mining Industries." *Water, Air and Soil Pollution* 148, no. 1–4 (2003): 167–77.

Pacheco-Vega, Raúl. "Agua embotellada en México: de la privatización del suministro a la mercantilización de los recursos hídricos." *Espiral: Estudios sobre Estado y Sociedad* 22, no. 63 (2015): 221–63.

Palacio, Germán. "An Eco-Political Vision for an Environmental History: Toward a Latin American and North American Research Partnership." *Environmental History* 17, no. 4. (2012): 725–43.

Parker, John E., and Gregory R. Wagner. "Silicosis." In *Encyclopaedia of Occupational Health and Safety: The Body, Healthcare, Management, and Policy.* Volume 1, edited by Jeanne Mager Stellman. 4th ed. Geneva, Switzerland: International Labor Organization, 1998.

Parsons, Arthur Barrette. "Revival of Zacatecas." *Engineering and Mining Journal* 122, no. 9 (1926): 324.

Pearson, Ron. "Preliminary Findings in Assessment of Soils and Crops in the Zacatecas Area, Mexico." In *North American Regional Action Plan for Mercury: Close-Out Report.* Montréal: Commission for Environmental Cooperation, May 2013.

Pérez Toledo, Sonia. "Introducción." In *Entre la tradición y la novedad: La educación y la formación de hombres 'nuevos' en Zacatecas en el siglo XIX,* edited by Sonia Pérez Toledo y René Amaro Peñaflores, 7–15. México DF: Universidad Autónoma de Zacatecas y Universidad Autónoma Metropolitana, 2003.

Piccato, Pablo. *City of Suspects: Crime in Mexico City, 1900–1931.* Durham: Duke University Press, 2001.

Pilcher, Jeffrey. *The Sausage Rebellion: Public Health, Private Enterprise, and Meat in Mexico City, 1890–1917.* Albuquerque: University of New Mexico Press, 2006.

Piper, Liza. *The Industrial Transformation of Subarctic Canada.* Vancouver: UBC Press, 2009.

Pletcher, David. "The Fall of Silver in Mexico, 1876–1910, and Its Effect on American Investments." *Journal of Economic History* 18, no. 1 (1958): 33–55.

Previsor (pseud.). "Prospects at Zacatecas." Letter to the editor, *Mining and Scientific Press,* 18 September 1909, 387–89.

Radkau, Joachim. *Nature and Power: A Global History of the Environment.* Oxford: Oxford University Press, 2008.

Raleigh, Clionadh. "The Absence of Water Conflicts in the Developing World: Evidence from Africa." In *The Oxford Handbook of Water Politics and Policy,* edited by Ken Conca and Erika Weinthal, 549–66. Oxford: Oxford University Press, 2018.

Ramazzini, Bernardino. *A treatise of the diseases of tradesmen, showing the various influence of particular trades upon the state of health . . . and now done in English.* London: printed for Andrew Bell et al., 1705. Gage Eighteenth Century Collections Online. eBook.

Ramírez, Santiago. *Datos para la historia del Colegio de Minería.* México DF: Impresa del Gobierno Federal, 1890.

"Regional Summaries: Mexico General Improvement, but Outlook Is Uncertain." *Engineering and Mining Journal* 117 (January–June 1924): 122.

Reports for Zacatecas, Mexico (1860–1888). Record Group 84, Records of the Foreign Service Posts of the Department of State, 1788–ca. 1991. Washington DC: National Archives and Records Administration. Microfilm.

Rice, Claude T. "Zacatecas, a Famous Silver Camp of Mexico." *Engineering and Mining Journal* 86 (29 August 1908): 401.

Ríos Molina, Andrés, ed. *Los pacientes del Manicomio La Castañeda y sus diagnósticos: Una historia de la clínica psiquiátrica en México, 1910–1968.* México DF: Instituto de Investigaciones Históricas e Instituto de Investigaciones Doctor José María Luis Mora, 2017.

Ríos Zúñiga, Rosalina. "Separar y homogeneizar: Instrucción pública y ciudadanía en Zacatecas, 1825–1845." In *Entre la tradición y la novedad: La educación y la formación de hombres "nuevos" en Zacatecas en el siglo XIX,* edited by Sonia Pérez Toledo and René Amaro Peñaflores, 87–132. México DF: Universidad Autónoma de Zacatecas y Universidad Autónoma Metropolitana, 2003.

Robins, Nicholas A. *Mercury, Mining, and Empire: The Human and Ecological Cost of Colonial Silver Mining in the Andes.* Bloomington: Indiana University Press, 2011.

Rodríguez, Martha E. "El tifo en la Ciudad de México en 1915." *Gaceta Médica de México* 152 (2016): 253–58.

Rosenberg, Charles. *The Cholera Years: The United States in 1832, 1849, and 1866.* 2nd ed. Chicago: University of Chicago Press, 1987.

Rosental, Paul-André, ed. *Silicosis: A World History.* Baltimore: Johns Hopkins University Press, 2017.

Rosental, Paul-André, and Bernard Thomann. "Silicosis and 'Silicosis': Minimizing Compensation Costs; or, Why Occupational Diseases Cost So Little." In *Silicosis: A World History,* edited by Paul-André Rosental, 140–72. Baltimore: Johns Hopkins University Press, 2017.

Rosner, David, and Gerald Markowitz. *Deadly Dust: Silicosis and the On-Going Struggle to Protect Workers' Health.* Ann Arbor: University of Michigan Press, 2006.

Roumagnac, Carlos. *Los criminales en México: Ensayo de psicología criminal.* México DF: Tipografía "El Fénix," 1904. Hathi Trust eBook.

Russell, H. L. *Outlines of Dairy Bacteriology: A Concise Manual for the Use of Students in Dairying.* Madison: University of Wisconsin, 1899.

Salinas, Salvador. *Land, Liberty, and Water: Morelos after Zapata, 1920–1940.* Tucson: University of Arizona Press, 2018.

Santiago, Myrna. *The Ecology of Oil: Environment, Labor, and the Mexican Revolution, 1900–1938.* Cambridge: Cambridge University Press, 2009.

———. "Extracting Histories: Mining, Workers, and the Environment." In "New Environmental Histories of Latin America and the Caribbean." Special issue, *Rachel Carson Center Perspectives* no. 7 (2013): 81–88.

Santoyo Alonso, Leonardo, and Thomas Hillerkuss. "Agua esperé y tarde sembré: La dotación de aguas de la hacienda de espíritu santo, Pinos, Zacatecas (1930–1967)." In *Medio ambiente y insustentabilidad en Zacatecas,* edited by Patricia Rivera y Guillermo Foladori. Tijuana: Colegio de la Frontera, 2012.

Schell, William, Jr. "Silver Symbiosis: ReOrienting Mexican Economic History." *Hispanic American Historical Review* 81, no. 1 (2001): 89–133.

Scott, James. *Weapons of the Weak: Everyday Forms of Peasant Resistance.* New Haven: Yale University Press, 1987.

Sedgwick, W. T., and J. L. Batchelder. "A Bacteriological Examination of the Boston Milk Supply." *Boston Medical and Surgical Journal* 126 (1892): 25–28.

Selee, Andrew. "Municipalities and Policymaking." In *The Oxford Handbook of Mexican Politics*, edited by Roderic Ai Camp, 101–18. New York: Oxford University Press, 2012.

Sellers, Christopher C. *Hazards of the Job: From Industrial Disease to Environmental Health Science*. Chapel Hill: University of North Carolina Press, 1997.

Sonneschmid, Federico. *Tratado de la amalgamación de Nueva España*. París: Galería de Bossange and México: Librería de Bossange, Antoran y Compañía, 1825.

Speckman Guerra, Elisa. *Crimen y castigo: Legislación penal, interpretaciones de la criminalidad y administración de justicia (Ciudad de México, 1872–1910)*. México DF: El Colegio de México e Instituto de Investigaciones Históricas, 2001.

Stein, Stanley, and Barbara H. Stein. *Silver, Trade, and War: Spain and America in the Making of Early Modern Europe*. Baltimore: Johns Hopkins University Press, 2000.

Stevens, Donald Fithian. *Mexico in the Time of Cholera*. Albuquerque: University of New Mexico Press, 2019.

Stoddard, John L. *John L. Stoddard's Lectures: Illustrated and embellished with the views of the world's famous places and people, being the identical discourses delivered during the past eighteen years under the title of the Stoddard Lectures*. Volume 7. Boston: Blach Brothers, 1898.

Studnicki-Gizbert, Daviken, and David Schecter. "The Environmental Dynamics of a Colonial Fuel-Rush: Silver Mining and Deforestation in New Spain, 1522 to 1810." *Environmental History* 15, no. 1 (2010): 94–119.

Suárez-Potts, William J. *The Making of Law: The Supreme Court and Labor Legislation in Mexico, 1875–1931*. Stanford: Stanford University Press, 2012.

Tarr, Joel. "The Metabolism of the Industrial City: The Case of Pittsburgh." In *City, Country, Empire: Landscapes in Environmental History*, edited by Jeffry M. Diefendorf and Kurk Dorsey, 15–37. Pittsburgh PA: University of Pittsburgh Press, 2005.

Thomas, David J., and Robert A. Gayer. "Effects of As, Pb, and Cd on the Cardiovascular System." In *Metal Toxicology*, edited by Robert A. Goyer, Curtis D. Klaasen, and Michael P. Waalkes, 265–85. San Diego CA: Academic Press and Harcourt Brace, 1995.

Tiberghien, G[uillaume]. *Código moral y tratado de urbanidad: Para uso de las escuelas del estado*. Zacatecas: Impresa y Literatura de N. Espinosa, 1890.

Tinajero, Araceli, and J. Brian Freeman, eds. *Technology and Culture in Twentieth-Century Mexico*. Tuscaloosa: University of Alabama Press, 2013.

Toner, Deborah. *Alcohol and Nationhood in Nineteenth-Century Mexico*. Lincoln: University of Nebraska Press, 2015.

Tortolero Villaseñor, Alejandro. *El agua y su historia: México y sus desafíos hacia el siglo XXI*. México DF: Siglo XXI editores, 2000.

———. "Entre las revoluciones y el desarrollo: El agua en México, siglos XIX y XX." In *México en tres momentos: 1810–1910–2010*, volume 2, edited by Alicia Mayer, 55–76. México DF: Universidad Autónoma de México, 2007.

———. "Transforming the Central Mexican Waterscape: Lake Drainage and Its Consequences during the Porfiriato." In *Territories, Commodities and Knowledges: Latin*

America Environmental History in the Nineteenth and Twentieth Centuries, edited by Christian Brannstrom, 121–47. London: Institute for the Study of the Americas, 2004.

———. "Water and Revolution in Morelos, 1850–1915." In *A Land between Waters: Environmental Histories of Modern Mexico*, edited by Christopher Boyer, 124–49. Tucson: University of Arizona Press, 2012.

Toxqui, Aurea, and Gretchen Pierce, eds. *Alcohol in Latin America: A Social and Cultural History*. Tucson: University of Arizona Press, 2017.

Turner, Victor. *The Ritual Process: Structure and Anti-Structure*. 1966. Chicago: Aldine, 1996.

Tutino, John. *The Mexican Heartland: How Communities Shaped Capitalism, a Nation, and World History, 1500–2000*. Princeton: Princeton University Press, 2018.

Valdez Aguilar, Rafael. *El cólera: Enfermedad de la pobreza*. Culiacán: Universidad Autónoma de Sinaloa, 1993.

Van Horssen, Jessica. *A Town Called Asbestos: Environmental Contamination, Health, and Resilience in a Resource Community*. Vancouver: UBC Press, 2016.

Velasco Murillo, Dana. *Urban Indians in a Silver City: Zacatecas, Mexico, 1546–1810*. Stanford: Stanford University Press, 2016.

Vidal, Salvador. *Bosquejo histórico de Zacatecas*. Volume 3, *Desde el año de 1857 a 1867*. 1943. Zacatecas: Instituto Zacatecano de Cultura "Ramón López Velarde," 2009.

Vitz, Matthew. *A City on a Lake: Urban Political Ecology and the Growth of Mexico City*. Durham: Duke University Press, 2018.

Voigt, Lisa. *Spectacular Wealth: The Festivals of Colonial South American Mining Towns*. Austin: University of Texas Press, 2016.

Wakild, Emily. *Revolutionary Parks: Conservation, Social Justice, and Mexico's National Parks*. Tucson: University of Arizona Press, 2011.

Walker, Brett. *Toxic Archipelago: A History of Industrial Disease in Japan*. Seattle: University of Washington Press, 2011.

Wasik, Bill, and Monica Murphy. *Rabid: A Cultural History of the World's Most Diabolical Virus*. New York: Penguin Books, 2013. Kindle edition.

Watt, Andrew. "Personal Experiences of Miners' Phthisis on the Rand, 1903 to 1916." In *Silicosis: Records of the International Conference Held at Johannesburg, 13–27 August 1930*. London: P. S. King, 1937.

White, Richard. "'Are You an Environmentalist or Do You Work for a Living?' Work and Nature." In *Uncommon Ground: Rethinking the Human Place in Nature*, edited by William Cronon, 171–85. New York: Norton, 1995.

———. *The Organic Machine: The Remaking of the Columbia River*. New York: Hill and Wang, 1995.

Williams, Rosalind. *Notes on the Underground: An Essay on Technology, Society, and the Imagination*. Cambridge MA: MIT Press, 1990.

Wolfe, Mikael D. "The Climate of Conflict: Political-Environmental Press Coverage and the Eruption of the Mexican Revolution, 1907–1911." *Hispanic American Historical Review* 99, no. 3 (2019): 467–99.

———. *Watering the Revolution: An Environmental and Technological History of Agrarian Reform in Mexico*. Durham: Duke University Press, 2017.

Worster, Donald. *Dust Bowl: The Southern Plains in the 1930s*. 1979. Oxford: Oxford University Press, 2004.

Zapata, Emiliano, et al. "Plan de Ayala." In *The Mexico Reader: History, Culture, Politics*, edited by Gilbert Joseph and Timothy Henderson, 339–43. Durham: Duke University Press, 2002.

Zarate, Francisco. *Apuntes sobre la minería del Estado de Zacatecas*. Urbana: University of Illinois, 2014.

Zetina Rodríguez, María de la Carmen. "La controversia ambiental en torno a la presa La Zacatecana, Guadalupe, Zacatecas." *Desacatos* 51 (May–August 2016): 160–79.

———. "La historia de un tesoro que se convirtió en un desastre ambiental, la Zacatecana, ejido de Guadalupe, Zacatecas." *Revista de El Colegio de San Luis* n.s. 2, no. 4 (2012): 160–94.

Index

A Revolution Unfinished: The Chegomista Rebellion and the Limits of Revolutionary Democracy in Juchitán, Oaxaca
Colby Ristow

Murder and Counterrevolution in Mexico: The Eyewitness Account of German Ambassador Paul von Hintze, 1912–1914
Edited and with an introduction by Friedrich E. Schuler

Deco Body, Deco City: Female Spectacle and Modernity in Mexico City, 1900–1939
Ageeth Sluis

Pistoleros and Popular Movements: The Politics of State Formation in Postrevolutionary Oaxaca
Benjamin T. Smith

Alcohol and Nationhood in Nineteenth-Century Mexico
Deborah Toner

Death Is All around Us: Corpses, Chaos, and Public Health in Porfirian Mexico City
Jonathan M. Weber

To order or obtain more information on these or other University of Nebraska Press titles, visit nebraskapress.unl.edu.